A QUIET REVOLUTION
IN INDIGENOUS
SERVICE DELIVERY

NEW PUBLIC MANAGEMENT AND ITS EFFECTS
ON FIRST NATIONS ORGANISATIONS

A QUIET REVOLUTION IN INDIGENOUS SERVICE DELIVERY

NEW PUBLIC MANAGEMENT AND ITS EFFECTS ON FIRST NATIONS ORGANISATIONS

EDITED BY DEIRDRE HOWARD-WAGNER

Australian
National
University

ANU PRESS

CENTRE FOR INDIGENOUS
POLICY RESEARCH (CIPR)
Monograph No. 41

Australian National University

ANU PRESS

Published by ANU Press
The Australian National University
Canberra ACT 2600, Australia
Email: anupress@anu.edu.au

Available to download for free at press.anu.edu.au

ISBN (print): 9781760466879
ISBN (online): 9781760466886

WorldCat (print): 1482902628
WorldCat (online): 1482905132

DOI: 10.22459/CIPR41.2025

WARNING: Readers are notified that this publication may contain names or images of deceased persons.

Cover design and layout by ANU Press. Cover artwork by Lani Balzan.

This book is published under the aegis of the Centre for Indigenous Policy Research (CIPR) editorial board of ANU Press.

Contents

Abbreviations   vii

List of images   ix

Acknowledgements   xi

Contributors   xiii

1. New Public Management, the Indigenous service market,
    and their effects   1
    Deirdre Howard-Wagner

2. The 'quiet revolution' in Indigenous affairs: How Australia
    ended up with a marketised Indigenous service delivery
    system in the New Public Management era   27
    Deirdre Howard-Wagner

3. 'You can have a voice but you gotta pay your own bus fare':
    The First Peoples Disability Network   59
    June Riemer, Karen Soldatić, and Kim Spurway

4. 'Moving with the times' and uncertain futures: Butucarbin
    in the New Public Management era   83
    Jennifer Beale, Jack Gibson, and Deirdre Howard-Wagner

5. 'If I don't prioritise that accountability back to my
    community ...': National Centre for Indigenous Excellence   113
    John Leha, Clare McHugh, Kim Spurway, and Karen Soldatić

6. Muru Mittigar: Country, culture, community, and contracts   133
    Janet Hunt, Cheryl Goh, Ros Fogg, and Christopher Galloway

7. The Glen Centre: A strength-based culturally immersive
    model of care hidden in plain sight   159
    Deirdre Howard-Wagner and Chris Mason

8. Decolonising the Indigenous service market   181
    Deirdre Howard-Wagner

Index   201

Abbreviations

ABS	Australian Bureau of Statistics
ADN	Aboriginal Disability Network
ATSIC	Aboriginal and Torres Strait Islander Commission
CAEP	Community Adult Education Program
CGC	Commonwealth Grants Commission
COAG	Council of Australian Governments
CTG 2020	National Agreement on Closing the Gap 2020
DEX	Data Exchange
DPO	Disabled People's Organisation
DSS	Department of Social Services
FPDN	First Peoples Disability Network
IAS	Indigenous Advancement Strategy
IBA	Indigenous Business Australia
ILSC	Indigenous Land and Sea Corporation
LALC	Local Aboriginal Land Council
NAIDOC	National Aborigines' and Islanders' Day Observance Committee
NCIE	National Centre for Indigenous Excellence
NCP	National Competition Policy
NDIS	National Disability Insurance Scheme
NIAA	National Indigenous Australians Agency
NILS	No Interest Loans Scheme
NPM	New Public Management
NSW	New South Wales

OCHRE	Opportunity, Choice, Healing, Responsibility, Empowerment: New South Wales Government plan for Aboriginal affairs
PLDC	Penrith Lakes Development Corporation
PWDA	People with Disability Australia
SUAs	Significant Urban Areas
TAFE	Technical and Further Education: Australian vocational training colleges
WSAAS	Western Sydney Area Assistance Scheme

List of images

Image 4.1. Butucarbin Aboriginal Corporation.   89

Image 7.1. Yarning around the campfire.   163

Image 7.2. The Glen T-shirt.   164

Acknowledgements

The authors thank the two anonymous referees for their comments.

The authors thank the senior position-holders who participated in the research through the First Nations Discussion Circles and the survey.

This research was fully supported by the Australian Government through the Australian Research Council's Discovery Projects funding scheme (project DP180103453). The views expressed herein are those of the authors and are not necessarily those of the Australian Government or the Australian Research Council.

Contributors

Jennifer Beale is a Gamillaroi woman who has worked extensively in Aboriginal and Torres Strait Islander communities in New South Wales (NSW) and interstate, bringing a community development focus to her work. She has extensive experience in Aboriginal health and community adult education in both remote and urban communities. For the past 30 years, Jennifer has lived and worked in the Dharug Aboriginal community in Western Sydney. She played the primary role in establishing Butucarbin Aboriginal Corporation, which delivers innovative and successful skill development programs to the Mt Druitt community, and is currently its Executive Officer.

Ros Fogg is a proud Dharug woman from the Buruberongal and Cannemegal clans of the Dharug nation, having lived on Country her whole life. Her family history predates colonisation and she is a direct descendant of Maria Lock, Yarramundi, and Gomberee. As the current Chair of the Muru Mittigar Board, she is passionate about her role which provides both education and employment opportunities to Aboriginal peoples in Western Sydney. She is a mother of three adult children and has five grandchildren. Her other passion is practising and teaching yoga, having completed her professional training over 20 years ago.

Christopher Galloway is the CEO of Muru Mittigar, providing strategic, operational, and financial leadership to this Aboriginal social enterprise. He has over 15 years of experience in executive roles and has a record of transforming businesses and driving revenue growth while maintaining quality, compliance and innovation standards. He has strong financial management expertise and is an ISO-certified auditor for quality, environmental and occupational health, and safety management systems.

Jack Gibson, a Wiradjuri man, has extensive experience in the First Nations organisations sector. He spent the past 30 years living and working on Dharug Country in Western Sydney. He has worked with and in First Nations organisations as a management consultant and at board, executive, and frontline worker levels, respectively. Jack is the Community Development Worker for Butucarbin and is also undertaking doctoral research at the Institute for Culture and Society, Western Sydney University, which explores the ways in which First Nations people negotiate their Indigeneity in the context of community-based First Nations organisations and services in Western Sydney.

Cheryl Goh is a Boorooberongal woman of the Dharug Nation. Her clan area is north-western Sydney along the Nepean/Hawkesbury river system. She is a descendant of Yarramundi, his father Goomberee, and his daughter, who became known as Maria after attending the Parramatta Native institution. Maria later married a convict Robert Lock, and from their nine (surviving to adulthood) children, is one of the many branches that form the Dharug nation today. Cheryl returned to formal education in her late 30s, graduating from Macquarie University with a *Bachelor* of Arts with a Diploma of *Education,* with majors in Aboriginal studies, history, and sociology, with the intention of teaching high school. However, she was approached to teach 'a few' units for TAFE (technical and further education colleges, the Australian vocational training institutions) in Western Sydney and found there she could fulfil most of her desires as an educator; it was, in the main, second-chance education. She retired from teaching, mainly at Mount Druitt College of TAFE, in January 2020, 25 years after taking those few units. Cheryl joined the board of Muru Mittigar some 17 years ago, with her main focus on cultural education.

Deirdre Howard-Wagner is a sociologist, socio-legal scholar, POLIS@ ANU Social Policy, Participation and Inclusion Program Lead, and former Director of Research and Associate Professor at the Centre for Indigenous Policy Research at The Australian National University. Her research focuses on historical and contemporary racial projects in Indigenous policy contexts, Closing the Gap policy, Indigenous care, Indigenous justice, urban Indigenous development, and self-determination.

Janet Hunt is an Honorary Associate Professor at the Centre for Aboriginal Economic Policy Research, at The Australian National University. Her research focuses on self-determination, governance, and community development.

John Leha has worked extensively in the Indigenous sector across all levels of government and community-controlled organisations. John is a proud Birri Gubba, Wakka Wakka, and Tongan man born and raised on Gadigal land, Sydney.

Chris Mason is a proud Ngemba man, his family is from Brewarrina in the far north-west of NSW. He has been employed in the community services sector for over 10 years and is very skilled and passionate about assisting people to turn their lives around. Chris has worked in various roles in the judicial, homeless, mental health, education, and employment sectors and is now working at The Glen Centre in the alcohol and other drugs (AOD) sector, believing the AOD system is the most dynamic of them all. Chris has worked at The Glen Centre as a counsellor, case manager, and program coordinator, and is now a senior counsellor, which offers the opportunity to utilise all the above-mentioned experience.

Clare McHugh is the CEO of the National Centre of Indigenous Excellence (NCIE) – a not-for-profit social enterprise based in Redfern – where she leads the delivery of a range of programs and enterprises that build capabilities and create life-changing opportunities for young Aboriginal and Torres Strait Islander peoples in Sydney, and across Australia. Clare is passionate about creating positive change for Australia's First Nations people and communities and has worked extensively in the NSW Land Rights system.

June Riemer is a Gumbaynggirr-Dunghutti woman and Deputy CEO of First Peoples Disability Network, the peak national disability systemic advocacy organisation for Aboriginal and/or Torres Strait Islander peoples living with disability. June has been one of Australia's leading Indigenous disability advocates over the last 20 years, driving change internationally through the United Nations and nationally through federal and state governments.

Karen Soldatić is a Canadian excellence research chair, Health Equity and Community Wellbeing at Toronto Metropolitan University, and Whitlam Fellow at Western Sydney University.

Kim Spurway is a Senior Research Associate with the Institute for Culture and Society at Western Sydney University. Kim's research focuses on critical approaches to humanitarian emergencies, natural disasters, artificial intelligence technologies, race, disability, and sexuality.

1

New Public Management, the Indigenous service market, and their effects

Deirdre Howard-Wagner

Introduction

In 2020, then Australian prime minister of a Coalition government, Scott Morrison, announced a new National Agreement on Closing the Gap (CTG 2020), conceding that '[First Nations] community-controlled services usually achieve better results, employ more [First Nations] people, and are often preferred over mainstream services' (Morrison, 2020; National Indigenous Australians Agency [NIAA], 2020). CTG 2020 marked the formal recognition of the importance of a strong and sustainable First Nations community-controlled sector[1] for delivering services to meet the needs of First Nations people across Australia (National Agreement on CTG, 2020, p. 8). Australian governments were recognising that the sector's capacity to build its workforce, capital infrastructure, and service provision should be strengthened. Australian governments were committing to 'community-controlled organisations hav[ing] a dedicated, reliable, and consistent funding model designed to suit the types of services required by communities', as well as to 'implement[ing] measures to increase the proportion of services delivered by [First Nations]

---

1   The terms 'First Nations community-controlled sector' and 'community-controlled First Nations organisations' are used throughout this edited collection as the term preferred by First Nations authors and partners in the collaborative research project from which the collection was produced.

organisations' (NIAA, 2020). With CTG 2020, Australian governments were reversing a policy decision and correcting a policy failure that had been in place for 15 years, since 2005.

Although policy failures are regularly understood to be unintended and atypical occurrences from which well-intentioned governments can learn, they can also signify the 'dark side' of policymaking (Leong & Howlett, 2022, p. 1379).[2] This volume explores the 'dark side' of policymaking, creating a space for recognising the adverse effects of a calculated 'quiet revolution' in government Indigenous services design and delivery, which saw Indigenous services mainstreamed and marketised under the Coalition government of a previous prime minister, John Howard.

The marketisation of Indigenous service delivery brought about significant institutional change: a new Indigenous service system was created, and the design and delivery of Indigenous services were fundamentally reformed. The approach was heavily influenced by thinking around the New Public Management (NPM). It promoted competition and enterprise between First Nations organisations and mainstream organisations, in which potential service providers competitively tendered to deliver government Indigenous services. Governments purposively designed the Indigenous service market as a social institution and social arena of exchange using competitive mechanisms to allocate Indigenous services to First Nations people to overcome disadvantage. The system created by the Howard Coalition Government thus narrowed the focus of government Indigenous service delivery to that of overcoming disadvantage. It also laid the foundations for an individualised system that adopted a person-centred approach. This approach was implemented across Indigenous service delivery in Australia through multilateral agreements between federal and state governments.

While CTG 2020 had much to recommend, the die had been cast in the Howard era. The government Indigenous service market created by the Howard Government embodied the principles of NPM, including the

---

2   Leong and Howlett argue that not all policymaking is well-intentioned, 'undertaken in a dispassionate, technical way in order to serve the public interest and, with respect to policy learning, that its aim is to learn the best way to improve policy and program delivery and avoid policy failures' (Leong & Howlett, 2022, p. 1379). As Leong and Howlett note:

> Even those studies which highlight the political and power-based nature of policy narratives and target constructions typically still hold out the hope that policy learning can contribute to the adoption of more evidence-based policy solutions and improved outcomes emerging from policy processes …
>
> (Leong & Howlett, 2022, p. 1380)

principle of cost-effectiveness, and encouraged a short-term, introspective, individualised, and transactional approach to the delivery of Indigenous services (Howard-Wagner, 2018). Howard-Wagner explains how the system has become multilayered, fragmented, and unnecessarily complex with services provided by federal, state or territory, and local governments through mainstream and First Nations not-for-profit organisations (2018).

As this volume shows, the imperative for policy change is unmistakable and, as CTG 2020 recognised, there is much work to be done. The government Indigenous service market that is now well entrenched in the public administration system has failed to 'close the gap'. It has operated to marginalise First Nations people and First Nations organisations, who have had very little say, if any, over the last 20 years, about how government services are designed to meet their needs.[3] The chapters in this volume comprehensively describe and illustrate how the government Indigenous market, and the Indigenous service delivery system created around that market, have failed and why system change is needed, drawing on the firsthand experiences of community-controlled First Nations organisations through organisational case studies in urban settings in New South Wales (NSW). The chapters map out the problem, its causes, and its consequences.

Instead of creating Indigenous market economies, the new Indigenous service system created during the Howard era has gone on to exacerbate economic inequalities, produce economic precarity and create organisational fragility in the community-controlled sector (Howard-Wagner et al., 2023). The new system has capitalised on Indigenous volunteerism and exploited the economic value of community-controlled First Nations organisations, Indigenous labour processes, and Indigenous expertise across the board. It has come to rely heavily on under-resourced First Nations organisations to do the job of government without community or organisational input into the design of Indigenous programs and services. Australian governments have controlled the supply of government services and programs to First Nations people, setting the demand and the prices in the Indigenous service economy.

While Jordan et al. argue that there is no easy way to outline the Indigenous service system or explain in detail the particularly complex multi-jurisdictional arrangements or multifaceted nature of Indigenous service delivery (Jordan et al., 2020, p. 11), or even explain easily the complex

---

3   See Closing the Gap Reports 2009–2022: www.closingthegap.gov.au/resources/reports.

multi-sector arrangements that have formed, as Howard-Wagner argues (Howard-Wagner et al., 2023), it is possible to represent this complexity through the experiences of individual community-controlled First Nations organisations operating on the ground. This is the objective of this edited volume. Importantly, the chapters reveal the variegated nature of the government Indigenous service market and the differentiated articulations of First Nations organisations operating within it through case studies of organisations operating in urban settings in NSW. Those case studies reveal not only how this market has intervened in the lives of First Nations people, but also how this market has failed to come to grips with the social reality of community-controlled First Nations organisations and what it takes for them to improve the lives of First Nations people.

This volume offers the expertise of individual community-controlled First Nations organisations operating in urban settings in NSW, which variously operate as social enterprises, businesses, community development organisations, social service providers, representatives, and advocacy organisations.[4] Concentrating on the experiences of individual First Nations organisations allows us to examine the complex, layered Indigenous service system as a multi-jurisdictional phenomenon on the ground in an

---

4   This volume is the culmination of a four-year Australian Research Council–funded research project co-designed by researchers from the Centre for Aboriginal Economic Policy Research at The Australian National University (CAEPR), the Institute for Culture and Society at Western Sydney University, and six urban First Nations organisations: First Peoples Disability Network, Butucarbin, The National Centre of Indigenous Excellence, Muru Mittigar, The Glen, and Tjillari Aboriginal Justice Corporation. Five of these organisations are the subject of the case studies presented in five of the eight chapters. The senior position-holders are partners and participants in the research and co-authors of those chapters. Tjillari Justice Aboriginal Corporation was not in a position to participate as a case study organisation. Deb Martin, its CEO, was a partner in the research, contributing strongly to its co-design, including the survey, and participating in First Nations Discussion Circles. In addition to these case studies, we conducted a statewide survey of 474 urban First Nations organisations in NSW, with a response rate of 11 per cent of First Nations organisations across 30 significant urban areas. This research sits alongside an in-depth place-based case study by Howard-Wagner of 14 First Nations organisations in the Greater Newcastle region (Howard-Wagner, 2021). One reviewer questioned our practice of co-authorship, pointing out that co-authoring with participants is not the ethical convention in Western publication practices and that there are set criteria and conventions around crediting communities and organisations, such as crediting partners as partners and for research permission, interest, and contributions (Castleden et al., 2010, p. 25). Scholars engaged in Indigenous research are increasingly challenging such conventions (Castleden et al., 2010, p. 25). Those scholars argue that shared authorship is a means to improve the research process as it strengthens Indigenous ownership, control, accessibility, and possession of information and data (Castleden et al., 2010; Giles & Castleden, 2008). In this volume, even though the academic researchers have done the writing, disrupting and decolonising Western conventions via sharing authorship recognises the expertise of our partners, their intellectual contribution, and the sovereignty of their data.

urban context.[5] Urban contexts are important, but often absent or given lower priority in government and public policy narratives, directions, and modelling about and for First Nations peoples. They are an important, and overlooked, context with nearly 80 per cent of First Nations people living in urban settings in Australia and over 90 per cent of First Nations people in the state of NSW living in major cities or inner regional areas (NSW Government, 2013, p. 5). The two largest populations of First Nations people are in Western Sydney and on the Central Coast of NSW (Australian Bureau of Statistics [ABS] 2016; Markham & Biddle, 2018). This means that community-controlled First Nations organisations operating in urban settings in NSW represent the largest population of First Nations people in Australia. While the gap in socio-economic disadvantage may be wider in remote localities, First Nations organisations in urban settings, by population, carry the bulk of responsibility for improving the lives of First Nations people in Australia.

Individually, the empirically grounded, interpretive case studies in this volume provide particular value: they expose the intense and complex matters of a highly fragmented and variable institutional landscape, involving the federal and state government departments and agencies, and contracted service providers, that make up the Indigenous service market.[6] They show the tremendous variation in funding arrangements and administrative requirements within this market and allow us to explore and gain explicit insight into the potential tensions, contradictions, and constraints of NPM systems for governments seeking to support and realise the full potential of community-controlled First Nations organisations in achieving community outcomes and CTG 2020.

The volume as a whole shows the overlooked but important strategic as well as operational function of the Indigenous service market in achieving multiple outcomes, not least its function of closing the gap. While

---

5   In 1967, section 51(xxvi) of the Australian Constitution was amended with the words 'other than the Aboriginal race in any State' deleted, giving the federal government the 'power to make laws for the peace, order and good government of the Commonwealth with respect to: … the people of any race for whom it is deemed necessary to make special laws'. The federal government has had concurrent power with the Australian states to make laws for Aboriginal and Torres Strait Islander peoples since.

6   By way of illustration, a community-controlled urban First Nations organisation in NSW may provide aged care, health services, programs and community support, and out-of-home care. Its funding partners may be NSW Health, NSW Families and Community Services, NSW Families and Community Services Ageing, Disability and Home Care, Department of the Prime Minister and Cabinet, Commonwealth Department of Health, National Authority on Aboriginal and Torres Strait Islander Health Care, and the NSW Primary Health Network.

Indigenous service delivery in Australia remains challenged by the need to overcome disadvantage, or what is simply now known as closing the gap, reform requires novel, value-creating approaches within the Indigenous service system. While the majority of this volume focuses on the problem, the final chapter focuses on system change.

Changing the rules of the game

From 2005, federal and state governments 'rolled out' (Peck & Tickell, 2017) the new rules of the game for a marketised government Indigenous service system (Sullivan, 2015, p. 7), in terms of what (laws, frameworks, and standards), how (the procedures, handbooks, and manuals), and with what (the tools, templates, forms, and guidelines). Over time, that Indigenous service system came to embody many of the characteristics of the neoliberalisation of government services, like maximising cost efficiency, effectiveness, and delivering measurable outcomes (Woolford & Curran, 2013, p. 49). It went on to treat program guidelines as rigid rules that would prevent innovation and fail to meet local needs. And, in keeping with the international trend, a complex Indigenous government service system came into existence. It came to be a highly decentralised, fractured, and complex multi-sector Indigenous service system with multiple regulated sectors. It resulted in community-controlled First Nations organisations having to comply with multiple layers of regulation, performance management, and accreditation. Like other government service markets in the neoliberal age, it came to be *systemically* uneven, or 'variegated' (Brenner et al., 2010).

The Indigenous service system created in the Howard era has gone on to deliver top-down government-designed and siloed sector-based programs and services through a form of public administration that is in keeping with the characteristics of NPM. The three tiers of government aside, even within government agencies this style of public administration has resulted in organisational fragmentation, disaggregation, and a high volume of single-purpose delivery entities around government Indigenous service delivery. Funding has become tied to highly specialised program outputs, with outcomes measured at the level of individualised service delivery.

In the disability area, for example, 2011–12 saw the commencement of the NSW Government's Stronger Together 2 policy (NSW Government, 2011). This state policy sat alongside the introduction of the federal National Disability Insurance Scheme, which represented a major reform in the disability sector. The person-centred approach of these policies has completely altered disability services in NSW. What were formerly government-controlled services are now provided through a market/consumer-driven model. These two intersecting policies, which have created the disability services market in NSW, require First Nations organisations to navigate complex administrative systems to sustain obligations to government departments and local community members.

NPM and Indigenous service delivery research

Studies of NPM in practice have found that, while it should improve government efficiency, it has not delivered better value (Lapsley, 2009) or increased economic efficiency, nor produced results through innovation fostered by competition (Melo et al., 2022, p. 1032). NPM has fragmented public services, which has caused problems with service delivery coordination (Howard, 2015 p. 237). NPM has produced disjointed and inconsistent service delivery arrangements (Howard, 2015, p. 237). NPM has failed to get holistic outcomes for communities or society. Importantly, NPM failed to address 'wicked problems', such as overcoming poverty (Christensen & Laegreid, 2017, Chapter 1; Meagher et al., 2022, p. 3) or, in Australia's case, overcoming Indigenous disadvantage. The effects of NPM and marketisation have thus been well documented.

This volume contributes to a small, but key, body of scholarship on the outcomes of NPM on First Nations organisations in Australia, Canada, and Aotearoa New Zealand (see, e.g., Howard-Wagner, 2018; McCaskill et al., 2011; Moran et al., 2014; Page, 2018; Snyder et al., 2015; Sookraj et al., 2012; Sullivan, 2018). Scholarship reveals that, since its deployment, NPM has had multiple effects on First Nations organisations, changing the relationships between them, the communities they serve and belong to, and governments (e.g., Marsh, 2015; Moran & Porter, 2014; Moran et al., 2016; Sullivan, 2015).

Research shows that the broader government service market is under-resourced and under-funded, and that the service delivery cost that contractors incur exceeds the revenue or funding provided (Australian Council of Social Services, 2013, p. 23). The research shows that there is little, or no, funding left for innovation, capacity building, professional development, or business development among not-for-profits in Australia or internationally (Muir & Salignac, 2017, p. 68). The chapters in this volume illustrate how the situation is far worse for community-controlled First Nations organisations. Of course, the case studies show that the effects of the marketisation of government Indigenous services are not the same for all First Nations organisations; much depends on their specific goals, the sector in which they operate, and their funding relationships.

While the effects of the marketisation of Indigenous services may differ, there are commonalities around how First Nations organisations encounter the market and elucidate the ongoing struggles they encounter under its strategies of governance to maintain their ethical commitments to culture and community (Howard-Wagner, Soldatić, et al., 2022, p. 211). Significantly, the chapters in this volume reveal how this complex, layered federal and state government funding system interacts with First Nations organisations as complex First Nations organisations. The chapters explain the ways in which funding arrangements radically diminish the capacity of First Nations organisations to achieve their other commitments to their communities, such as through the experiences of the First Peoples Disability Network (FPDN) (Chapter 3) and Butucarbin Aboriginal Corporation (Chapter 4). Only in exceptional cases do First Nations organisations find ways to flourish, such as in the case of The Glen (Chapter 7).

In many areas of social service delivery federally, as well as in NSW, First Nations organisations have had to adopt new financial models of business operation to sustain the delivery of specialised services to their communities, while simultaneously integrating the compliance demands of two tiers of government. Research presented in the chapters, and other research conducted by its authors, show that First Nations organisations in urban NSW 'struggle to compete for limited, short-term funding rounds with each other and larger non-Indigenous mainstream not-for-profits' (Howard-Wagner et al., 2023, p. 24). This research shows that current funding and administrative arrangements are at odds with government efforts to support and build the community-controlled sector under CTG 2020 (Howard-Wagner et al., 2023). The research shows that 'unstable short-term funding too often fails to keep pace with rising costs and evolving community needs' (Howard-Wagner et al., 2023, p. 24).

What government inquiries found

Alongside the research findings in this area, a 2013 NSW Inquiry into the Outsourcing of Community Service Delivery found that funding agreements and contract conditions themselves have become a source of variability across service delivery in NSW (NSW Legislative Assembly, 2013, p. 28). Even within agencies and departments, there can be a high degree of variability. For example, the inquiry found that the Department of Families and Community Services (FACS) NSW tailors schedules in funding agreements around location, duration, target group, and other conditions of service delivery. It found that 'smaller providers are often subject to short-term contractual arrangements, which compromises stability and client confidence in continuing service provision' (NSW Legislative Assembly, 2013, p. 28). The inquiry also found that:

> problems relating to the duration of contracts and funding continuity were also stressed by service providers during the Committee's visits to service providers in Western Sydney, Walgett, and Narrabri. Uncertainty about continued funding levels, compromising the need for long-term stability to build client relationships, is a major concern, particularly for Indigenous community providers.
>
> (NSW Legislative Assembly, 2013, p. 28)

The criteria vary for determining 'appropriate levels of remuneration for service delivery' (NSW Legislative Assembly, 2013, p. 26). Importantly, the NSW Legislative Assembly found that:

> … the arrangements used for allocating funding do not constitute procurement in any traditional sense, in that they do not reflect a fee for service. Rather, the expectation in the funding agreement is that a co-contribution will be required through 'fees and other sources'.
>
> (NSW Legislative Assembly, 2013, p. 28)

Chapter 5 demonstrates the devastating implications of co-contribution on Butucarbin Aboriginal Corporation. Overall, too, the chapters in this volume point to the extractive limitations of co-contribution. The conclusion details important considerations in this regard.

Key findings from this project

This edited volume is the product of a four-year collaborative research project. The project is a collaboration between three academic researchers, Deirdre Howard-Wagner, Karen Soldatić, and Janet Hunt, as well as nominated representative senior position-holders from six partner First Nations organisations. Our research team included: Jack Gibson, Butucarbin; June Riemer, FPDN; Cheryl Goh, Muru Mittigar; John Leha, formerly the NCIE and now CEO of AbSec; Deb Martin, Tjillari Aboriginal Justice Corporation;[7] and Chris Mason, The Glen. All nine team members remained dedicated and engaged in the research throughout the life of our project.

Our iterative critical co-design approach has entailed collective decision-making on all details of the research throughout the project with First Nations people in the driver's seat of data governance (i.e., collection, analysis, dissemination, and ownership) over four years. It entailed the fusion of comparative methods and strategies to co-create knowledge. The intention of our practices has been to decolonise our methodology, transform power relations, build a relational collaboration, and privilege Indigenous ways of being, knowing, and doing (Hernandez-Ibinarriaga & Martin, 2021). The research is premised upon a model of co-determination, where First Nations partner organisations and researchers come together to identify shared processes, goals, and outcomes, and work together with a shared goal of improving our knowledge and understanding of the effects of the NPM era on First Nations organisations in Significant Urban Areas (SUAs) in NSW. The research process included First Nations Discussion Circles, a statewide survey, in-depth case studies of First Nations organisations in SUAs in NSW, and desktop research that compared similar issues in other settler colonial contexts including Canada, Aotearoa New Zealand, and the United States of America.

Through the collection and analysis of survey data, the research identified characteristics that related across community-controlled organisations in SUAs in NSW. Surveys were directed to senior position-holders across identifiable federal and state-incorporated urban community-controlled organisations across 35 SUAs, as defined by the Australian Bureau of

---

7   Deb Martin's contributions did not result in a specific chapter, but she contributed more broadly to understanding the context in which First Nations organisation are working.

Statistics (ABS) in the Australian jurisdiction of NSW (ABS, 2016). We also included Queanbeyan because, although it is part of the Australian Capital Territory's Significant Urban Area, it is in NSW.

Fifty-two of the 474 First Nations organisations from the 35 SUAs in NSW participated in the survey, which is an 11 per cent response rate. The 52 survey respondents represented incorporated community-controlled First Nations organisations in NSW SUAs in that they proportionally reflected the different characteristics exemplified in the target population. While this is a low response rate, the data are representative samples across nearly all SUAs in terms of organisational type and size, sectoral focus, and spread of SUAs (see Howard-Wagner et al., 2023). The results show that this era has affected the capacity of community-controlled organisations to act in the interests of First Nations people (Howard-Wagner, Riemer et al., 2022). The ability to act in the interests of First Nations people depends on the capacity of organisations to act autonomously and to be self-determining. It concerns, as Howard-Wagner, Riemer et al. point out, 'the capacity to autonomously make decisions appropriate for their organisation and appropriate for the community that an organisation serves' (2022, p. 21). In the context of the communities that they serve, the case studies illustrate that obligation to the community is a core organisational value and a principle that dictates organisational behaviour.

It is a finding of the overarching research project, of which these case studies form part, that self-determination is expressed not only as organisational autonomy but also the autonomy of urban First Nations people to pursue collective, community-orientated visions and agendas through community-controlled First Nations organisations (Howard-Wagner, Riemer et al., 2022). Self-determination refers to the ability of First Nations organisations to create enabling conditions for First Nations people living in urban localities beyond simply delivering services to individuals. Howard-Wagner, Riemer et al. explain elsewhere that:

> First Nations people come together to create organisations that are multifaceted societal, cultural and political actors whose function is to improve the cultural, social, political, and economic life outcomes of First Nations people. The intergenerational visions and agendas of those who create First Nations organisations are directed beyond service delivery to Indigenous recovery, cultural continuity, development, and self-government. This is the place of First Nations organisations in Indigenous society.

(2022, p. 3)

The statewide survey confirmed that this ability to act or to have agency is associated with the ability to be autonomous and self-determining, which concerns the ability of community-controlled First Nations organisations to fulfil their missions, empower, give voice to First Nations people, and fulfil their societal function (Howard-Wagner et al., 2023, p. 3).

Importantly too, the results of that same statewide survey identified that the ability to act was inhibited by funding arrangements (Howard-Wagner et al., 2023). While their doors remained open, not only do the majority of community-controlled organisations in urban settings in NSW find it increasingly difficult to get funding, but they also report being under-funded and under-resourced. The results suggest that co-contribution is a prominent feature of how Indigenous services are currently funded at the state and federal levels.

The survey findings revealed high levels of fragility within the Indigenous sector and again identified that the primary source of that fragility is funding arrangements (Howard-Wagner et al., 2023, p. 22). The findings indicate that 90 per cent of participant First Nations organisations are in a fragile state, decreasing the capacity of those organisations to address the adversity of First Nations people and operate at the frontline of their communities (Howard-Wagner et al., 2023, p. 21). If not addressed, that fragility will have long-lasting effects, not only on government service delivery but on the resilience and recovery of First Nations people, hindering the agendas of Australian governments around closing the gap (Howard-Wagner et al., 2023, p. 24). This is a critical finding in light of the objective of CTG 2020.

Strengthening those findings is the discovery of a significant relationship between organisational strength and income, and the transformative capacity of organisations, 'particularly their ability to act autonomously and to be self-determining in a way that transforms the lives of First Nations people, their communities, and Indigenous society in a deliberate, conscious way' (Howard-Wagner et al., 2023, p. 22). That is, survey data analysis showed a significant relationship between autonomy, antifragility, and the ability to generate an income and fulfil those societal obligations (Howard-Wagner, Riemer et al., 2022, p. 22). To move from reactive adaptation and fragility to antifragility, a transformation of funding processes for autonomous and self-determining organisations is needed (Howard-Wagner et al., 2023, p. 22). As Howard-Wagner et al. note, 'This is an important public policy finding of our research' (2023, p. 22).

Going forward, the chapters in this volume are important for understanding the way that the Indigenous service market hinders the capacity to close the gap. The focus of this volume is on funding arrangements. While some First Nations organisations, like The Glen, have managed to navigate funding processes, move from a precarious to an antifragile state, and become an autonomous and self-determining organisation, this is not the only takeaway message of this volume. Funding processes are a significant barrier, but so too is the entrenched way that NPM has shaped the way that the Indigenous service delivery operates. There are many other problems with the Indigenous service delivery market, including, not least, the following: That government Indigenous service delivery has turned to focusing on the needs of the individual disadvantaged First Nations person (Coalition of Peaks, 2023). The creation of a government Indigenous service market saw the transfer of decision-making about services out of the hands of First Nations communities and organisations and into the hands of white bureaucrats who, on the whole, fail to understand local needs and priorities and who operate within a deficit-based and often paternalistic mindset (Coalition of Peaks, 2023).

This is why initiatives like CTG 2020, Local Decision Making in NSW, the Northern Territory and Queensland, and Empowered Communities are so critical. Such initiatives have the potential to elevate local and regional voices to ensure that Indigenous service design and delivery is focused on local needs and priorities. Efforts around transforming government under Priority Reform Three and the *OCHRE* Local Decision Making in NSW initiative align with broader efforts to transform government internationally in what is now commonly described as the post-NPM period. 'Post-NPM' concerns the decade or so of widespread international reconfiguring of New Public Management.

Transforming the way government works at the interface between First Nations communities and organisations and government domains introduces many new considerations. If implemented as intended, such initiatives could potentially improve engagement with First Nations organisations and communities or lead to shared decision-making and the delivery of services in partnership with First Nations organisations and communities, or better still devolve decision-making to local communities. To work, government agencies would truly need to transform the way that they do business with First Nations communities and organisations, abandoning those deeply entrenched NPM principles and practices that shape the very way they think, practice, and operate in relation to First Nations communities and organisations.

The key barrier to transforming government is that the Indigenous service market as it presently operates is structurally still government-centric with the hierarchical state system of government and administration dominating Indigenous non-hierarchical forms of governance and accountability. The practice of Western non-Indigenous ways of being, knowing, and doing continue to dominate the decisions and actions of government agencies and their employees, and tokenistic inclusion of Indigenous representation in decision-making, not only perpetuates power relations but is a form of institutional racism (Howard-Wagner & Markham, 2023). Such practices continue, despite initiatives like *OCHRE* Local Decision Making and CTG 2020.

To illustrate, within months of the Commonwealth Implementation Plan 2023 being released, the Australian Productivity Commission released its 'Review of the National Agreement on Closing the Gap Draft Report' (Productivity Commission, 2023a) along with 'Priority Reform 3: Transforming Government Organisations Information Paper No. 4 Draft Report' (Productivity Commission, 2023b). In those two reports, the Productivity Commission makes a number of critical observations about the actions of all governments to date around CTG 2020, including in relation to Priority Reform Three – transforming mainstream organisations. The Productivity Commission identifies that 'the primary concern about the [CTG] Agreement is that implementation has not moved beyond "business as usual"' (Productivity Commission, 2023b, p. 4). This too is a key finding of the *OCHRE* Local Decision Making stage one and two evaluations (Howard-Wagner & Markham, 2023).

Chapter outlines and insights

The premise of this volume is that the adverse effects of the Indigenous service market and the associated system created by the Howard Coalition Government were not a case of a well-conceived policy failing to deliver where it counts. Retrospectively, and arguably, as this volume illustrates, the Howard Coalition Government made an avoidable policy error in which something good or of value was eliminated when it mainstreamed and marketised government Indigenous service delivery in 2005. At points within this volume, the dark sides of policymaking are examined and interpreted as acts of wilful ignorance on the part of the government (Howlett, 2022).[8]

The volume illustrates how the quiet revolution in Indigenous affairs changed the rules of the game (Howard-Wagner, 2016, 2018; Hunt, 2016; Moran & Porter, 2014; Moran et al., 2014; Sullivan, 2009, 2015). In Chapter 2, Deirdre Howard-Wagner considers the federal Howard Coalition government's quiet revolution as a far more complex government agenda. Drawing on Peck and Tickell's (2017) analysis of 'actually existing neoliberalism', the chapter identifies observable 'roll-back' neoliberal moment of 'active destruction and discreditation' (Peck & Tickell, 2017, p. 384). It explains the period between 1996 and 2004 as a period of highly politicised federal Indigenous policy, which culminated in the mainstreaming of Indigenous affairs and the formation of a new Indigenous service market for the delivery of government services to First Nations people. The rationale for government intervention in Indigenous service delivery was provided by the neoliberal theory of welfare failure. One implication of the Howard Coalition Government viewing Indigenous policy as separatism is that, in mainstreaming Indigenous service delivery to overcome Indigenous disadvantage, it was arguably applying a malevolent policy to fix what it saw as the excesses of the state. From the outset, the government Indigenous service system operated within a deficit logic towards community-controlled First Nations organisations. There was also the wilful ignorance of Indigenous interests by the Howard Coalition Government.

Chapter 2 situates the rationale for policy change within the context of neoliberalism Howard-style. Neoliberalism Howard-style extended beyond the realm of the economic to the social, ensuing a radical restructuring of Australian society and the welfare state that resulted in what Rose and Miller observe in other contexts as a 'profound transformation in the mechanisms for governing social life' (Rose & Miller, 1992, p. 200).

Chapter 3 is a case study of Australia's peak First Nations disability advocacy organisation, the FPDN, a community-controlled organisation based in Sydney South, NSW, by June Riemer, Kim Spurway, and Karen Soldatić.

---

8   In considering the 'dark side' of policymaking, Michael Howlett examines the motivations for wilful ignorance (2022). He describes wilful ignorance as '… intentional ignorance, the phenomenon of burying one's head in the sand or purposely ignoring existing evidence and persisting with false beliefs which support pre-established positions' (Howlett, 2022, p. 308).

This case study of FPDN illustrates the unique contribution FPDN makes as an advocate for Australia's First Nations people living with a disability. Over time, FPDN has become the leading national Indigenous disability advocacy organisation. It has received international recognition across multiple United Nations institutions for its strategic advocacy. The in-depth case study in Chapter 3 provides an overview of FPDN's history, the impacts of changing government funding and procurement structures, and the ongoing struggle for formal recognition of the unique Indigenous knowledge, know-how, and skills that are required to effectively advocate for First Nations people with disabilities. In the chapter, Riemer, Spurway, and Soldatić explain how funding and grant contracting have unique and novel implications for small representative advocacy organisations such as FPDN, which remains significantly under-funded and under-represented across all spheres of national policy. Chapter 3 reveals how funding has led to the extraction and colonisation of the unique knowledge held by First Nations organisations, which is grounded in their ongoing community relationships of trust, respect, and dignity. The intensive time and work FPDN puts into building collaborative and respectful knowledge practices with local community members and partners with whom they work is not priced into market funding models. The chapter also reveals how it navigates the ideological differences between its Indigenous-centric values and the conventions of Australian governments around both disability and funding, which are rooted in Western conceptions, as it strives to fulfil its obligations to First Nations people living with disability.

Chapter 4 presents the case of one of Western Sydney's longest-standing community-controlled not-for-profit First Nations organisations: Butucarbin Aboriginal Corporation. Butucarbin was founded in 1993 at the tail end of the era of self-determination and community development. It was established in a different policy and funding environment, its costs were covered, and this enabled innovation and self-determination. Today, Butucarbin operates in a funding environment that not only undervalues its time and labour but in which its basic costs are not factored into the unit price for the services it delivers. Chapter authors Jennifer Beale, Jack Gibson, and Deirdre Howard-Wagner attribute these current conditions in part to the competitive undercutting of costs by large not-for-profit organisations. But importantly, the authors explain how this funding model is poorly matched to the needs of a small-scale community-controlled First Nations organisation. They also explain how expectations set for the delivery of services by funding bodies are not matched to the needs of local

First Nations people and are not helping to reach CTG targets. In the last 20 years, Butucarbin has had no opportunity to build capacity, build reserves, or initiate long-term planning. These 20 years of administrative and regulatory change, scarcity of resources, increased workloads, and instability have fatigued Butucarbin. This has suppressed self-determination and agency and led to passive resignation among Butucarbin's executive and board about its future as a community-controlled organisation engaged in service provision to Aboriginal people living in Western Sydney. Butucarbin's board is faced with an unsustainable funding situation. While Butucarbin does not plan on closing, further change will likely mark its end as a community-controlled First Nations organisation engaged in service provision. This would represent a further whittling away of Indigenous community infrastructure in an urban locality in dire need of community-focused and community-driven initiatives.

The pressure of the competitive marketplace on community-controlled social enterprises and businesses, evident in Chapter 5, is also shown in Chapter 6. Chapter 5 presents a case study of the National Centre of Indigenous Excellence (NCIE), an Indigenous not-for-profit social enterprise located on the former site of the Redfern Public School in Sydney, NSW. To draw out its unique contribution to the Indigenous sector, authors John Leha, Clare McHugh, Kim Spurway, and Karen Soldatić review the history of the NCIE, its governance structures, and its unique role in working with, and for, First Nations communities in Australia. The case study interrogates some of the challenges and successes this unique First Nations organisation faces in the era of NPM. As a social enterprise, NCIE was 'driven by a public or community cause'. Leha et al. explain how NCIE obtained most of its funding from commercial operations, not from grants or donations. It has mostly used these funds for its social mission. The organisation has expanded considerably since 2010, developing and testing a gamut of unique, diverse business strategies to develop a sustainable governance model and long-term financial independence from the government. These strategies have been shaped by its parent body, the Indigenous Land and Sea Corporation, within the confines of the NPM policy environment. Despite these efforts, NCIE remained commercially unviable. This chapter will show that the NPM approach prioritises neoliberal rationality, managerialism, market-driven frameworks, and the supposed quick-time efficiency of modern organisations. This neo-colonial approach emphasises commerciality over place-based, embedded First Nations knowledge, community governance processes, and longer-term community-focused productivities. This creates tensions for the NCIE, as it balances the demands placed on it by funding and governance bodies with the expectations of First Nations communities. The NCIE continues to work at a grassroots level as a not-for-profit social enterprise that places community needs before those of the market.

Chapter 6 is a case study of Muru Mittigar, a Dharug social enterprise that has been operating on Dharug Country in Western Sydney since 1999, authored by Janet Hunt, Cheryl Goh, Ros Fogg, and Christopher Galloway. Muru Mittigar currently employs 39 staff, 62 per cent of them Aboriginal. As many of the First Nations people who live in Western Sydney come from other parts of NSW and Australia, Muru Mittigar's First Nations staff come from diverse backgrounds. Over its 22-year history, Muru Mittigar shifted from essentially being a subsidiary of the Penrith Lakes Development Corporation to becoming an independent, self-reliant organisation. Muru Mittigar focuses on three areas of work: community, Country, and culture. However, to sustain the cultural education and community work it values, which includes increasing rates of Indigenous employment, Muru Mittigar has to win contracts in the commercial market. As the case study shows, Muru Mittigar has held a diverse range of contracts procuring its land management, bushfire mitigation, and similar services. These contracts have enabled people to work on Dharug Country and, increasingly, on the Country of others. Although Muru Mittigar benefits from opportunities for Indigenous procurement under NSW policies discussed above, it is clear that the work it has to undertake is always defined by the institution (government or private sector) procuring the work. Muru Mittigar delivers on these externally defined contracts and thereby creates employment for First Nations people, yet these arrangements limit its capacity to be self-determining. Furthermore, Muru Mittigar competes with mainstream organisations which, without the same social goals, do not have the same costs. As Muru Mittigar seeks to engage First Nations people who have often been unemployed for some time, it has to provide a great deal of personal support and training at extra cost. This case study shows how the expectation, characteristic of NPM, that First Nations organisations can achieve their social objectives (of community development and self-determination) through commercial market mechanisms, is incorrect. While Muru Mittigar has survived and achieved a lot, the NPM framework within which it tries to achieve its goals does not make it easy to do so.

The case study in Chapter 6 reveals how legislative frameworks that are intended to enhance Indigenous opportunity around procurement, like those in NSW and at the federal level, are insufficient. As Chapter 6 shows, while operating within the Indigenous business sector and relying heavily on Indigenous procurement in a market-based contracting environment, Muru Mittigar struggles to realise its community goals. In Chapter 6, Hunt et al. illustrate how Indigenous procurement operates as a weakly defined social procurement environment that is not only cost-competitive to the detriment of community-controlled First Nations organisations but also currently fails to fully remunerate cultural skills and knowledge. Hunt et al. point to the 'hidden subsidy' that Muru Mittigar provides, as a social enterprise, to enable the social goals of closing gaps to succeed. They also explain how Muru Mittigar operates in a short-term and increasingly uncertain contract environment, in which there is growing competition from other First Nations organisations and non-Indigenous organisations that use 'black cladding'. Hunt et al. conclude that remunerating for cultural skills and knowledge, and resourcing important cultural and community work that an organisation like Muru Mittigar undertakes, would not only be an important step in correcting Indigenous procurement but would also recognise that those operating in this market are not Indigenous for-profit businesses alone but also social enterprises whose goals include broader community benefit with associated costs, pointing to the vast inequality of power in this market.

In Chapter 7, Deirdre Howard-Wagner and Chris Mason illustrate the point that even those organisations that are antifragile today, like The Glen, have gone through a difficult journey. A decade ago, The Glen struggled to get recognition for its expertise. It lost considerable federal and state funding sources. The Glen did not simply adapt to its funding cuts but strategically tailored its response to these challenges. Like many First Nations organisations, Chapter 7 shows that The Glen has accomplished extraordinary things in the NPM era despite chronic underfunding and considerable scrutiny. Today, The Glen's outstanding efforts mobilising its story as a successful alcohol and drug rehabilitation centre, and its significant contribution to addressing drug and alcohol dependency, are well recognised. The Glen takes a holistic approach to rehabilitation, with a focus on cultural strength. The heart of its program has not changed much in the last decade. Its expertise in addressing drug and alcohol dependence among Aboriginal and Torres Strait Islander men illustrates how Indigenous practices benefit men from non-Indigenous backgrounds, and it has become a leader in developing a 'model of care' for its sector. Over the last decade, it has also become a leading community-controlled First Nations enterprise. The story of how The Glen has navigated the NPM era illustrates how organisations can interact with a government Indigenous market system without compromising their organisational values and systems. While The Glen is an example of how an organisation can go from fragility to antifragility in this market, it also provides important insights around particular models of funding and how government investment in infrastructure, along with fee-for-services, factors significantly in building antifragility for community-controlled First Nations organisations (Howard-Wagner et al., 2023).

In concluding, Chapter 8 returns to an analysis of the overarching effects of funding arrangements, explaining what needs to change in Australia. The chapter returns to the proposition that a purely NPM approach was never suitable for government Indigenous service delivery in Australia, but reflects more deeply on what it is about the system that needs to be reformed. In doing so, it focuses on the institutional practices that operate as extractive and exploitative, explaining why the system needs to be not only reconfigured but decolonised. To make such a contribution, the concluding chapter considers the key findings across the volume, which illustrate how what is valued, and by what measure, has been a point of tension in the way governments and others have done business with First Nations organisations in the NPM era. It revisits the findings in the chapters about the economising, exploitative, and racialised effects of the existing government Indigenous service delivery market, particularly its funding arrangements. The chapter argues that fundamental change needs to be made to the way governments fund Indigenous service delivery and points to some of the practical changes needed.

References

Australian Bureau of Statistics (2016). Australian statistical geography standard (ASGS): Volume 4 – Significant Urban Areas, Urban Centres and Localities, section of State, July 2016. www.abs.gov.au/ausstats/abs@.nsf/Lookup/by%20Subject/1270.0.55.004~July%202016~Main%20Features~Design%20of%20SUA-15

Australian Council of Social Services (2013). Australian community sector survey 2013: National report. ACOSS Paper 202. www.acoss.org.au/images/uploads/Australian_Community_Sector_Survey_2013_ACOSS.pdf

Brenner, N., Peck, J., & Theodore, N. (2010). Variegated neoliberalization: Geographies, modalities, pathways. *Global Networks, 10*(2), 182–222. doi.org/10.1111/j.1471-0374.2009.00277.x

Castleden, H., Morgan, V. S., & Neimanis, A. (2010). Researchers' perspectives on collective/community co-authorship in community-based participatory Indigenous research. *Journal of Empirical Research on Human Research Ethics*, *5*(4), 23–32. doi.org/10.1525/jer.2010.5.4.23

Christensen, T., & Laegreid, P. (2017). Introduction – Theoretical approach and research questions. In P. Laegreid (Ed.), *Transcending New Public Management: The transformation of public sector reforms*. Routledge.

Coalition of Peaks (2023). *A new way of working: Talking about what's needed to close the gap in life outcomes between Aboriginal and Torres Strait Islander people and other Australians*. Resources. www.coalitionofpeaks.org.au/resources

Giles, A. R., & Castleden, H. (2008). Community co-authorship in academic publishing: A commentary. *Canadian Journal of Native Education*, *31*(1), 208–213.

Hernandez-Ibinarriaga, D., & Martin, B. (2021). Critical co-design and agency of the real. *Design and Culture*, *13*(3), 253–276. doi.org/10.1080/17547075.2021.1966731

Howard, C. (2015). Rethinking post-NPM governance: The bureaucratic struggle to implement one-stop-shopping for government services in Alberta. *Public Organization Review*, *15*, 237–254. doi.org/10.1007/s11115-014-0272-0

Howard-Wagner, D. (2016). Child wellbeing and protection as a regulatory system in the neoliberal age: Forms of Aboriginal agency and resistance engaged to confront the challenges for Aboriginal people and community-based Aboriginal organisations. *Australian Indigenous Law Review*, *19*, 88–102.

Howard-Wagner, D. (2018). Aboriginal organisations, self-determination, and the neoliberal age: A case study of how the 'game has changed' for Aboriginal organisations in Newcastle. In D. Howard-Wagner, M. Bargh, & I. Altamirano-Jiménez (Eds), *The neoliberal state, recognition and Indigenous rights: New paternalism to new imaginings*. ANU Press. doi.org/10.22459/CAEPR40.07.2018.12

Howard-Wagner, D. (2021). *Indigenous invisibility in the city: Successful resurgence and community development hidden in plain sight*. Routledge. doi.org/10.4324/9780429506512

Howard-Wagner, D. (2025). Urban First Nations organisations and the effects of new funding rationalities and technologies of governing in the New Public Management era. In E. Strakosch, J. Lahn, & P. Sullivan (Eds), *Bureaucratic occupation: Government and First Nations peoples.* Springer.

Howard-Wagner, D., Riemer, J., Leha, J., Mason, C., Soldatić, K., Hunt, J., & Gibson, J. (2022). *The Indigenous service market: Conflicting ways of seeing urban First Nations organisations in the era of NPM* (CAEPR Discussion Paper 296). The Australian National University.

Howard-Wagner, D., Soldatić, K., Spurway, K., Hunt, J., Harrington, M., Riemer, J., Leha, J., Mason, C., Fogg, R., Goh, C., & Gibson, J. (2022). Indigenous organisational resistance in the NPM era. In K. Soldatić & L. St Guillaume (Eds), *Social suffering in the neoliberal age: State power, logics and resistance*. Routledge.

Howard-Wagner, D., Soldatić, K., Riemer, J., Leha, J., Mason, C., Goh, C., Hunt, J., & Gibson, J. (2023). Organisational fragility among urban FNOs in the era of New Public Management. *Australian Journal of Social Issues*, *58*(3), 523–549. doi.org/10.1002/ajs4.243

Howard-Wagner, D., & Markham, F. (2023). *Preliminary findings of the OCHRE local decision making evaluation stage 2* (CAEPR Commissioned Paper 01/23). Centre for Aboriginal Economic Policy Research, ANU College of Arts and Social Sciences. doi.org/10.25911/YPGB-E627

Howlett, M. (2022). Avoiding a Panglossian policy science: The need to deal with the darkside of policy-maker and policy-taker behaviour. *Public Integrity*, *24*(3), 306–318. doi.org/10.1080/10999922.2021.1935560

Hunt, J. 2016. *Let's talk about success: Exploring factors behind positive change in Aboriginal communities* (CAEPR Working Paper 109/2016). Centre for Aboriginal Economic Policy Research, ANU College of Arts and Social Sciences. caepr.cass. anu.edu.au/sites/default/files/docs/Working_Paper_16-046-%2824May16% 29_0.pdf

Jordan, K., Markham, F., & Altman, J. (2020). *Linking Indigenous communities with regional development: Australia overview* (CAEPR Commissioned Report No. 5). Centre for Aboriginal Economic Policy Research, ANU College of Arts and Social Sciences. doi.org/10.25911/5f7edceea4190

Lapsley, I. (2009). New Public Management: The cruellest invention of the human spirit? *Abacus*, *45*(1), 1–21. doi.org/10.1111/j.1467-6281.2009.00275.x

Leong, C., & Howlett, M. (2022). Policy learning, policy failure, and the mitigation of policy risks: Re-thinking the lessons of policy success and failure. *Administration & Society*, *54*(7), 1379–1401. doi.org/10.1177/00953997211065344

Markham, F., & Biddle, N. (2018). *Indigenous population change in the 2016 Census* (CAEPR 2016 Census Papers, 1/2016). Centre for Aboriginal Economic Policy Research, ANU College of Arts and Social Sciences. caepr.cass.anu.edu.au/sites/ default/files/docs/2024/11/CAEPR_Census_Paper_1_2018.pdf

Marsh, I. (2015). The malfunctions of New Public Management: A case study of governance in Indigenous affairs. In J. Wanna, E. A. Lindquist, & P. Marshall (Eds), *New Accountabilities, New Challenges*. ANU Press. doi.org/10.22459/NANC.04.2015.09

McCaskill, D. N., FitzMaurice, K. D., & Cidro, J. (2011). *Toronto Aboriginal research project*. Toronto Aboriginal Support Services Council.

Meagher, G., Perche, D., & Stebbing, A. (2022). *Designing social service markets: Risk, regulation and rent-seeking*. ANU Press. doi.org/10.22459/DSSM.2022

Melo, S., De Waele, L., & Polzer, T. (2022). The role of post-New Public Management in shaping innovation: The case of a public hospital. *International Review of Administrative Sciences*, *88*(4), 1032–1049. doi.org/10.1177/002085 2320977626

Moran, M., Porter, D., & Curth-Bibb, J. (2014). *Funding Indigenous organisations: Improving governance performance through innovations in public finance management in remote Australia* (Closing the Gap Clearinghouse Issues Paper No. 11). Australian Institute of Health and Welfare. www.aihw.gov.au/getmedia/cc5909f4-869f-4a75-aed9-e170d1e0a5b8/ctgc-ip11.pdf

Moran, M., & Porter, D. (2014). Reinventing the governance of public finances in remote Indigenous Australia. *Australian Journal of Public Administration*, *73*(1), 115–127. doi.org/10.1111/1467-8500.12064

Moran, M., Porter, D., & Curth-Bibb, J. (2016). The impact of funding modalities on the performance of Indigenous organisations. *Australian Journal of Public Administration*, *75*(3), 359–372. doi.org/10.1111/1467-8500.12192

Morrison, S. (2020, 12 February). Prime Minister's national Closing the Gap statement [speech]. Parliament House, Canberra. web.archive.org/web/2020 0226122910/www.pm.gov.au/media/address-closing-gap-statement-parliament

Muir, K., & Salignac, F. (2017). Can market forces stimulate social change? A case example using the national disability insurance scheme in Australia. *Third Sector Review*, *23*(2), 57–80. search.informit.org/doi/10.3316/informit.2005 39427687469

National Agreement on Closing the Gap (2020). *Closing the Gap in partnership: National agreement on Closing the Gap*. www.closingthegap.gov.au/sites/default/files/files/national-agreement-ctg.pdf

National Indigenous Australians Agency (NIAA) (2020). Priority reforms. *Closing the Gap in partnership: National agreement on Closing the Gap*. www.closingthegap.gov.au/priority-reforms

NSW Government (2011). *Stronger together 2: Annual report 2011–2012*. Families and Community Services, Ageing, Disability and Homecare, data.gov.au/dataset/ds-nsw-4015325e-0513-47ad-95c1-040844bce753/details?q=

NSW Government (2013). *NSW Aboriginal health plan 2013–2023*. www1.health.nsw.gov.au/pds/ActivePDSDocuments/PD2012_066.pdf

NSW Legislative Assembly (2013). *Outsourcing community service delivery*. Committee on Community Services Final Report, Report 2/55–November 2013.

Page, A. (2018). Fragile positions in the new paternalism: Indigenous community organisations during the 'Advancement' era in Australia. In D. Howard-Wagner, M. Bargh, & I. Altamirano-Jiménez (Eds), *The neoliberal state, recognition and Indigenous rights: New paternalism to new imaginings*. ANU Press. doi.org/10.22459/CAEPR40.07.2018.10

Peck, J., & Tickell, A. (2017). Neoliberalizing space. In R. Martin (Ed.), *Economy. Critical essays in human geography*. Routledge. doi.org/10.4324/9781351159203

Productivity Commission (2023a). *Review of the National Agreement on Closing the Gap: Draft report*. www.pc.gov.au/inquiries/current/closing-the-gap-review/draft/closing-the-gap-review-draft.pdf

Productivity Commission (2023b). *Review of the National Agreement on Closing the Gap Priority Reform 3: Transforming government organisations*. Information Paper 4: Draft report. www.pc.gov.au/inquiries/current/closing-the-gap-review/draft/ctg-review-draft-information4.pdf

Rose, N., & Miller, P. (1992). Political power beyond the state: Problematics of government. *British Journal of Sociology*, *43*(2), 173–205. doi.org/10.2307/591464

Snyder, M., Wilson, K., & Whitford, J. (2015). Examining the urban Aboriginal policy gap: Impacts on service delivery for mobile urban Aboriginal peoples in Winnipeg, Canada. *Aboriginal Policy Studies*, *5*(1), 3–27. doi.org/10.5663/aps.v5i1.23259

Sookraj, D., Hutchinson, P., Evans, M., Murphy, M., & Okanagan Urban Aboriginal Health Research Collective (2012). Aboriginal organizational response to the need for culturally appropriate services in three small Canadian cities. *Journal of Social Work*, *12*(2), 136–157. doi.org/10.1177/1468017310381366

Sullivan, P. (2009). Reciprocal accountability: Assessing the accountability environment in Australian aboriginal affairs policy. *International Journal of Public Sector Management*, *22*(1), 57–72. doi.org/10.1108/09513550910922405

Sullivan, P. (2015). *Reciprocal relationship: Accountability for public value in the Aboriginal community sector*. The Lowitja Institute.

Sullivan, P. (2018). The tyranny of neoliberal public management and the challenge for Aboriginal community organisations. In D. Howard-Wagner, M. Bargh, & I. Altamirano-Jiménez (Eds), *The neoliberal state, recognition and Indigenous rights: New paternalism to new imaginings*. ANU Press. doi.org/10.22459/CAEPR40.07.2018.11

Woolford, A., & Curran, A. (2013). Community positions, neoliberal dispositions: Managing nonprofit social services within the bureaucratic field. *Critical Sociology*, *39*(1), 45–63. doi.org/10.1177/0896920512439728

2

The 'quiet revolution' in Indigenous affairs: How Australia ended up with a marketised Indigenous service delivery system in the New Public Management era

Deirdre Howard-Wagner

In the 1980s, the Australian Government embarked on a package of sweeping economic reforms under the leadership of then Labor prime minister Bob Hawke and treasurer Paul Keating. In 1983, Australia became a fully fledged participant in the international financial market when the Hawke Government decided to 'float' the Australian dollar and deregulate the financial market to allow the free movement of financial capital in and out of Australia (Capling et al., 1998, p. 47). This was a process of deregulation, trade liberalisation, and industry restructuring. Deregulation meant that rural towns lost services, including banking and health services. Trade liberalisation had a significant effect on pastoralism. Industry restructuring affected the steel, passenger, motor vehicle, textile, clothing, and footwear industries, which impacted major regional areas such as Newcastle (Capling et al., 1998, p. 57).

In the early 1990s, the succeeding Labor prime minister Keating took these reforms a step further, with a wave of privatisation that saw public assets, for example, Qantas and the Commonwealth Bank, sold off (Chandler-Mather, 2021, p. 1). In 1992, the Keating government established the National Competition Policy Review, also known as the Hilmer Review, which inspired the National Competition Policy (NCP) and expanded the reach of competitive markets into more sectors of Australia's economy and society. In 1996, the federal Keating Labor Government endorsed the *Competitive Tendering and Contracting by Public Sector Agencies* report (Chandler-Mather, 2021, p. 1). As Chandler-Mather notes, the report 'recommended a massive expansion of outsourcing in the public sector, via contracting and competitive tendering, the further marketisation of public administration, and a hollowing out of government agencies' (Chandler-Mather, 2021, p. 1).

The state and territory governments followed suit (Chandler-Mather, 2021, p. 1). Chandler-Mather argues that this period saw governments across the nation 'aggressively enforcing a competitive, market logic in crucial sectors like electricity, gas, aviation, finance, transport, and communications' (2021, p. 1). Australian governments were adopting an Australian style of neoliberalism to address Australia's economic problems (Chandler-Mather, 2021, p. 1). Further, Kruk and Bastaja argue that the NCP committed NSW to the creation of competitive markets for public sector goods and services (2002, p. 65). They indicate that 'with the concentration of revenue and taxation powers held at Commonwealth level, the federal government had played an increasingly influential role in the delivery of services at state level' (2002, p. 63). However, they also point out that NSW adopted an approach that integrated 'more strategic partnerships, increased community involvement, integrated service outcomes and the use of electronic technology' (Kruk & Bastaja, 2002, p. 62).

After coming to power in 1996, the Howard Coalition Government continued on the path of major economic reform, which extended from the privatisation of Telstra through to industrial relations. The Australian Public Service was gradually reformed and reduced in 1996. Approximately 15,000 public service positions were made redundant (Taylor, 1996). Many positions were reclassified. Departments were restructured and service delivery was overhauled. Management and accountability regimes changed. The reforms to the provision of government services initiated by Keating continued, emulating international changes to public administration known as NPM. This period of economic reform in Australia marked the introduction of reforms related to NPM across the public sector and government service delivery.

Neoliberalism Howard-style extended beyond the realm of the economic to the social, ensuing a radical restructuring of Australian society and the welfare state that resulted in what Rose and Miller observe in other contexts as a 'profound transformation in the mechanisms for governing social life' (Rose & Miller, 1992, p. 200). Society was governed for economic efficiency, and market-like relations transformed the social, welfare, and public sectors (Beeson & Firth, 1998, p. 6). At the same time as reforming the public sector and bringing the NPM into effect, the Howard Coalition Government problematised Keynesian social democracy and began restructuring the Australian welfare state. For Howard, Keynesian welfarism hampered economic growth, bred passivity and dependence, and undermined individual freedom.

A distinct difference between the Howard Government's neoliberal reform agenda and that of the previous two federal Labor governments was in these welfare reforms, including changes to assistance for the unemployed. Howard put in place markets where markets had not previously existed or did not have a foothold in welfare sectors, through mechanisms that effectively privatised welfarism. The Howard Government introduced a 30 per cent rebate as an incentive for those aged 30 and above to encourage Australians to take out private health insurance, creating a two-tier health system in Australia. In 1997, the Howard Government introduced the *Aged Care Act*, opening the way for aged care to become a for-profit industry.

The role of the Australian Public Service in the provision of social services, welfare, and other public services was restructured: rather than the privatisation of the public sector, this was the marketisation of services, including the promotion of competition and enterprise. The Howard Government did not advocate the full privatisation of social or welfare services. Instead, as Connell, Fawcett, and Meagher point out, the Howard Government created 'markets for things whose commodification was once almost unimaginable: water, body parts, pollution and social welfare among them' (2009, p. 331).

In 2003, the then secretary of the Department of the Prime Minister and Cabinet, Peter Shergold, announced 'the new public management' that would 'have marked generational change in the APS' (Shergold, 2003).

Shergold described NPM as a 'quiet revolution', increasing 'competition in the delivery of services to government and on behalf of government' (Shergold, 2003). NPM was the instrument that Australian governments used to change public sector management and the expenditure of public funds. NPM was applied for a similar purpose internationally and its use has seen major changes to government service delivery (Salamon, 2002). In Australia, NPM was applied to create government service delivery markets across various sectors, such as the employment and disability sectors. The Australian Government's rationale for this approach was that it benefited consumers who gained increased choice, higher-quality services, and more diverse and innovative providers (Meagher et al., 2022, p. 2). As Meagher, Perch, and Stebbing point out, 'Australian policymakers put great faith in market mechanisms, invoking this faith in support of extending contracts, competition, and choice to more and more service areas' (2022, p. 2). Chandler-Mather observes that the state and territory governments all followed suit (2021, p. 1).

The rolling out of NPM was characterised by changes in funding structures and contractual arrangements (such as competitive tendering and so-called results-based management) and by new forms of government monitoring and regulation (such as accreditation, auditing, and corporate governance training) (Barrett, 2004). Performance targets would measure the provision of services based on performance indicators often referred to as 'outcomes' and 'outputs'. Furthermore, as Deakin and Michie observe:

> if there is a single strand that runs through the changes wrought by the neoliberal revolution … it is the revival of contract as the foremost organising mechanism of economic activity.
>
> (1997, p. 1, cited in O'Flynn, 2007, p. 355)

The contract encouraged competition and the doctrine of competition was central to the market's development, along with competitive tendering and contracting by governments as popular NPM instruments (O'Flynn, 2007, p. 355–356).

It was through NPM that neoliberal market mechanisms became 'general-purpose tools for public policy' (Muir & Salignac 2017, p. 58). It is for such reasons that NPM in Australia has been described by anthropologist Patrick Sullivan, who has studied this period closely, as 'neoliberal public management' (Sullivan, 2018). NPM is seen as the neoliberalisation of government service delivery because it entails the marketisation of those services.[1] NPM takes its principles and cues from the free market economy and *Homo economicus*. The principles of NPM are applied to the public realm with the view to it running in an entrepreneurial or businesslike manner (Fatemi & Behmanesh, 2012). As leading social policy scholars who have written widely on the effect of the NPM across the social service sectors more broadly, Connell, Fawcett, and Meagher point out, NPM concerns the expansion of the principles of neoliberalism, such as a free market, competition, best value for money, and optimum cost efficiency, across government services (2009, p. 331). Governments restructured the delivery of those services to enable and promote economic competition. Governments also put in place policies and regulations to remove all obstacles to the functioning of this competitive and efficient market and transform the way business is done through the inculcation of enterprising values and market-like relations across it (Howard-Wagner et al., 2018, p. 22). Stuart Hall (2005) refers to this type of reform as 'entrepreneurial governance' in that 'it promotes competition between service providers … focuses not on inputs but on outcomes … and prefers market mechanisms to administrative ones' (Hall, 2005, p. 1). The marketisation of government services is an economic model based on value for money in which potential service providers competitively tender for the contracting out of social, welfare, and other public services.

Prime minister Howard continued what his predecessor, prime minister Keating, started, but under his leadership Australian neoliberalism took new twists and turns (Howard-Wagner, 2018, p. 1335). There were important distinctions in the relationship between economic and social reform between the Hawke/Keating and Howard governments. Arguably, the distinction came down to what Brenner, Peck, and Theodore refer to as variegations in neoliberal agendas (2010). In this context, the variegations in neoliberalism under successive Hawke and Keating Labor governments compared with the Howard Coalition Government manifested in the marked distinctions in national policymaking in Indigenous affairs.

In 1990, the Aboriginal and Torres Strait Islander Commission (ATSIC) was established under the Hawke government as a vehicle for the realisation of self-determination, and in accordance with a driving principle of his government that First Nations peoples should have greater control over their

---

1   While Australia has seen many variants of neoliberalism at the federal and state and territory levels (Dean, 2004, p. 159), the central tenet of all variants is a 'market society' – the market is seen as the means to bring about a just and efficient society.

affairs. ATSIC's dual role was the administration of Indigenous programs and the representation of Indigenous or First Nations' interests, allowing First Nations people to participate in decisions about policies and programs that affected them.

In 1992, Keating's momentous Redfern speech on 10 December 1992, six months after the High Court *Mabo* decision, acknowledged the violence of colonisation, recognised Indigenous rights, and accepted the importance of reparation. In contrast, Howard's speeches denied the history of colonisation and redefined Indigenous rights. In 1997, then prime minister John Howard asserted in an interview on national television that 'the pendulum had swung too far in favour of Aboriginal people' (Howard, 1997b, p. 1). Howard was referring to the special measures in Australian law and policy aimed at addressing past injustices and granting Aboriginal and Torres Strait Islander peoples separate Indigenous rights (Howard-Wagner, 2006, 2018). Howard not only denied racial difference (Winant, 1997), but went as far as to construct racial difference as a privileged state and set out to erase it (Howard-Wagner, 2018, p. 1337).

Many of the chapters in this volume highlight the adverse effects of specific Indigenous policy moments under the Howard Coalition Government, such as the abolition of ATSIC and mainstreaming of Indigenous services in 2005. This chapter provides important context on the dark side of policymaking that led to the marketisation of Indigenous service delivery under the Howard Government. It considers Howard's agenda and his intent, arguing that Howard did not simply roll out NPM in Indigenous service delivery. Howard's aim was to wind back Indigenous rights.

The chapter is written from the standpoint that ignorance in Indigenous policymaking at this time was not neutral or incidental, but what Samson (2013), Sullivan and Tuana (2007), Howlett (2022) and others describe as 'wilful'. It considers the strategic application of wilful ignorance as a deliberate, cultivated, and sustained act of prejudice in relation to Indigenous policymaking under the Howard Government (Godlewska et al., 2010, p. 417; Lawrence & O'Faircheallaigh, 2022, p. 93).

Neoliberalism and its application to Indigenous affairs, Howard-style

Neoliberalism Hawke- and later Keating-style was along the lines of what is known as the Ordoliberal model of neoliberalism. A key feature of Ordoliberalism is that it does not abandon the policy of social justice. The Ordoliberal model promotes a form of 'government constructivism', especially government intervention in the realm of the social to maintain and support the market (Kendall, 2003, p. 9; see also Dean, 2004). Hawke and Keating established foundational policies of social justice in Australia while pursuing economic reform. The Hawke Government had put in place universal health care through Medicare, overhauled education, launched the Higher Education Contribution Scheme, known commonly as HECS, and introduced compulsory employer superannuation payments. It introduced tax cuts and increased welfare payments for low-income families (Redden, 2019, p. 715). As Redden writes, 'the Hawke-Keating reforms came with a collectivist Australian accent' (2019, p. 715). In Indigenous affairs, Hawke created the ATSIC. Keating had established the Council for Aboriginal Reconciliation in February 1992 and in 1993 his government passed the *Native Title Act* in response to the High Court's Mabo decision. Keating was the first Australian prime minister to acknowledge the damage done by invasion, dispossession, and assimilation policies (*The Guardian*, 2022).

On the other hand, while in opposition, Howard had voiced his hostility to the establishment of ATSIC, a treaty, and land rights, arguing that such initiatives were separatist and divisive (Howard, 1989, p. 1328, 1995, p. 410). For example, in a speech to parliament on 11 April 1989, Howard argued the following as opposition leader:

> … I say to the Minister and to his guilt-ridden Prime Minister that the present generation of Australians has every reason to be concerned about the fact that the Aboriginals [sic] are the most disadvantaged cultural group in our midst. We on this side of the House will yield to nobody in this Parliament or elsewhere in our concern to improve the lot of Australia's Aborigines [sic]. I also say to the Government and to the Minister that they will never improve the lot of Aborigines [sic] in 1989 and beyond by empty symbolic gestures such as treaties. I take the opportunity of saying again that if the Government wants to divide Australian against Australian, if it wants to create a black nation within the Australian nation, it should

go ahead with its Aboriginal and Torres Strait Islander Commission (ATSIC) legislation and its treaty. In the process it will be doing a monumental disservice to the Australian community …

If there is one thing, above everything else, that we in this Parliament should regard as our sacred and absolute duty, it is the preservation of the unity of the Australian people. The ATSIC legislation strikes at the heart of the unity of the Australian people. In the name of righting the wrongs done against Aboriginal people, the legislation adopts the misguided notion of believing that if one creates a parliament within the Australian community for Aboriginal people, one will solve and meet all of those problems.

(Howard, 1989, p. 1328)

In this speech, Howard lays the foundations for the future of Indigenous public policy, and his concern with overcoming Indigenous disadvantage and abolishing ATSIC as a form of separatism. He regards his sacred and absolute duty as that of preserving the unity of the Australian people.

Howard also not only problematised what he referred to as 'passive welfare', but he distanced himself from Indigeneity as a collective racial identity, which permitted and forced the integration of Indigenous Australians into the mainstream. Howard argued that his objective was to 'unite' Australia (Howard, 1996a, p. 8218), and any collective claims to rights, such as Indigenous rights, operating outside of his core unified framework were rendered invidious. Indigenous rights were positioned outside history and social context.

As I noted elsewhere, it was not only the standardising and homogenising tendencies of neoliberalism Howard brought into Indigenous policymaking at this time, but Howard did so through the blatant denial of social and historical white colonial dominance (Howard-Wagner, 2006, 2018). In various other speeches to parliament, Howard denied the violence of colonisation and subsequent Commonwealth policies, such as the removal of Aboriginal children. Reparation for past wrongs was progressively reframed as political indulgence. Howard declared such viewpoints as 'the black armband view of history' (Howard, 1996, p. 1). He not only engaged in what Samson (2013), Sullivan and Tuana (2007), and Howlett (2022) call 'wilful ignorance', but he also reordered Australian history through national reconciliation, recognition, and reparation laws in relation to First Nations peoples (Howard-Wagner, 2018, p. 1338). Howard ignored the relevance of the past to the present (Howard-Wagner, 2018, p. 1338). His systematic sidelining of Indigenous narratives involved reinvigorating racialised practices by sanitising Australia's past, diminishing the credibility of Aboriginal and Torres Strait Islander peoples as epistemic agents in their attempts to be heard (Howard-Wagner, 2018, p. 1338). His position was not new. Dating back to 1972, Howard had expressed strong objections to many of the Commonwealth statutory laws and policies introduced into the Australian Parliament to progress Indigenous rights over a period of 24 years.

While the Howard Coalition Government's purported motivation for reform would be the wicked problem of long-term and entrenched Indigenous disadvantage, at the crux of this problem for Howard were welfarism, separatism, and self-determination. Howard orchestrated a grand and powerful paternalistic intervention in the lives and social reality of First Nations peoples through mainstreaming and individualising Indigenous service delivery in 2005. He took Indigenous infrastructure, program, and service design out of the hands of communities and community-controlled First Nations organisations.

For Howard, separate rights, institutions, and practices, such as a legal treaty or native title, were in effect antithetical to the epistemological and moral codes underpinning his neoliberal style of governing. The discursive construction of the pendulum having swung too far in the direction of Indigenous Australians allowed for a neoliberal intervention. The political objective was to wind back the perceived benefits that Indigenous rights and self-determination had unfairly bestowed on Indigenous Australians. Separate rights were to eventually be replaced by mainstreaming. Howard's reform agenda not only led to the abolition of ATSIC but also the rolling out of a government Indigenous service market nationally.

Howard's intervention in Indigenous affairs, including his duties to Indigenous Australians, was limited to removing the impediments to market forces, restructuring the welfare state, denying all privileges, and promoting individualism. Howard abandoned social justice, stipulating that it was only the state's duty to the poor or minorities to provide social services (see Hayek's *The Constitution of Liberty*, 1960). Under Howard, separate institutions, such as ATSIC, were problematised as excesses of the welfare state. Yet, the marketisation of government Indigenous services took much longer to achieve.

Later, Shared Responsibility Agreements would enact Howard's neoliberal model of governance, 'reducing dependency on passive welfare' (Vanstone, 2004a; and Howard, 2004a). The Indigenous citizen would be reconstituted as the prudent neoliberal subject. The objective was to 'boost employment and economic development in Indigenous communities' (Howard, 2004b). On the one hand, Howard constructed First Nations people as free agents who can escape disadvantage via the market, but at the same time deficit discourses constructed First Nations people as lacking the capacity to take full responsibility for their own fate. It is through policy initiatives such as Shared Responsibility Agreements, the Northern Territory Intervention, and the cashless debit card, that this attitude of Howard, and the sustained effect of his attitude in the Indigenous policy space, becomes apparent.

It is these key characteristics of Howard's style of neoliberalism that aligned it with the thinking of Friedrich von Hayek. The work of Friedrich von Hayek influenced renowned neoliberal political architects American president Ronald Reagan (1981–89) and British prime minister Margaret Thatcher (1979–90). Thatcher's notion of society as an 'artefact' that can be constituted is a direct quotation of Hayek's (1960, 1976) argument; it is the idea that society can be artificially constituted. Hayek was also extremely critical of 'social justice' and its moral effects (see Karl Popper, 1966). Separate rights and state welfare interfere with the operation of the market (Hayek, 1960, 1976). Hayek was critical of the demands of special interest groups who required special privileges (Hayek, 1976). For Hayek, individuation served certain purposes; yet it stemmed from a moral basis. As Hayek stated:

> the essence of the liberal position … is the denial of all privilege if privilege is understood in its proper and original meaning of the state. It is an ethic in which its normalising impulse is individualism and formal equality.
>
> (quoted in Lloyd, 1997, p. 79)

For Hayek, neoliberalism was a major socio-political-moral project that featured traditional doctrines of classical liberalism but differed in terms of its political practice (Kendall, 2003, p. 6). Kendall explains this as being: 'A more authoritative state … concentrate[ing] on providing the conditions under which individual entrepreneurship, self-government, freedom and responsibility can be possible' (2003, p. 6).

On the one hand, neoliberalism positively conceives of the poor as free agents who have the ability to escape poverty via the market (Katz 2013). In this sense, it rejects pathological theories of poverty and sees the poor as equal to the rest of mainstream society. Since everyone is expected to make market-based decisions that would improve their lives, the poor are logically called out to do the same. On the other hand, neoliberalism constructs the poor, especially women, as deficient and immoral individuals who do not take full responsibility for their own fate.

Importantly, once elected to power, the political imperative of the Howard Coalition Government was to respond to what Howard saw as the excesses of previous federal policy in Indigenous affairs. The discursive construction of 'the pendulum having swung too far' in the direction of Indigenous Australians legitimated intervention (Howard, 1997a, p. 1). Howard's political objective was to wind back the perceived so-called 'benefits' that Indigenous rights and self-determination had unfairly bestowed on First Nations people (Howard, 1997, p. 1). Howard's position concerning an apology to the Stolen Generation, his rejection of the High Court *Wik* decision and its review, and his restructuring, and eventual abolition, of ATSIC were sustained by a view towards redressing the privileged status of First Nations people. Howard rejected the special status of First Nations people under international law, which became evident in several law and policy reform decisions, such as those relating to reconciliation, Indigenous heritage protection, and Indigenous legal services. Howard realigned the pendulum with the passing of the *Native Title Act 1998* (Cth). Howard also attempted to realign the pendulum through the introduction of the Aboriginal and Torres Strait Islander Heritage Protection Bill 1998 but failed. Later, Howard would not only refuse to sign the United Nations Declaration on the Rights of Indigenous People, but he would actively campaign the governments of the United States, Canada, and New Zealand to do likewise.

These policies conformed to the view that 'the pendulum had swung too far' (Howard, 1997a) and that the state was resetting policy to align with the general interest. Howard's reform agenda was based on the assertion that all Australians be treated equally, ensuring that no one group of Australians was privileged over another. Howard's policy of 'practical reconciliation' decoupled the practical needs of First Nations peoples for health, education, and employment, from the broader issue of Indigenous rights and self-determination (Howard-Wagner, 2021, p. 115). He realigned the pendulum through his move away from issues of racism and native title. He turned to governing social inequality with an emphasis on Indigenous disadvantage and what Howard referred to as 'practical outcomes'.

In a speech given at the 1997 Reconciliation Convention, Howard announced he was giving 'priority to programmes that directly target Indigenous disadvantage in health, housing, education, and employment' (Howard, 1997a, p. 1). He declared that this is 'why we are focussing government resources on these areas in a way that will achieve the best outcome' (Howard, 1997a, p. 1). His government's mission was to 'reduce dependency on passive welfare' (Vanstone, 2004a; Howard, 2004a).

Howard moved away from social justice and turned instead to governing poverty, or in this case, governing Indigenous disadvantage. This was consistent with the Organisation for Economic Co-operation and Development pushing for governments to create the conditions and deliver the services necessary to reduce poverty internationally. Howard set about bringing into effect a mainstream way for Indigenous service delivery to overcome disadvantages. Howard's focus turned to governing the disadvantaged individual. Howard's reform in the public administration of Indigenous social services would ultimately centre around market enablement (Howard-Wagner, 2018).

In Indigenous affairs, market enablement entailed moving service provision out of the hands of ATSIC and communities and into the hands of the government. From 2002, the Council of Australian Governments (COAG) promoted initiatives to improve outcomes in identified areas of Indigenous disadvantage through the cooperative efforts of governments at all levels. While not immediate, this policy of 'practical' reconciliation eventually culminated in significant changes to the regulation and funding of government services for First Nations people. However, the turn to governing Indigenous disadvantage was more than an opposition to welfarism. Howard opposed separatism. Governing through Indigenous disadvantage has operated as a complex, overt racial project in which Aboriginal and Torres Straits Islander peoples in Australia are invented, constituted, and assimilated into the neoliberal body politic through the positive paternalistic governing of Indigenous socio-economic disadvantage (Howard-Wagner, 2018).

Elsewhere, I argue that, intrinsically, the governing of First Nations people through their socio-economic disadvantage is a powerful racial project in which the neoliberal state arbitrates in Indigenous politics and, in fact, reconfigures Indigenous politics (Howard-Wagner, 2018). During the years that Howard was prime minister, there was little room for First Nations peoples to move politically (even within the politics of poverty governance) in terms of overcoming Indigenous disadvantage. The National CTG Agreement signed in 2020 marks a significant departure from Howard's agenda. It is not only indicative of a move towards a post-NPM era, aligning itself internationally, but it is a recognition of the failure of neoliberalism Howard-style to address Indigenous disadvantage. The case studies in this volume show how Howard-style neoliberal governance affected the agency and agendas of community-controlled First Nations organisations and thus contributed to their political stymieing.

Abolishing ATSIC to advance the mainstream way: How and why ATSIC was problematised

It became apparent within its first year of coming to power that the Howard Coalition Government planned to wind back and even potentially abolish ATSIC. Once in power, ATSIC itself was problematised by Howard, and other key members of his government, such as Pyne, Costello, and Vanstone, through the smoke-and-mirrors of purported conflicts of interest, poor governance, excessive bureaucracy, and the failure to deliver services. The calculations and strategies of neoliberalism undermined ATSIC. In 1996, the Howard Government's appointment of an external special auditor, Klynveld, Peat, Marwick, and Goerdeler (KPMG), was for the express purpose of examining accountability within ATSIC (Pratt, 2003, p. 8). The KPMG audit cost ATSIC nearly $1 million. In addition to the KPMG audit, between 1998 and 2003, the Federal Office of Evaluation and Audit conducted 243 audits of ATSIC. As Cunningham and Baeza explain, the 243 audits occurred:

> despite ATSIC's status as perhaps the most audited and monitored organisation of its kind, and the only one with its own internal audit office … and that 95% of the 1122 organisations assessed by the special auditor [Klynveld, Peat, Marwick and Goerdeler (KPMG)] were approved for funding [and] … of the remaining 60, most were found to have minor technical irregularities.
>
> (Cunningham & Baeza, 2005, p. 463)

From its inception, ATSIC's accountability matrix subjected it to a complex web of scrutiny. This scrutiny intensified considerably following the election of the Howard Government in 1996.

After a barrage of attacks, not only from the Howard Coalition Government, ATSIC was slowly dismantled. In 1996, the Howard Coalition Government commissioned the Taylor Report (1997). The Taylor Report was a review of the policy functions of ATSIC, which resulted in the transfer of major policy sections of ATSIC to the newly established Office of Indigenous Policy within the Australian Government Department of the Prime Minister and Cabinet. The Howard Coalition Government appropriated considerable funds from ATSIC's budget to set up the Office of Indigenous Policy (Cunningham & Baeza, 2005, p. 463; Ivanitz, 2000. p. 9). It 'mainstreamed' functions relating to education and health (Malezer, 1997, p. 9) and reduced ATSIC's spending. For example, $470 million worth of cuts were made to ATSIC over four years that affected programs such as the Commonwealth Development Employment Project (CDEP) Scheme and Housing infrastructure (Malezer, 1997, p. 9). The Howard Government mainstreamed the administration of Aboriginal and Torres Strait Islander cultural heritage protection, transferring the administration of the *Aboriginal and Torres Strait Islander Heritage Protection Act 1984* (Cth) from ATSIC to the Australian Government Department of the Environment in 1998.

In 2004, the Howard Government announced that ATSIC would be abolished altogether. Howard was quoted in *The Daily Telegraph* on 1 April 2004, stating that he believed the way forward for Aboriginal Australia was to deliver programs and services in 'a mainstream way':

> I don't believe that anything is achieved by abolishing ATSIC and replacing it … with other forms of representative bodies … I think what we have to do is have the principle that everybody is treated equally, but you do have special programmes to address particular disadvantage.
>
> (Phillips, 2004, p. 1)

At the time of its abolition, most of the areas for which ATSIC had previously had fiscal responsibility had already been mainstreamed (Behrendt, 2005). Howard intended to mainstream funding for Indigenous programs by relocating that funding to relevant mainstream line departments. In hindsight, it becomes apparent that Howard needed to abolish ATSIC, including all of its regional and state structures, to achieve his overarching agenda of mainstreaming Indigenous affairs. As Larissa Behrendt points out:

> … at the time of its abolition, [ATSIC did not] have fiscal responsibility for the areas of health and education and was only a supplementary funding provider on issues such as domestic violence, languages, heritage protection and housing. In addition to this, there has also been a failure to understand that a large percentage (almost 80 per cent) of the ATSIC budget was quarantined for programs such as the Community Development Employment Program (a work-for-the-dole scheme) and the Community Housing and Infrastructure Program. These misconceptions about ATSIC's role directed attention away from government departments (federal and state and territory) with the actual responsibility for Indigenous policy and service delivery.
>
> (2005, p. 4)

The abolition of ATSIC tied in with the 'quiet revolution' in Indigenous service delivery.

Laying the foundations for a quiet revolution in Indigenous service delivery

It is within this context of the broader rolling out of NPM in Australia that significant change to Indigenous service delivery began. The Howard Coalition Government began laying the foundations for a national fully functioning NPM Indigenous service delivery system, with its decisions to:

- abolish ATSIC
- introduce a 'quiet revolution' in Indigenous affairs
- endorse the COAG National Framework of Principles for Government Service Delivery to Indigenous Australians
- initiate the replacement of the *Aboriginal Councils and Associations Act 1976* (Cth) with the *Corporations (Aboriginal and Torres Strait Islander) Act 2006* (Cth).

Through the abolition of ATSIC, the Howard Coalition Government 'reassigned all of its programmes to mainstream government departments and announced a policy of whole-of-government service delivery across these various departments and agencies' (Sullivan, 2009, p. 59). It is for such reasons that Sullivan found that this new Indigenous affairs policy 'was founded in a highly politicised environment' in which 'past practices of directly funding Aboriginal communities and community organisations was rejected' (Sullivan, 2009, p. 61). Reforms would not only see the mainstreaming of Indigenous services but also extend the marketisation of government Indigenous service delivery across Indigenous health and social services, Indigenous procurement, and commercial tendering.

At the federal level, these policies represented a pivotal policy transition away from the policies that defined the preceding self-determination era. This transition was solidified in 2006 when the *Aboriginal Councils and Associations Act 1976* (Cth), which was intended to engender self-government through the formation of Aboriginal Councils and Associations, was replaced with the *Corporations (Aboriginal and Torres Strait Islander) Act 2006* (Cth). The new act was designed to strengthen and improve governance in First Nations organisations to 'align corporate governance requirements with modern standards of corporate accountability', as well as allow 'for a range of assistance from training to a rolling program of "good governance audits"' (Entsch, 2005, p. 12). This approach assisted with the marketisation of government Indigenous service delivery. It also assisted with shifting the role of community-controlled First Nations organisations from that of community development and service provision and design with and for communities, to that of highly regulated third-party not-for-profit corporate players. The capacity of First Nations organisations to perform this new role, which required them to operate in the service market and fulfil contractual obligations to roll out government-designed programs and services, needed to be developed.

The Howard Coalition Government had already begun to create the conditions for entrepreneurship among First Nations organisations, for example through the establishment of Indigenous Business Australia, which would eventually lead to the development of an Indigenous business sector in Australia. In 2001, the Aboriginal and Torres Strait Islander Commercial Development Corporation (CDC), which was established in March 1990, became Indigenous Business Australia (IBA) through an amendment to the *Aboriginal and Torres Strait Islander Commission Act 2005* (Cth). While CDC's initial functions were to engage in commercial activities and promote and encourage Indigenous self-management and self-sufficiency, IBA shifted that focus towards improving Indigenous participation in viable businesses (Ellison, 2004, p. 1). In 2005, responsibility for the Indigenous Home Ownership Program and the Indigenous Business Development Program passed to IBA with the abolition of ATSIC (Ellison, 2004, p. 1).

The Commonwealth Development Employment Program was later abolished and replaced by the Commonwealth Development Program, which came to be seen as a highly punitive program (Finance and Public Administration References Committee, 2017). In 2007, a review of the Community Housing Infrastructure program conducted by Price Waterhouse Cooper (PWC) recommended that it too be abolished and replaced with alternative Indigenous service delivery initiatives (PWC, 2007). PWC recommended that the framework for housing and associated infrastructure:

> … should be reformed and modernised and refocused so that all participants ranging from governments through to tenants are part of a new practical era – one based on national, state, regional, community and individual responsibilities and accountabilities which delivers appropriate accommodation for those most in need.
>
> (PWC, 2007, p. 17)

In that same period, through COAG, all Australian governments pledged to 'close the gap' in Indigenous disadvantage. In 2002, COAG commissioned the Steering Committee for the Review of Commonwealth/State Service Provision to produce a regular report against key indicators of Indigenous disadvantage. The first Overcoming Indigenous Disadvantage framework would outline targets to reduce inequality in First Nations peoples' life expectancy, children's mortality, education, and employment. Three years later, COAG approved the National Indigenous Reform Agreement, which would commit governments to deliver programs across six 'building blocks' (Dawson et al., 2021). In 2002, COAG announced an initiative to improve outcomes in identified areas of Indigenous disadvantage through a whole-of-government approach, whereby governments worked with communities, known later as the COAG trials. COAG anticipated that the lessons learned from the COAG trials would be rolled out across Indigenous affairs to achieve better long-term outcomes (Morgan Disney Associates, 2006, p. 4).

While the 'quiet revolution' would increase 'competition in the delivery of services to government and on behalf of government' (Shergold, 2003, p. 1), the mainstreaming of Indigenous service delivery differed from a traditional NPM approach. With mainstreaming, Shergold stressed the difference between 'old' and 'new' mainstreaming, in which collaboration and a whole-of-government approach would be adopted for the delivery of infrastructure, services, and programs to Indigenous communities and peoples to ensure an integrated government response to Indigenous disadvantage (Shergold,

2004; cited in Pratt & Bennett, 2004, p. 9; Senate Select Committee on Administration of Indigenous Affairs, 2005, Chapter 5). Shergold's whole-of-government approach had five key characteristics. These were as follows:

- collaboration between the key agencies
- a focus on regional needs, worked out with regional voices
- flexibility of operation to enable administrative innovation to be undertaken free from the restraint of rigid program guidelines
- annual reporting against a series of socio-economic indicators
- an insistence upon the importance of joint leadership – 'a true test of collegiality' (Shergold, 2004; cited in Pratt & Bennett, 2004, p. 9).

A new taskforce was to be chaired by the Minister for Aboriginal and Torres Strait Islander Affairs. Other members would include the Minister for Transport and Regional Services, the Attorney-General, the Minister for Health and Ageing, the Minister for Family and Community Services, the Minister for Employment and Workplace Relations, the Minister for Education, Science and Training, the Minister for Communications, Information Technology and the Arts, the Minister for the Environment and Heritage, and the Minister for Justice and Customs.

The final iteration of what became COAG's National Framework for Government Indigenous Service Delivery identified that effective collaboration between Australian Government departments around service delivery to Indigenous communities and regions required the 'flexible use of funds which may involve pooling them from cross-agency projects or transferring them between programs' (COAG, 2004, p. 14). This would necessitate a 'moving away from treating program guidelines as rigid rules – [program guidelines would] be revised if they prevent innovation or fail to meet local needs' (COAG, 2004, p. 14).

As I note elsewhere, post-ATSIC the Howard Coalition Government heralded mainstreaming, mutual obligation, and shared responsibility as the way forward for Indigenous affairs. These operating principles underpinned the whole-of-government approach. However, the whole-of-government approach did not achieve its aims. Despite efforts at collaboration, silos were created, and service delivery stayed fragmented. There was no evidence of flexible approaches to funding or government accountability around Indigenous service delivery.

What's more, the government Indigenous service market was opened up to mainstream not-for-profit and for-profit organisations, as government agencies increasingly engaged mainstream not-for-profit organisations and funded them to deliver those services (Howard-Wagner et al., 2018). Indigenous services were no longer delivered as community services through community organisations, but as fragmented government services through a mix of predominantly non-Indigenous mainstream and community organisations. This change, along with short-term funding and the discontinuation of successful Aboriginal programs, resulted in the loss of local capacity, knowledge, and experience in Aboriginal service delivery in NSW. On the surface, the Howard Coalition Government's motivation for the 'quiet revolution' centred around the wicked problem of long-term and entrenched Aboriginal and Torres Strait Islander disadvantage. The 'quiet revolution' was 'heralded as a new way of doing business' (Vanstone, 2005, p. 1). Yet, Indigenous service delivery reform was approached from a political and normative standpoint. Community organisations were politicised. The 'quiet revolution' was presented as a panacea to First Nations organisations acting as 'intermediaries' and 'claiming to speak for Indigenous Australians' (Vanstone, 2005, p. 1). Community organisations were discursively constructed as the problem, with statements about how they 'may be controlled by one family group that doesn't necessarily speak with or for the others in the community' (Vanstone, 2005, p. 1).

According to proponents, true neoliberal market economy service delivery procurement has the potential to provide significant employment, capacity building, economic opportunities, and even wealth creation. While the creation of a government Indigenous service market encouraged the productive participation of First Nations organisations in the market economy and promoted entrepreneurial initiatives, changes to government Indigenous service delivery were not simply aimed at projecting Indigenous people into the market economy. As this chapter illustrates, the Howard Coalition Government's aim to institute and provide the foundations for this new economic and social order was highly interventionist, once again attempting to restructure the cultural, communal, and place-based origin of First Nations organisations. The Howard Coalition Government sought to shape and regulate First Nations organisations, targeting their systems and governance structures.

Through its 'quiet revolution' in Indigenous service design and delivery, the Howard Coalition Government not only abolished ATSIC and mainstreamed Indigenous service delivery, but it also created a government

Indigenous service market. The Howard Coalition Government wound back the capacity of community organisations to be self-determining (Howard-Wagner et al., 2022). It took decisions about service design and delivery out of the hands of First Nations communities, who had been designing social infrastructure, programs, and services to meet the needs of local First Nations people through community First Nations organisations since the 1970s. Up to that point, community control had been situated in Australian policy as an act of self-determination (Howard-Wagner, 2021). For First Nations people, the objective of community control was to strengthen and empower First Nations communities and people. In receiving government grants to design and deliver their own programs and services, some First Nations communities had even been charting the way to a self-determined economy in urban settings (Howard-Wagner, 2021). Policy reform not only diminished the capacity of community organisations to design their own social and economic infrastructure, programs, and services, but also the capacity of First Nations people to privilege Indigenous ways of knowing, being, and doing. Policy reform diminished the capacity of those organisations to act in the wider interest of collective care and wellbeing at the local and regional levels. Policy reform diminished the capacity of communities to develop a workforce, capital infrastructure, and service provision through community organisations. Policy reform diminished the capacity of First Nations people to chart the way to self-determined economies in urban settings (Howard-Wagner, 2021).

Conclusion

The Howard Coalition Government's motivation for Indigenous policy reform centred around the wicked problem of entrenched Indigenous disadvantage, which it sought to solve through a 'quiet revolution' in Indigenous service delivery. In so doing, the Howard Coalition Government was applying a mainstream solution to a complex problem and approaching the problem from a political and normative standpoint. While the Howard Coalition Government laid the foundations for a complex Indigenous service system, at the same time its solution to overcoming Indigenous disadvantage through mainstreaming Indigenous services and creating a government Indigenous service market remained contested by First Nations people. First Nations people had their own ideas and preferences around how the complex problem of entrenched disadvantage experienced by First Nations people should be addressed, as well as the policy cause of 'Indigenous disadvantage'.

The Howard Coalition Government wilfully ignored the recommendations of various government inquiries, which had argued and substantiated why the community-controlled sector should be bolstered through greater autonomy and authority to make decisions about services and better financing. The approach of block funding had been suggested for community-controlled First Nations organisations by the Royal Commission into Aboriginal Deaths in Custody in 1991 (1991, Paragraph 27.3: Recommendation 190). In 2001, the Commonwealth Grants Commission (CGC) Indigenous Funding Inquiry recommended that Aboriginal and Torres Strait Islander people should have authority to make decisions about the services they receive, be involved in decision-making for mainstream services, and ideally, even control the funds to provide the services (CGC, 2001, p. xiii). The intent was for funding arrangements to change to 'enable community control of service provision as far as practicable' (CGC, 2001, pp. xv–vi).

In abolishing ATSIC and mainstreaming the Indigenous service system, the Howard Coalition Government took control of Indigenous services out of the hands of communities and their organisations. First Nations community organisations were intended to be self-determining, and community control over the establishment and running of First Nations organisations had built the strength and empowerment of First Nations communities and people. Howard not only narrowed the focus of that system to that of closing the gap, but he also laid the foundations for a system that focused on individual needs and compartmentalised those needs into specific areas. While driven federally, the person-centred approach of the system has completely altered Indigenous services nationally, including in NSW.

This is not to say that Indigenous rights cannot exist within the context of an Indigenous service market (Howard-Wagner et al., 2018, p. 12). What happened in Australia was unique. As Howard-Wagner, Bargh, and Altamirano-Jiménez point out,

> historically excluded, First Nations peoples are encouraged to integrate into the global economy and realise their newly recognised rights to development via the market and self-government, which fit well with the reduction of the state and the transfer of administrative responsibilities.

> (2018, p. 12)

In a true market economy, service delivery procurement has the potential to provide significant employment, capacity building, economic opportunities, and even wealth creation, if it operates in the Indigenous interest. Instead, Indigenous service delivery procurement and contracts have been highly restrictive, with Australian governments focused on maximising cost-effectiveness. Australian governments have controlled the supply of government services and programs to First Nations people, setting the demand and prices in the Indigenous service economy top-down. The Indigenous service market has not only been highly paternalistic, but a strong disconnect has existed between local needs and priorities and what the Indigenous service market provides. The problem is that not only have Australian governments largely failed to integrate the right to self-determination, development, and self-government into the framework of the government Indigenous service market, but they have also failed to work with communities to determine community needs and priorities.

The Howard Coalition Government also ignored developments in Indigenous service delivery internationally. In Aotearoa New Zealand, 'policy opportunities to decrease the size of the state created opportunities for Māori to increase their collective wealth and build the Māori asset base' (O'Sullivan, 2018, p. 241). As O'Sullivan notes, 'Māori have also been able to take greater responsibility for their delivery of public services, which has, in turn, enhanced self-determination' (2018, p. 242). In Aotearoa New Zealand, 'agency is privileged over subservience and perpetual victimhood' (O'Sullivan, 2018, p. 242). In that context, as O'Sullivan writes, 'Māori economic entities have positioned themselves to pursue collective interests and challenge the constraints of a neoliberal order while simultaneously pursuing its possibilities' (2018, p. 242). This was not the case in Australia.

The marketisation of Indigenous service delivery disregarded self-determination, local decision-making, and Indigenous governance. It stifled growing urban Indigenous economies, such as in Newcastle and Western Sydney (Howard-Wagner, 2021). It ignored the 30-year-old movement for community control in urban settings that started in Redfern in the 1970s. First Nations peoples in cities had created community-controlled corporations whose functions inhabited multiple economic, political, social, and cultural spaces, and, as a result, created various connections with disparate elements of the broader economy (Howard-Wagner, 2021).

First Nations corporations were founded on Indigenous principles and their governance and operations were guided by Indigenous principles, values, and practices.[2]

The marketisation of Indigenous service delivery did not eliminate First Nations organisations; however, the Howard Government mainstreamed the delivery of government Indigenous services, resulting in the high involvement of white not-for-profit providers and for-profit providers in government Indigenous service delivery. The Howard Government stopped listening to the voice of representatives of community-controlled First Nations organisations, who had long been lobbying on the part of their communities. These two changes alone curtailed First Nations peoples' capacity to be engaged in decision-making about First Nations service delivery. On top of this, policy, funding, and regulation meant that market principles now permeated First Nations business practices, constituted them as market actors, and inculcated them into a market culture. In the eyes of the Howard Government, First Nations organisations were now seen as businesses, enterprises, and government social and health care providers in an open, competitive market. They were now in funding competition with white organisations to deliver individualised government initiatives, including social and health care, to First Nations people (Howard-Wagner, 2018a, 2018b; Howard-Wagner et al. 2018). At the same time, in designing the market, government departments defined the Indigenous services and programs to be exchanged, and constructed the social arenas and rules for market exchange (Meagher et al., 2022, p. 21; Vogel, 2018, p. 15).

In line with this agenda, the federal Indigenous Advancement Strategy was introduced in 2014, under the Abbott Coalition Government, seeing 65 per cent of federal funding for Indigenous service delivery going to large mainstream not-for-profits and the corporate sector, and only 21 per cent to community-based First Nations organisations (Howard-Wagner, 2018; Page, 2018). These policy changes were intended to shift the focus not only onto service delivery, but also to a market discipline in the creation

2   The first appointed Chair of ATSIC, Lowitja O'Donoghue, stated in 1995:
     The most significant achievement in this area [move toward self-determination] has been the establishment in March 1990 of the Aboriginal and Torres Strait Islander Commission (ATSIC), of which I am the Chairperson. For the first time in Aboriginal and Torres Strait Islander affairs, Indigenous Australians were given the right to make decisions affecting their lives. ATSIC was the culmination of almost 20 years of Commonwealth Government involvement in Indigenous affairs and represents a radical departure from the bureaucracies and advisory committees of the past. No other country has a similar body to allow Indigenous people to determine the public administration of their own affairs. (O'Donoghue, 1995)

of a government Indigenous service market that strongly aligned with overcoming Indigenous disadvantage, or what in 2008 came to be known simply as 'closing the gap'. In keeping with a market mentality, Indigenous service providers were judged solely on their ability to carry out the provision of services in an efficient and cost-effective way.

In many areas of Indigenous service delivery, predominantly non-Indigenous not-for-profit and for-profit organisations moved further into the business of Indigenous communities in urban NSW (Howard-Wagner, 2018a, p. 93). And, increasingly, large national organisations with existing infrastructure, head offices, and national policy departments, which are better equipped to offer the best value for money, have won contracts and pushed small community-controlled First Nations organisations out of the market or onto its fringes (Howard-Wagner, 2011, p. 93; 2016). The delivery of Indigenous services by non-Indigenous organisations has been reinforced through federal Indigenous policy and funding practices. For example, under the first round of the federal Indigenous Advancement Strategy in 2014, mainstream organisations were encouraged to apply for funding, but to 'focus on delivering measurable outcomes for Indigenous people in the Government's priority areas' and to 'encourage service providers to look at the grant round and consider how their proposals may fit' (Scullion, 2014, p. 1). It has been argued that 'almost 600 non-Indigenous organisations, charities and corporations are being given hundreds of millions of Australian taxpayer dollars under [the Australian federal government's] Indigenous Advancement Strategy (IAS)' (Cross, 2021, p. 1). That is:

> over $1.6 billion is currently being paid to 589 non-Indigenous entities under the Strategy – approximately 39 per cent of IAS funds – with many wealthy organisations taking on extra taxpayer dollars to deliver strategies with minimal results.

> (Cross, 2021, p. 1)

This chapter has shown how Howard-style neoliberalism, continued by the Abbott Coalition Government in more recent years, repositioned Indigenous rights in Australia. The government Indigenous service market became the means by which to bring this into effect.

References

Barrett, P. (2004, October). *Results based management and performance reporting an Australian perspective*. UN Results Based Management Seminar. Australian National Audit Office. citeseerx.ist.psu.edu/document?repid=rep1&type=pdf& doi=a513347cf15ec01ac521d112ebd6de079c067650

Beeson, M., & Firth, A. (1998). Neoliberalism as a political rationality: Australian public policy since the 1980s. *Journal of Sociology*, *34*(3), 215–231. doi.org/ 10.1177/144078339803400301

Behrendt, L. (2005). The abolition of ATSIC – implications for democracy. *Democratic Audit of Australia*. Research School of Social Sciences, The Australian National University.

Brenner, N., Peck, J., & Theodore, N. (2010). Variegated neoliberalization: Geographies, modalities, pathways. *Global Networks*, *10*(2), 182–222. doi.org/ 10.1111/j.1471-0374.2009.00277.x

Capling, A., Considine, M., & Crozier, M. (1998). *Australian politics in the global era*. Addison Wesley Longman Australia.

Chandler-Mather, M. (2021, 29 March). How the Labor Party sold Australia's public assets for a song. *Jacobin*. jacobin.com/2021/03/australian-labor-party-paul-keating-privatization-neoliberalism

Commonwealth Grants Commission (2001). *Indigenous funding inquiry final report*.

Connell, R., Fawcett, B., & Meagher, G. (2009). Neoliberalism, New Public Management and the human service professions: Introduction to the special issue. *Journal of Sociology*, *45*(4), 331–338. doi.org/10.1177/1440783309346472

Council of Australian Governments (2004). *National framework of principles for government service delivery to Indigenous Australians*.

Cross, H. (2021, 13 April). Non-Indigenous organisations receiving 40% of Indigenous Advancement Strategy funding. *National Indigenous Times*. web.archive.org/web/20210922183614/https://nit.com.au/non-indigenous-organisations-receiving-40-of-indigenous-advancement-strategy-funding/

Cunningham, J., & Baeza, J. L. (2005). An 'experiment' in Indigenous social policy: The rise and fall of Australia's Aboriginal and Torres Strait Islander Commission (ATSIC). *Policy and Politics, 33*(3), 461–473. doi.org/10.1332/ 0305573054325684

Dawson, J., Augoustinos, M., Sjoberg, D., Canuto, K., Glover, K., & Rumbold, A. (2021). Closing the Gap: Examining how the problem of Aboriginal and Torres Strait Islander disadvantage is represented in policy. *Australian Journal of Social Issues*, *56*(4), 522–538. doi.org/10.1002/ajs4.125

Deakin, S., & Michie, J. (1997). Contracts and competition: An introduction. *Cambridge Journal of Economics*, *21*(2), 121–125. doi.org/10.1093/oxford journals.cje.a013662

Dean, M. (2004). *Governmentality: Power and rule in modern society*. Sage Publications.

Ellison, C. (2004, 1 December). Aboriginal and Torres Strait Islander Commission Bill 2004 Second Reading Speech. *Senate Hansard*.

Entsch, W. (2005, 23 June). Corporations (Aboriginal and Torres Strait Islander) Bill Second Reading Speech. *House of Representatives Official Hansard* No. 12.

Fatemi, M., & Behmanesh, M.R. (2012). New Public Management approach and accountability. *International Journal of Management, Economics and Social Sciences*, *1*(2), 42–49. papers.ssrn.com/sol3/papers.cfm?abstract_id=2236141

Finance and Public Administration References Committee (2017). *Report of an Inquiry into the appropriateness and effectiveness of the objectives, design, implementation and evaluation of the Community Development Program (CDP)*. Australian Senate.

Fricker, M. (2007). *Epistemic injustice: Power and the ethics of knowing*. Oxford University Press. doi.org/10.1093/acprof:oso/9780198237907.001.0001

Godlewska, A., Moore, J., & Bednasek, C. D. (2010). Cultivating ignorance of Aboriginal realities. *The Canadian Geographer/Le Géographe canadien*, *54*(4), 417–440. doi.org/10.1111/j.1541-0064.2009.00297.x

Hall, S. (2005). New Labour's double-shuffle. *Review of Education, Pedagogy, and Cultural Studies*, *27*(4), 319–335. doi.org/10.1080/10714410500338907

Hayek, F. A. (1960). *The constitution of liberty*. Routledge and Kegan Paul.

Hayek, F. A. (1976). *The road to serfdom*. Routledge. doi.org/10.4324/978020399 1718

Howard, J. (1989, 11 April). Ministerial statement: Administration of Aboriginal Affairs. *House of Representatives, Debates*.

Howard, J. (1995, 2 March). ATSIC Amendment (Indigenous Land Corporation and Land Fund) Bill 1994: Consideration of Senate Message. *House of Representatives Hansard*.

Howard, J. (1996, 11 December). Ministerial Statements: 1996 Progress Report to the People. *House of Representatives Hansard*.

Howard, J. (1997a, 4 September). Transcript of the prime minister, the Hon John Howard, television interview with Kerry O'Brien. *The 7.30 Report*. ABC TV. web.archive.org/web/20060826063226/http://pm.gov.au/news/interviews/1997/730rep.html

Howard, J. (1997b, 29 March). Mining. *House of Representatives Hansard*.

Howard, J. (1999, 28 January). Transcript of the prime minister's Federation Address, The Australian Way, presented to the Queensland Chamber of Commerce and Industry, Brisbane.

Howard, J. (2004a). Government report card: Indigenous Australians. web.archive. org/web/20051212052859/http://pm.gov.au/gov_rep_card/indigenous.htm

Howard, J. (2004b, 16 April). Transcript of the prime minister, the Hon John Howard MP, interview with John Laws, Radio 2UE. web.archive.org/web/2004 0614230237/http://www.pm.gov.au/news/interviews/Interview797.html

Howard-Wagner, D. (2006). *Post Indigenous rights: The political rationalities and technologies governing federal Indigenous Affairs in Australia in the contemporary period* [PhD thesis]. University of Newcastle.

Howard-Wagner, D. (2018a). Aboriginal organisations, self-determination and the neoliberal age: A case study of how the 'game has changed' for Aboriginal organisations in Newcastle. In D. Howard-Wagner, M. Bargh, & I. Altamirano-Jiménez (Eds), *The neoliberal state, recognition and Indigenous rights: New paternalism to new imaginings*. ANU Press. doi.org/10.22459/CAEPR40.07. 2018.12

Howard-Wagner, D. (2018b). Governance of indigenous policy in the neo-liberal age: Indigenous disadvantage and the intersecting of paternalism and neo-liberalism as a racial project. *Ethnic and Racial Studies*, *41*(7), 1332–1351. doi.org/10.1080/01419870.2017.1287415

Howard-Wagner, D. (2021). *Indigenous invisibility in the city: Successful resurgence and community development hidden in plain sight*. Routledge. doi.org/10.4324/9780429506512

Howard-Wagner, D., Bargh, M., & Altamirano-Jiménez, I. (2018). From new paternalism to new imaginings of possibilities in Australia, Canada and Aotearoa/New Zealand: Indigenous rights and recognition and the state in the neoliberal age. In D. Howard-Wagner, M. Bargh, & I. Altamirano-Jiménez (Eds), *The neoliberal state, recognition and Indigenous rights: New paternalism to new imaginings*. ANU Press. doi.org/10.22459/CAEPR40.07.2018.01

Howard-Wagner, D., Riemer, J., Leha, J., Mason, C., Soldatić, K., Hunt, J., & Gibson, J. (2022). *The Indigenous service market: Conflicting ways of seeing urban First Nations organisations in the era of NPM* (CAEPR Discussion Paper 296). The Australian National University.

Howlett, M. (2022). Avoiding a Panglossian policy science: The need to deal with the darkside of policy-maker and policy-taker behaviour. *Public Integrity, 24*(3), 306–318. doi.org/10.1080/10999922.2021.1935560

Ivanitz, M. (2000). The demise of ATSIC? Accountability and the Coalition government. *Australian Journal of Public Administration, 59*(1), 3–12. doi.org/10.1111/1467-8500.00135

Kendall, G. (2003). *From liberalism to neoliberalism*. Paper presented to the Social Change in the 21st Century Conference, 21 November 2003, Centre for Social Change Research, Queensland University of Technology.

Kruk, R., & Bastaja, A. (2002). Emerging directions in public sector management in New South Wales. *Australian Journal of Public Administration, 61*(2), 62–68. doi.org/10.1111/1467-8500.00273

Lawrence, R., & O'Faircheallaigh, C. (2022). Ignorance as strategy: 'Shadow places' and the social impacts of the ranger uranium mine. *Environmental Impact Assessment Review, 93*. doi.org/10.1016/j.eiar.2021.106723

Lloyd, M. (1997). Foucault's ethics and politics: A strategy for feminism? In M. Lloyd & A. Thacker (Eds), *The impact of Michel Foucault on the social sciences and humanities*. Palgrave Macmillan. doi.org/10.1007/978-1-349-25101-8_5

Malezer, L. (1997). Australia's race record attacked. *Land Rights Queensland*, September.

Meagher, G., Perche, D., & Stebbing, A. (2022). *Designing social service markets: Risk, regulation and rent-seeking*. ANU Press. doi.org/10.22459/DSSM.2022

Morgan Disney and Associates. (2006). *Synopsis review of the COAG trial evaluations*. Report to the Office of Indigenous Policy Coordination (OIPC). formerministers. dss.gov.au/wp-content/uploads/2012/06/COAGsynopsisreport_220207.pdf

Muir, K., & Salignac, F. (2017). Can market forces stimulate social change? A case example using the national disability insurance scheme in Australia. *Third Sector Review, 23*(2), 57–80. search.informit.org/doi/10.3316/informit.200539427 687469

O'Donoghue, L. (1995). 'Recognition, rights, reform', speech by Lowitja O'Donoghue, Chairperson of ATSIC at the presentation of the ATSIC report on 'Native Title social justice measures' to the government, 25 March 1995, *Canberra Survey*, *48*, 1–4.

O'Flynn, J. (2007). From New Public Management to public value: Paradigmatic change and managerial implications. *Australian Journal of Public Administration*, *66*(3), 353–366. doi.org/10.1111/j.1467-8500.2007.00545.x

O'Sullivan, D. (2018). Māori, the state and self-determination in the neoliberal age. In D. Howard-Wagner, M. Bargh, & I. Altamirano-Jiménez (Eds), *The neoliberal state, recognition and Indigenous rights: New paternalism to new imaginings*. ANU Press. doi.org/10.22459/CAEPR40.07.2018.13

Page, A. (2018). Fragile positions in the new paternalism: Indigenous community organisations during the 'Advancement' era in Australia. In D. Howard-Wagner, M. Bargh, & I. Altamirano-Jiménez (Eds), *The neoliberal state, recognition and Indigenous rights: New paternalism to new imaginings*. ANU Press. doi.org/10.22459/CAEPR40.07.2018.10

Phillips, M. (2004, 1 April). PM to make Aborigines mainstream. *Daily Telegraph*.

Popper, K.R. (1966). *The open society and its enemies* (5th edition). Routledge and Kegan Paul.

Pratt, A. (2003) *Make or break? A background to the ATSIC changes and the ATSIC Review.* Current Issues Brief No. 29 2002-03. Australian Parliamentary Library. apo.org.au/sites/default/files/resource-files/2003-05/apo-nid6836.pdf

Pratt, A. & Bennett, S. (2004). *The end of ATSIC and the future administration of Indigenous affairs*. Current Issues Brief No. 4, 2004-05, Australian Parliamentary Library. parlinfo.aph.gov.au/parlInfo/search/display/display.w3p;query=Id:%22library/prspub/FXED6%22

Price Waterhouse Cooper (2007). *Living in the Sunburnt Country – Indigenous Housing: Findings of the Review of the Community Housing and Infrastructure Programme*. classic.austlii.edu.au/au/journals/AUIndigLawRw/2007/23.html

RCIADIC (1991). *Royal Commission into Aboriginal deaths in custody*. Australian Government.

Redden, G. (2019). John Howard's investor state: Neoliberalism and the rise of inequality in Australia. *Critical Sociology*, *45*(4–5), 713–728. doi.org/10.1177/0896920517745117

Rose, N., & Miller, P. (1992). Political power beyond the state: Problematics of government. *British Journal of Sociology*, *43*(2), 173–205. doi.org/10.2307/591464

Salamon, L. (ed.) (2002). *The tools of government: A guide to new governance.* Oxford University Press.

Samson, C. (2013). *A world you do not know: Settler societies, Indigenous peoples and the attack on human diversity.* School of Advanced Studies Press.

Scullion, N. (2014). A new era of Indigenous grant funding commences [press release]. Commonwealth Minister for Indigenous Affairs News and Media.

Senate Select Committee on Administration of Indigenous Affairs. (2005). *After ATSIC – Life in the mainstream?* Commonwealth of Australia. www.aph.gov.au/~/media/wopapub/senate/committee/indigenousaffairs_ctte/report/final/report_pdf.ashx

Shergold P. (2003, 13 June). *Two cheers for the bureaucracy: Public service, political advice and network governance.* Paper presented at the Australian Public Service Commission Lunchtime Seminar, Canberra. pandora.nla.gov.au/pan/53903/200511090000/www.pmc.gov.au/speeches/shergold/australian_bureaucracy_2003-06-13.htm

Shergold, P. (2004). Connecting Government: Whole of government responses to Australia's priority challenges [Speech].

Sullivan, P. (2009). Reciprocal accountability: Assessing the accountability environment in Australian aboriginal affairs policy. *International Journal of Public Sector Management*, *22*(1), 57–72. doi.org/10.1108/09513550910922405

Sullivan, P. (2018). The tyranny of neoliberal public management and the challenge for Aboriginal community organisations. In D. Howard-Wagner, M. Bargh, & I. Altamirano-Jiménez (Eds), *The neoliberal state, recognition and Indigenous rights: New paternalism to new imaginings.* ANU Press. doi.org/10.22459/CAEPR 40.07.2018.11

Sullivan, S., & Tuana, N. (Eds). (2007). *Race and epistemologies of ignorance.* Suny Press. doi.org/10.1353/book5200

Taylor, M. (1996, 29 December). The cuts which kept on coming. *Canberra Times.*

The Guardian (2022, 10 December). 'Keating told the truth': Stan Grant, Larissa Behrendt and others remember the Redfern speech 30 years on. *The Guardian.*

Vanstone, A. (2004a, 15 April). New service delivery arrangements for Indigenous Affairs [media release]. www.atsia.gov.au/media/media04/v04012.aspx (site discontinued).

Vanstone, A. (2005, 23 February). Address to National Press Club, Canberra.

Vogel, S. K. (2018). *Marketcraft: How governments make markets work*. Oxford University Press. doi.org/10.1093/oso/9780190699857.001.0001

Winant, H. (1997). Racial dualism at century's end. In W. Lubiano (Ed.), *The house that race built*. Random House.

3

'You can have a voice but you gotta pay your own bus fare': The First Peoples Disability Network

June Riemer, Karen Soldatić, and Kim Spurway

Introduction

This case study focuses on Australia's peak First Nations disability advocacy organisation, the FPDN, an Aboriginal community-controlled organisation based in Sydney South, NSW, Australia. This chapter was co-produced by FPDN and two Western Sydney University researchers. The chapter represents the firsthand accounts from the lead author, June Riemer, Deputy CEO of FPDN, and members of the FPDN board of directors on co-managing a First Nations organisation in the NPM era, situating these experiences within the broader context of intersectional challenges within the disability and Indigenous sectors. Riemer and co-author Karen Soldatić, Australian Research Council Chief Investigator, worked together to coordinate the interviews with the FPDN board and executive team members from late 2019 through to the end of 2020, with interviews occurring both face to face and online due to the COVID-19 pandemic. Soldatić and Riemer were involved in the initial design of the research project and Riemer was the co-chair of the Indigenous Advisory Research Group throughout the four-year study, therefore taking a leadership role in the study's research design, survey, and implementation throughout.

This chapter, while led by Riemer as Deputy CEO of FPDN, incorporates the voices of FPDN board members who were interviewed separately by Soldatić either face to face or online, who then provided feedback on their transcripts to ensure clarification of meaning and understanding, in line with Indigenous data sovereignty principles.

The aim of the chapter is, first, to describe the important representational work of FPDN as Australia's peak disability advocacy organisation for First Nations people and second, to explain the unique impact of NPM on small First Nations advocacy peak organisations working in an area that remains significantly under-funded and under-represented across all spheres of national policy. The chapter will start by outlining the significance of disability conjointly with racial governance under practices of settler coloniality, to situate the unique struggles faced by FPDN in its work. Then the chapter moves to describe the origins and history of FPDN as the only peak Disabled People's Organisation (DPO) representing First Nations peoples with disabilities in Australia. FPDN has managed to sustain and grow as an organisation while simultaneously advocating for Indigenous disability rights both internationally, at the United Nations, and nationally, with federal and state governments. FPDN might be an organisation that is small in terms of staff and funding, yet it has managed to achieve significant outcomes for First Nations people living with disability, even with compounding constraints passed in the NPM era. Throughout the chapter, we document that, despite the constraints on its operation, the structural disadvantages imposed by the current 'neoliberal public management' regime (Sullivan, 2018), and the resulting challenges in its operating environment, FPDN has successfully maintained its community-focused values and identity since it was first established in 1999 by three First Nations people working out of a small room in People with Disability Australia's (PWDA) offices.

As this case study demonstrates, while the FPDN organisation and its advocates have increased the profile of disability First Nations claims to rights and justice both internationally and nationally, it has done so against the hegemony of NPM in policy discourse and practice, against which it constantly struggles. The focus of NPM policies on direct service delivery, and the imposition of 'efficient', market-based mainstream service delivery and grant contracting has unique and novel implications for small, representative advocacy organisations such as FPDN. The case study reveals that in practice, NPM policies are inconsistent and counterproductive for organisations such as FPDN, whose mandate is beyond mere service provision and is focused upon the elevation of disability rights-based claims by First Nations peoples. The case study discusses how the Network's implicit, embedded community knowledge is often ignored as legitimate or, worse still, becomes coopted and colonised by non-Indigenous institutions and systems. The lack of recognition given to the Network's experience, skill sets, and know-how in culturally respectful and inclusive disability knowledge and rights often undermines the organisation's capacity to realise its full community-articulated mandate.

In this chapter, we therefore argue that the way NPM is currently enacted is a continuation of longstanding historical processes of colonisation and expropriation, which aims to extract Indigenous knowledge for settler colonial advantage. The chapter also illustrates that the assumptions of efficiency, as articulated in NPM policy discourses, are embedded in settler colonial temporalities, which do not address substantive issues of disability disadvantage and inequality. This is despite the well-documented relationship between the prevalence of First Nations disability and settler coloniality (Avery, 2018). This preoccupation with short-termism and market-based efficiencies sidelines and discounts First Nations knowledge formations that rely on deep cultural understandings and relational knowledge systems. First Nations approaches necessitate a substantial commitment of time and resources in order to progressively build trust, develop relationships, and create meaningful connections with First Nations peoples and their informal, community-embedded care networks. The rush for outcomes within NPM governance systems often conflicts with First Nations temporal ontologies and epistemologies that are created through embedded relational networks of community.

The intersection of disability, First Nations peoples, and settler coloniality

The Network's advocacy for disability rights is a significant point of contention within the settler colonial state of Australia. While First Nations peoples have the highest rates of disability across all settler colonial contexts globally (United Nations Department of Economic and Social Affairs, 2015), this is particularly pronounced in Australia (Soldatić, 2018). The prevalence of disability and chronic illness among Australia's First Nations peoples is almost twice that of settler Australians (ABS, 2017), and the highest of all First Nations peoples globally (Avery, 2018). The prevalence of disability experienced by First Nations communities, particularly across settler colonial contexts, is well recognised as the outcome of longstanding regimes of settler colonial rule and dispossession (Soldatić, 2020).

It is well documented by Indigenous scholars, such as Madi Day (2021), that notions of the 'body, health and wellness' have longstanding significance for settler colonial regimes of racialised power and practices of governing. First established under imperial Britain and its colonial regimes of local population management, eugenics was a core discursive practice of biopolitical governance (see Foucault, 2002) across the British empire to assert the authority of white coloniality upon First Nations peoples and normalise settler colonial practices of power (Bashford, 2004). Eugenics had two purposes (Blacker, 1952). First, it was used to control and contain the reproduction of First Nations peoples with the aim of elimination (Wolfe, 2006). Second, eugenics was employed to advance the 'physical fitness' of the settler population, whereby a raft of educational programs, border regimes, and reproductive controls were designed to contain and eliminate the possibility of disability (Wyndham, 2003). Thus, these longstanding historical settler colonial biopolitical regimes map across the bodies and minds of First Nations peoples living with disability, their care networks, and their communities (Beaupert & Bielefeld, 2020).

The work of this case study is set within this historical context. As a First Nations advocacy organisation for First Nations people living with disabilities, FPDN has had to confront the unique and nuanced discursive practices of racialisation and ableism that operate across the singular categories of 'Indigenous' and 'disability', as defined by the settler colonial state. First Nations peoples living with disabilities are required to simultaneously work across and through these two singular categories of population management to ensure that they have some access to the resources that they need in their everyday lives. FPDN seeks to address this by disrupting and intervening in three policy fields – disability, Indigenous, and mainstream – to promote inclusive accessibility for First Nations peoples living with disability. Moreover, given the distinct settler colonial history of biopolitical population management, FPDN has had to invest time, resources, and personal energy into building its representational legitimacy as a cultural knowledge broker. FPDN has had to do this across three spheres that are central to the everyday life worlds of the Network's constituents: the settler colonial state, the predominately white middle-class disability community, and finally, their own First Nation communities. The complex navigation that this requires has led to a sophisticated organisational strategy that enables the FPDN to build on its values and community mandate to gain traction towards the realisation of disability rights and justice for First Nations peoples.

'He was an Aboriginal guy with one leg'

FPDN came out of years of work by Aboriginal and Torres Strait Islander disability activists. This began in 1999 when Uncle Lester Bostock was volunteering as a board member with the mainstream, non-Indigenous PWDA representative organisation. After his volunteering stint, Uncle Lester decided that First Nations people with disabilities were not adequately represented in the disability sector, nor were their needs being met in mainstream organisations. Uncle Lester decided that there was a real need for an organisation that represented the interests and needs of First Nations people with disabilities. Uncle Lester started to work on setting up the Aboriginal Disability Network (ADN) while volunteering with PWDA. This pioneering work was founded on his lived experiences as a Bundjalung man with disabilities:

> And he was an Aboriginal guy with one leg, so he, you know, he was that he could see that there was need and there was work to be done for not only him, not just looking after himself, but looking after other people with disabilities.
>
> (FPDN Board Member 1)

Uncle Lester and other advocates established the first national conference for First Nations people with disabilities in Alice Springs in 1999, with the aim of discussing the need for a national First Nations DPO (FPDN, 2021a). Aboriginal and Torres Strait Islander disability advocates and representatives from all states and territories attended the conference. From this conference, ADN was officially incorporated in 2002, 'to give Aboriginal people with disability living in New South Wales a voice of their own' (FPDN, 2021a). Uncle Lester was the Network's first Chairperson, and Damian Griffis was its first executive officer (FPDN, 2021a).

Like many other First Nations organisations, this First Nations DPO started out small and slowly grew through the hard work, determination, and passion of its founders and supporters. To support ADN, PWDA gave them a room to work and access to the boardroom for meetings. The room in the PWDA offices was so small there was only room for one desk, with Damian sitting on one side and Uncle Lester on the other. Despite limited resources, Damian and Uncle Lester started to organise and advocate for First Nations peoples with disabilities. They were later joined by Aunty Maureen (FPDN Board Member 1) to start building the organisation.

From the very start, finding funding for ADN was difficult:

> they tried everywhere … they got down on hands and knees almost to beg for money. You know to help set them up. And they were always writing and put a submission in and all this and that.
>
> (FPDN Board Member 1)

From 2002 onwards, Uncle Lester, Damian, and Aunty Maureen started to travel around NSW to consult with Aboriginal people with disabilities about their needs. They also started a recruiting drive, asking for support and for people to join ADN and help fund it. The membership fee at that time was $2. ADN worked hard, as a board member said: 'Putting out the word about what we wanted to start up' (FPDN Board Member 1). The campaigning and lobbying were eventually successful, and the organisation managed to attract about 50 members statewide. ADN was also starting to be recognised as an important new First Nations organisation by other Aboriginal disability activists from other states. Uncle Lester, Aunty Maureen, and Damian travelled to other states to pass on their experiences and skills to local disability advocates. From this, several states also started to organise and advocate for the needs and rights of First Nations peoples with disabilities.

At first, ADN did not have much success finding funding. To build its legitimacy as a representative organisation with the cultural authority to articulate the concerns of community members living with disability, ADN undertook high-level policy advocacy with local political actors across the major parties in NSW. First, ADN approached NSW politicians for support. ADN met with the NSW Liberal Shadow Minister for Ageing and Disability Services, Andrew Constance, who promised ADN funding if the Liberal-National party won the next state election. Even though the Coalition did win, ADN never received funding at the state level. So, Uncle Lester, Damian, and Aunty Maureen felt that their funding strategy was not getting any support at the state level and began to identify other potential political allies among the major parties at a national level. As a result, in 2010, they decided to go to Canberra to meet with Bill Shorten and Jenny Macklin from the federal Labor Government. At the time, Bill Shorten was the Parliamentary Secretary for Disabilities and Children's Services, and Jenny Macklin was the Minister for Families, Housing, Community Services and Indigenous Affairs. At the end of the meeting, Bill Shorten said that he would support the organisation if ADN could demonstrate to him what it was doing. Shorten also asked for ADN to expand its mandate from the state to the national level:

> To help kick start this new national organisation, the then federal Labor government gave the organisation funding to hold a national conference of all First Nations disability advocates to meet in Sydney. Each state and territory sent two delegates to the conference, and, from this first meeting, First Nations Peoples Disability Network was formed.
>
> (FPDN Board Member 1)

Although informally constituted in 2010, FPDN has officially operated as a charity and a registered public company since 2014 (FPDN, 2021a). FPDN is now a nationwide peak organisation that acts as 'the custodians of the narratives of First Peoples with disability, their families and communities' (FPDN, 2021b). FPDN is a small nonprofit organisation with 13 staff nationwide and five board members. FPDN staff are predominantly First Nations people, and its governance body is wholly composed of First Nations people with lived experiences of disability. The FPDN navigates several social service sectors including disability, Indigenous affairs, and human rights. In addition, the organisation has international commitments as a member of the United Nations Committee on the Rights of Persons with Disabilities, and often attends meetings of the Committee. FPDN depends almost completely on state and federal government support, with almost 95 per cent of their running costs and revenue stream coming from NSW or Australian Government grants (Australian Charities and Not-for-profits Commission, 2021).

'We're gatherers of information, we don't just keep to our lane'

Formally incorporated in 2014 as the national peak body advocating for the rights of First Nations people with disability, their families, and their communities, FPDN lobbies the government, the private sector, and community organisations on the needs and rights of First Nations peoples with disabilities. FPDN also provides information to and supports First Nations people with disabilities to help them navigate the complexities of the current welfare and legal systems. As a First Nations organisation with First Nations peoples with disabilities on its board and within its staff, FPDN has positioned itself as an organisation with a unique knowledge base. It is able to draw on the unique lived experiences and implicit, embedded understandings of being both First Nations and a person with an impairment. Consequently, FPDN understands in a fine-grained and nuanced way the needs and everyday challenges of First Nations peoples with disabilities. This enables an effective, culturally and disability-appropriate approach to working with First Nations communities that mainstream, non-Indigenous organisations lack.

From its very beginnings as a three-person team sharing a space in PWDA offices, this personal, embedded, intersectional understanding of First Nations culture and disability gave FPDN a unique perspective that shaped the ways it developed its programs, and the ways it did business with community, non-Indigenous organisations, and government:

> No, that was his [Uncle Lester's] motto, that was he tells everybody. He was doubly disadvantaged. First of all being an Aboriginal person, second of all being a disabled person. And then that all comes against him before he starts talking about, you know, in other words, he's not getting the same treatment being an Aboriginal guy as the next person who was a white guy that's getting that.
>
> (FPDN Board Member 1)

As an organisation that is predominantly composed of First Nations people with disabilities and with a robust knowledge of the social service sector and policies affecting First Nations people living with disabilities, FPDN is a critical knowledge broker and intermediary. First Nations people living with disabilities are among the most economically disadvantaged and socially marginalised groups in Australia (Riemer & Soldatić, 2021). The cost of disability often increases First Nations economic precarity as household economic wealth is absorbed into the additional costs associated with disability care and support (Soldatić et al., 2021). In addition, First Nations people living with disabilities can have multiple impairments, some of which are acquired due to the lack of available public health services in regional and remote areas of Australia (Soldatić, 2018). For example, it is well noted within the research that many services have limited capacity to take on persons living with a range of different impairments, as they only offer specialised services, or they lack the expertise necessary to be responsive to the multiple supports required (Fitts & Soldatić, 2020).

This lack of capacity in services can make navigating ableist environments extremely challenging, especially for those people living in remote and rural towns with poor infrastructure and service provision. If services are available in the town in which they are living, which is not always a given, many people do not understand the rules, their rights to access such services, or the kinds of services and supports for which they are eligible from government, private, and community sector providers. Although FPDN itself has limited capacity, it attempts to provide support and advice that enable First Nations people with disabilities and their families to better navigate the complex, ableist institutions that can marginalise them. A woman Elder on the FPDN board explains how FPDN provided critical information about social service eligibility and accessibility for a First Nations Elder with disabilities and her family:

> Well, it's getting the right thing done for our people, you know. A lot of Aboriginal people don't know what they, uh, what they're involved in. One case scenario that we had was when we had an elderly lady, she was living with her son and his family. And it was a burden on him it was a burden on him because he had disabled teenage daughter, that's for instance. And had the mother living with him, mother was in her 70s, and she needed medical care, she needed being looked after as much as the kid did. And so, they were finding it really, really hard and struggling financially as well as mentally. And so, we went in and had a look at her case and everything. And Damian says, 'Oh does your mum get the pension?' And he said, 'No, he said, 'she looked after us when we were kids so' he said. 'It's our turn to look after her', he said. 'So', he [Damian] said, 'She's entitled to a pension, she could get a pension, an old age pension.' 'Oh, no she can't because she needed to work, you know she always stayed at home and looked after us. Now it's our turn to look after her.' 'Come on, let's go down to Centrelink'. He was surprised that she was able to and not only that the fact that for a couple of months from the time she applied for it to the time that she got it, but it was also a couple of months and eh. Oh, he couldn't thank Damian enough. It was you know something that, he didn't know that she was entitled to because she needed to work, she looked after herself, looked after the kids, stayed at home and looked after the kids while the husband went out to work, yeah. So, it was something they didn't know, and I'd say wouldn't be the only one who wouldn't know, there'd be a lot of them that didn't think that. Oh, you know, didn't pay any taxes, went out and looked after people's homes, cleaned

> people's homes, did this and did that. I didn't pay the taxes, I'm not due a pension. And uhm because they don't know the scheme you know, only get the pension if you worked and paid taxes.
>
> (FPDN Board Member 1)

Not only is the FPDN there to support and provide advice on eligibility and access to essential services, but it also acts as an essential frontline intermediary between non-Indigenous service providers and First Nations communities. The Network's Deputy CEO talks about how non-Indigenous service providers often do not understand First Nations ways of being in the world, such as the relational nature of respectful Indigenous service delivery (see Prout, 2018). Nor, according to June Riemer, the Deputy CEO, do non-Indigenous service providers understand how First Nations persons with disabilities experience the everyday difficulties in which they operate, particularly in rural and remote communities (Avery, 2018). The Deputy CEO explains that First Nations people often have periods with little money and no access to services, resulting in little available food in communities – community members end up sharing what little they have. Even in communities with very little, First Nations people will give their food away to others even if they themselves are living off very little. In this case, she also stresses how important it is to take your time, to sit and talk to people to understand their point of view and not judge them based on non-Indigenous ways of being in the world. As the peak national representative organisation for First Nations people with disabilities, organisational staff have to regularly move in and out of their urban environment and directly engage with community members in rural and remote settings. As June Riemer, the Deputy CEO, outlines below, this includes having the cultural knowledge of localised practices that often differ from those of urban-based First Nations peoples. To learn such knowledge requires engaging in the time-intensive practice of deep listening to learn about the importance of family, community, and dogs, for First Nations communities in rural and remote regions, something that would not necessarily occur in their urban locales as national policy advocates:

> I remember going into one community in NT, near Utopia it's called Murray Downs. No one had any money, they'd all been cut off Centrelink,[1] no one had petrol or food, because they're 250 kms from

---

1   Centrelink, now renamed Services Australia, is the federal government agency responsible for income support payments and social services such as Disability Support Pension, Age Pension and Unemployment Benefits: www.servicesaustralia.gov.au/.

nearest shop, and that's where the Centrelink outreach office is … But then there wasn't a big community, 10 or 15 aging people there, and they had the Meals on Wheels[2] coming in, so they got their meals every day, the problem with that what I saw they were either givin' 'em away, cause that's what grandparents do … so they [Meals on Wheels] give 'em their meals in paper bags and cause she had lots of dogs, she fed it to them, so she was like this … So if I was that health care worker, I'd sit there and have a conversation, cause that's what I did, I sort of, cause we're out there a while, and I saw it a few times with this lady, she was giving all her food to her dogs. When we walked up, sat with her, made sure she ate, what she wanted and then give it to the dogs … but dogs look after the kids, older people, keep the snakes away, and all that sorta stuff, you know and in those particular communities the dogs save them … just goes back in history, from the dingo, so there's a story of that community, they told me, where they camped around the camp fires, they'd been camping, travelling across Country, so you know the Devils Marbles, yeah, so it happened there, so an old lady had rolled into the fire, on their journey forward, so they left her behind with aunts, cause she was completely burnt, but they went and killed a dingo, several dingoes, got the blubber around of the dingoes, and wrapped her in the blubber, and stayed behind, till she got better, Aboriginal family. So that's the Dreaming story, the dingoes are protective …

(FPDN Deputy CEO)

It is reasonable to assume that the Network's specialist know-how, and the importance of this know-how in approaching communities, would mean that FPDN is highly successful in grant rounds. This is not the case under the current regime of NPM. From the interviews with FPDN staff, it is clear that funding bodies value organisations that can meet the finite criteria as stipulated in NPM frameworks, rather than the embedded intersectional knowledge that occurs from longstanding relationships of respect, culture, and lived experience. The Network's experiences with government funding bodies suggest that the criteria used in the assessment of funding applications are not responsive to the unique expertise and know-how of First Nations organisations, and are obscure to them. Lack of transparency has long been an issue in public policy, but it is the view of FPDN that funding bodies do not reward the embedded specialist knowledge held by FPDN when deciding on funding grants. According to FPDN staff and board members,

---

2   Meals on Wheels provides meals, social connection, and a wellbeing check for older and socially isolated people: mealsonwheels.org.au/learn-more/about/.

a key issue is that non-Indigenous organisations seldom have the capacity to substantively understand the realities of living as a First Nations person with disabilities, or the relational nature of First Nations systems of kinship care and inclusion.

Curiously, non-Indigenous organisations working in the Indigenous sector recognise the importance of the Network's deep cultural knowledge of disability and kinship care relations. Interviews with FPDN board members and staff clearly identify that non-Indigenous organisations, before and after they receive a grant, will seek out and use the Network's expertise to meet their grant outcomes. In particular, the deep intersectional knowledge that FPDN offers is not only requested directly by such organisations but often exploited to ensure that the non-Indigenous organisations have participant take-up upon service implementation. The FPDN is frequently expected to provide this information and expertise free of charge, even when the organisation was not awarded funding within the same grant round.

One woman Elder on the FPDN board told the story of how another organisation used information gathered by FPDN to put together a proposal to a funding body without acknowledging that this information came from FPDN:

> Look that's the thing, we know you're doing a really very important work. The statistics they've [FPDN] gathered, although they'll [other organisation] flog 'em, it's plagiarism, that's okay but it's our work that we put in, they've got the statistics, and they take it and thank you very much. Like they don't fund us for this very important work, but they'll take our information. They're good, aren't they?
>
> (FPDN Board Member 3)

Continuing this line of thought, another board member illustrates how difficult it can be for an organisation such as FPDN to challenge such neoliberal practices, despite the fact that private firms and consultants would be financially renumerated for offering this type of advice and expertise:

> … this is intellectual property and there's federal legislation on intellectual property if you're a registered business or you're … person. But if you're an Aboriginal, your intellectual property is like whatever. But guess what you can't cop someone out for plagiarism if you're Indigenous. It's very difficult, you need to pay a lawyer about $900 bucks an hour to do that in the Supreme Court.
>
> (FPDN Board Member 2)

The Deputy CEO, June Riemer, also raised the issue of how the Network's expertise is pursued and used by large non-Indigenous organisations, with very little compensation for their work. This knowledge becomes critical and feeds into the success of these non-Indigenous organisations in obtaining large government grants:

> So, obviously we were happy to be involved [in the project] and they had a project then that was a data collection thing, so they asked us to be involved ... At that time – and they [non-Indigenous organisation] weren't – they did pay but it was very minimal, it was nothing for the expertise they got. So, what happened, a few of our colleagues worked with them, so they went to different remote regions nationally ... [staff member] wrote this amazing report for them, you can imagine the data ... they got ... another project after that for over a million dollars, and they would never have got it without [staff member's] report. So, what they got for $400 or something they paid us, you know what I mean, that skillset and expertise, it's – if [staff member] had charged or we had charged a consultancy fee, [firm], or what they got they would have got from any of the Big 4. So, sometimes it's a bit one-sided if you understand.
>
> (FPDN Deputy CEO)

Despite expectations within the sector that everyone can use their expertise without paying for it, the Deputy CEO demonstrates how the FPDN team are frustrated with the significant amount of time and resources spent supporting non-Indigenous organisations. Importantly, FPDN is now considering how to set up a fee-for-service model to ensure that this expertise and know-how is appropriately funded and respected:

> How much – so, there's a certain element we're supposed to do as the Peak, but it's not for every – which we get every service provider, every Peak, every whatever, contacting us daily, weekly ... So, it was interesting, yesterday, I was at something else out at Orange, and you forget, and I've noticed this a lot lately, the intel and the information and the skillsets we have that have just grown organically because we're this microcosm of information, it's amazing other people don't know. Yeah, yeah, I find that all the time. Because if you had to put a cost on what our intel is, it's what Damian was saying the other day, you know, what ... They're [government and other organisations] used to paying big money. We did it as a joke between me and [Damian] – I didn't think they'd – I thought they'd come back and go, no, and they did. So, the same project that I'm currently, not the same, but a similar project that I'm currently doing, Damian

> got $19,000 from DSS [Department of Social Services]. This other
> project that we're just about to – it won't start until September, that
> I just put in, got $120,000.

(FPDN Deputy CEO)

Ultimately, it is the everyday lived experience and embedded intersectional knowledge that sets it apart from other non-government organisations (NGOs) working in the sector:

> You forget how much you actually know too … not being a
> government organisation, we wear many hats, and we have many
> conversations, and we collect internally and personally a lot of data.
> So, we're the experts on the NDIS [National Disability Insurance
> Scheme], we're the experts on the National Disability Strategy,
> we're experts on every cohort of an individual's who you may come
> in contact. It's just like with the – what I was telling them about
> schools. That's not my avenue, but I listen and hear when I'm out in
> community. The stuff I told them about Coonamble, I heard that
> five years ago and then recently was talking again to people and had
> said to me they've involved the girls now, because back then, five
> years ago, it was a boys' program only. So, all the teachers and the
> girls were going, well, why – we've just got as many issues with the
> girls. Then I ran into someone somewhere else and just Coonamble
> came up, and I go, oh, whatever happened out at the high school
> there? They went, oh no, they've done the program for girls now
> too and it's made retention rates … But also, that's what we – we're
> gatherers of information, we don't just keep to our lane. Whereas
> government entities, they have one lane all the time. That's the
> difference I think we bring to the table, isn't it?

(FPDN Deputy CEO)

'You gotta pay your own bus fare'

Despite the Network's embedded knowledge of living at the intersection of Indigeneity and disability, FPDN encounters significant difficulties obtaining funding to continue with its work in First Nations communities. Unlike larger non-Indigenous organisations, FPDN is resource-poor, both in terms of its number of staff and ongoing financial status. Given that FPDN is a relatively new organisation, it does not have the depth of resources of large non-Indigenous organisations working across the area of disability service delivery. These larger organisations are often able to draw on diverse funding sources including philanthropy, membership fees, and so forth. Moreover, the cost of ensuring that the organisation and its programs are inclusive and accessible to members, clients, staff, and board members living at the intersections of disability and Indigeneity is high. As an Aboriginal community-controlled organisation, the Network's board of directors and staff are all First Nations peoples, many of whom have disabilities, and who lack the kind of resources required to, for example, make up funding shortfalls for travel or inefficient bureaucratic processes that delay grant tranche payments.

FPDN runs on a very limited budget of about $300,000 annually and does not have the same liquidity as larger organisations, which can subsidise program activities such as travel for staff in addition to paying for board members' time and participation while waiting for the next funding tranche. As the Deputy CEO stated, FPDN often 'don't know when the money's coming in'. This creates high levels of stress for staff who, despite FPDN management's commitment to maintaining its current workforce, live from contract to contract with no guarantee of ongoing employment. FPDN is constantly looking for money to keep people employed and keep the core functions of the organisation operating. Essentially, there is no extra money to allow FPDN to subsidise board and staff members to support their work beyond explicit contracted periods.

This problem is exacerbated by the Network's increasing reliance on highly competitive, small, short-term grants, that are highly targeted at explicit contracted outcomes. Consequently, FPDN staff use a lot of their scarce time and resources competing with large non-Indigenous not-for-profits (NFPs) and private corporations for these small grants. These grants provide only short-term support for the activities and often have burdensome reporting requirements. For example, the 2019 NDIS transition grant awarded a maximum of $20,000 for organisations to transition to the individualised funding structure of the new disability support scheme. As a small, urban-based national peak which operates in urban, rural, and remote areas across Australia, FPDN were particularly disadvantaged as the resources were largely designed for single-site organisations located in a single geographical area. Additionally, these types of one-off transitional grants have such onerous application and reporting requirements that some organisations, including FPDN, have refused to apply for them.

Even when applications are successful, the high-level of reporting expected from government agencies means that even a small grant is 'micromanaged into, like an inch of its life' (FPDN Deputy CEO). The reliance on small tranches of money also makes the organisation's internal operations riskier and more complex. They mean that all of the staff are on three-month contracts because the organisation cannot take the risk of contracting staff for longer periods in case they are unable to find funds to pay them. Adding to this problem is the fact that payments from federal government agencies, such as the Department of Social Services and the NDIS, can often be as much as six months late.

These grants, federal, state, and local government, also do not provide funding for essential items such as travel, which increases the complexity of their operational management. The additional costs associated with travel accessibility are a particular problem for a board composed of First Nations people with disabilities. While the board is often required to travel to meet with other organisations and governments, doing so often means paying for carers to travel. Covering these costs can be very difficult given the longstanding Indigenous economic disadvantage that has come with colonial dispossession. Some FPDN board members travel thousands of kilometres, from the Northern Territory and Queensland, for meetings in Sydney and Canberra. As one board member articulates: 'you have your own voice, but you have to pay your own train fare to get there'. It takes longer for board members to travel given their disabilities. They often require assistance from support networks to do so, and this doubles the cost of fares and accommodation. As a community-controlled organisation that is managed and staffed by people living with disability who have limited financial resources, the costs of inclusive representation are considerable. As noted by one of the board members, a First Nations person living with disabilities, this makes FPDN 'more expensive' and 'less competitive' (FPDN Board Member 3) than larger non-Indigenous NFPs and corporations that do not need to meet the disability accessibility and travel costs associated with being a national representative organisation. FPDN has to include provisions for disabled staff and board members in its planning and budget, and these costs remain under-recognised in NPM competitive funding models:

> … when the family and community services manager wants to go to FPDN, because we get told two weeks before a consultation is in Sydney and they want to speak to people, they want to speak to people from Bourke, Broken Hill … isolated communities where they'd be better off walking to Sydney than catching a plane … it's a $600 return plane fare, now if you have a person with high needs disability, you have to arrange a lot of things …
>
> (FPDN Board Member 3)

FPDN staff and board members are also frustrated that significant block funding is granted to larger non-Indigenous organisations who, with more resources and large economies of scale, have a competitive advantage. Within the grant process, consolidated administrative structures mean that these larger organisations can absorb some of their operational costs into other areas of their budgets. This trumps the expertise and lived experience required to work in First Nations communities that First Nations organisations in general, and FPDN in particular, bring. Indeed, FPDN provides information free of charge to non-Indigenous organisations and is used by many non-Indigenous organisations, disability services, and social services, to enter First Nations communities. This places more strain on an organisation with limited resources, as visiting non-Indigenous organisations often rely on FPDN staff, cars, and time to travel to meet with communities. FPDN is not always reimbursed for the time and resources expended on these trips, even though government organisations and large NFPs have considerable resources. As representatives of First Nations communities, the FPDN management team is also asked to sit on advisory boards and committees without compensation, despite the fact that non-Indigenous board members are often paid for the time they commit to external organisational governance as board members. As a consequence, a resource-poor First Nations organisation, and the critical knowledge practices it has developed through a deep connection to the community as an Indigenous disability advocacy organisation, is being appropriated by well-resourced, non-Indigenous organisations to do the work for which these organisations are funded, through free advisory sessions, community access, and information provision.

Unlike non-Indigenous organisations, FPDN has a commitment to communities that goes beyond service delivery and representation. The organisation is deeply connected to First Nations communities and, as such, has to participate and engage at a much deeper level. This impacts FPDN staff's professional and personal time in ways not experienced by many non-Indigenous people. Ironically, it is the Network's know-how and experience in communities that make it so effective in getting good outcomes for the First Nations communities. The real strength of First Nations organisations, such as FPDN, is that the members are drawn from the communities they represent. This enables First Nations organisations like FPDN to work with the community, understand their needs, and respond appropriately. However, even though this knowledge and expertise may be exploited by non-Indigenous players, these qualities are not recognised by the government when it comes to funding First Nations community-based programs. This indicates a complete lack of understanding about the real value added by the Network's expertise and experience:

> … in those processes, there's not that cultural knowledge and understanding that we wear many hats as workers. How do you put that in a policy? It's not taken into account … I'm just waiting till the program comes to an end, because [partner organisation] go all the time to me, oh, we want feedback, we want to work with you. But I think, well, you're not listening though.
>
> (FPDN Deputy CEO)

Throughout the interviews, it became apparent that there were clear differences in the treatment of large non-Indigenous organisations, which often have a limited geographical reach, and FPDN. As a national peak organisation based in urban Sydney, FPDN is unable to seek cost recovery for the work necessary to critically understand the experiences, needs, and advocacy concerns of rural and remote First Nations peoples living with disabilities:

> Even this [non-Indigenous organisation's name] project, that was our issue. So, our workers are using their own car, most of them, for smaller jobs. Long distance stuff they'd hire. But it was the same issue. The funding we got, originally Damian looked at leasing a fleet of cars, but we didn't get enough money in the contract to do it, which would have made much more – we did lease in the beginning for the first three months. The workers, we had leases for them, because – but then, we can't pay you this money and lease you a car and buy you a laptop and buy you a phone and buy this. Because there was no back-end assets funding support. They just assumed, that's the problem with DSS and this contract, they assume, [non-Indigenous organisation's name] have all that back-end stuff. But as a small NGO, we don't. We have to go out and buy laptops and phones. Then again, going back to our workforce, most of them may not have green slips and comprehensive insurance, or the readily available funds to put a tank of petrol in every week, or two tanks of petrol.
>
> (FPDN Deputy CEO)

This ableist attitude is also cultural and based on a fly-in, fly-out model that does not account for First Nations community needs:

> … if you want to go to an isolated area and you wanted to talk to local community member with a disability [name removed to protect identity], I'm gonna say isolated. He doesn't have an aeroplane, he doesn't fly aeroplanes, so you gotta go see him up in the Torres Strait.

So, there's [board member's name] up there … You want to go and talk to him, and you might know this already, you're not just talking to Serea, and I'll just put letters for it, A for Aunty, Uncle, and his mum's here, his dad's there, but that's his aunts and uncles, it's not just his mum and dad's brothers and sisters, it's everyone on his island. You don't go to his island, it's his mob … what's that gubba model on board here, gubba model of consultation [interjection from another board member: gubba is 'white man'] … He's going to talk to Serea. FPDN way … FPDN will see them there on social media. Gubbas will see that too and go straight to talk to him. But FPDN will go and speak to the whole island. So, mums, dads, aunties, uncles and everything if you know what I mean?

(FPDN Board Member 2)

Board members spoke about the considerable cost, time, and effort required to travel to meetings with the government and to fulfil their mandate as board members. One board member spoke about the cost and time needed for travel for another member with cerebral palsy:

You can have a voice but you gotta pay your own bus fare to get there if you're goin' at all half the time, you know, $600 plane fare for not just me as an advocate, [board member's name] is from Torres Strait Islands, that's nearly 3,000 kilometres right from Sydney … ferry, ferry to mainland, it's a shithouse route to go in that chair but this fella's been to the United Nations, haven't you, talkin' and that's what I wanted to say, not for him, but just to introduce that aspect of how difficult it is.

(FPDN Board Member 3)

Another board member spoke of the difficulties of travel and attending meetings:

It is hard because I can't stand for too long, I can't walk for too far, I forgot my cane so if I, you know, like access to go to up and down stairs like that. I mean I look like an abled person, if you stand me up, if I stood maybe 10 minutes in the same spot, I can hardly move and there's nowhere to sit, so therefore that's a big thing as well. Yeah, so if you go to a meeting then there's not enough chairs and I'm standing around, I'm stuffed … Driving long hours and that, you know. To be in a car, now if I've gotta go somewhere it's a three hour trip, my leg won't last. Oh, I've got to go, can someone come with me. And, so, if my sister doesn't come, or someone doesn't come for a drive with me, I'm buggered.

(FPDN Board Member 2)

One board member also spoke about how their work is often in rural and remote First Nations communities, and the challenges for people with disabilities travelling to communities and navigating rural spaces with inferior infrastructure, such as a lack of sidewalks, restricting wheelchair access:

> I don't know what these people [government] think, they think we're just going to be hobbling around in the CBD. We're not, our work is out in community, now community is like 4,000 miles away, 8,000 miles away, it's not around the corner. Until they work out the special needs of actual travel and the expenses of getting people there, uhm, yeah, it is very restrictive … If we want to go to a conference, say down in Melbourne, you know for all of us to get down there, they say, 'Oh well, you don't, we can't go, we're restricted as a board for non-participation because no funding to get you there.' So, yeah, as a board, we are behind the eight ball.
>
> (FPDN Board Member 2)

At the time of writing, FPDN has been successful in securing 2-year funding through CTG, which has doubled the organisation in size and significantly increased its capacity under a new agreement between the federal government and First Nations organisations. This was the first time that disability had been recognised as a priority by CTG, demonstrating a change in attitudes that reflects to some degree an understanding that people with disabilities have the 'right to a good life' (FPDN Deputy CEO). This substantial funding tranche enables FPDN to have a presence in all state and territory jurisdictions; to reinforce the First Nations disability sector; to work on attitudinal change about First Nations disability within government, the wider Aboriginal community-controlled organisation sector, and First Nations communities; to develop a policy and research team; to develop a training team; and to undertake a comprehensive evaluation of their programs. Riemer points out that this opportunity did not just land in the Network's lap. FPDN built on decades of work in the sector, building allies 'to walk alongside us' within the public sector and within the disability sector to become the only First Nations peak body representing disability Aboriginal community-controlled organisations. The funding process was long, arduous, and time-consuming, with the team's resources stretched to the limit through hours of weekly conversations with different jurisdictions to negotiate buy-in to the proposal. Riemer points out, 'I've still got my day job', and 'the amount of time we put into it, fully equates to the funding we got'. However, even though 'this is not a two-year conversation, we'll only be just touching the peak in two years', Riemer is confident that the grant will help highlight the successes and challenges of FPDN as Australia's only First Nations disability peak body.

Conclusion

As this case study illustrates, First Nations peoples' embedded intersectional, embodied knowledge of disability is located in a historical contextual relationship of settler colonialism. Settler colonial practices continue to have power over their lives, communities, and organisations in contemporary Australia. While there have many gains for First Nations Australians living with disability as a direct outcome of the advocacy work of FPDN, the struggle for Indigenous disability rights and justice is uniquely placed, in that it sits 'somewhere in between' and in 'close proximity to' longstanding settler colonial regimes of biopolitical population management. Living, working, and advocating across the assemblage of these biopolitical practices requires constant reflexive negotiation to create, and where possible, open out, new and novel potentialities, while doing the work required to realise Indigenous disability justice claims. Despite government discourses in relation to disability policy and disability rights, settler colonial regimes of power to contain and control Indigenous bodies and minds still remain pivotal to the racialisation of the Australian settler colonial state. Australia was not only a racialised settler colonial project, but it was also deeply enmeshed with notions of white capability that worked to erase the presence of disability (Soldatić, 2020).

The residual effects of settler colonial biopolitical management and its systems of internal population governing resonate with NPM strategies of competitive tendering and the marketisation of social services. In the latter, predominantly non-Indigenous able-bodied social services are increasingly gaining access to the necessary resources to deliver Indigenous disability services on the ground. Within this process, embodied Indigenous disability experiential knowledge claims are devalued in NPM practices and yet coopted to inform the competitive bids of mainstream service providers. The chapter has described how embodied Indigenous disability experiential knowledge claims are actively sought out by much larger, more successful services, with almost no acknowledgement of the impact on FPDN time and resources as an under-funded Indigenous disability advocacy organisation. FPDN is deeply connected to First Nations communities across Australia. Within its team, FPDN has lived experience of both Indigeneity and disability, with a significant proportion of the FPDN team embodying this very intersectionality in their everyday lives. However, this deep, connected experiential embodied knowledge is not acknowledged or rewarded in the current NPM grant system. In effect, non-Indigenous organisations take this knowledge, reconfigure it, and make it 'materialise as having real value' through the NPM competitive process of governing. By demonstrating their understanding of First Nations people with disabilities' needs and experiences, these organisations appear more effective to funding bodies and become more competitive for future funding rounds. This has important consequences for the day-to-day work of FPDN. Today, FPDN is dominated by competitive funding submission processes, administrative and financial reporting processes, and providing expertise at no cost to non-Indigenous organisations. FPDN continues to provide these services to successful mainstream service providers, even when they themselves have been unsuccessful within the same funding round, to ensure that their communities and community members receive the support they need. This chapter demonstrates the ways in which this neo-colonisation of First Nations knowledge plays out in the current NPM environment. As one board member so aptly pointed out in our interviews, this is a 'gubba model' that does not recognise the foundational community principles that have sustained FPDN since Uncle Lester Bostock first decided to organise, mobilise, and advocate for the rights of First Nations peoples with disabilities in Australia.

References

Australian Bureau of Statistics (2017). Aboriginal and Torres Strait Islander people with disability. In *Disability, Ageing and Carers, Australia: Summary of Findings*.

Australian Charities and Not-for-profits Commission (2021). *First Peoples Disability Network (Australia) Limited*. www.acnc.gov.au/charity/charities/7a151d4a-3aaf-e811-a962-000d3ad24a0d/profile

Avery, S. (2018). *Culture is inclusion*. First Peoples Disability Network.

Bashford, A. (2004). *Imperial hygiene: A critical history of colonialism, nationalism and public health*. Palgrave Macmillan.

Beaupert, F., & Bielefeld, S. (2020). Fixated persons units: A disability studies and critical race theory (DisCrit) analysis. In C. Spivakovsky, C. Steele, & P. Weller (Eds), *The legacies of institutionalisation: Disability, law and policy in the 'deinstitutionalised' community*. Hart Publishing. doi.org/10.5040/97815 09930760.ch-011

Blacker, C. (1952). *Eugenics: Galton and after*. Duckworth.

Day, M. (2021). Remembering Lugones: The critical potential of heterosexualism for studies of so-called Australia. *Genealogy*, *5*(3), 71. doi.org/10.3390/genealogy 5030071

First Peoples Disability Network (2021a). *History of our movement*. fpdn.org.au/ organisational-history/

First Peoples Disability Network (2021b). *Our vision and purpose*. fpdn.org.au/ vison-and-purpose/

Fitts, M., & Soldatić, K. (2020). Who's caring for whom? Disabled Indigenous carers experiences of Australia's infrastructures of social protection. *Journal of Family Studies*, *28*(2), 477–492. doi.org/10.1080/13229400.2020.1734478

Foucault, M. (2002). *Archaeology of knowledge*. Routledge.

Meals on Wheels Australia (n.d.). *About*. mealsonwheels.org.au/learn-more/about/

Prout, S. (2008). *The entangled relationship between Indigenous spatiality and government service delivery*. CAEPR Working Paper No. 41/2008. Centre for Aboriginal Economic Policy Research, The Australian National University. caepr.cass.anu.edu.au/sites/default/files/docs/CAEPRWP41_0.pdf

Riemer, J., & Soldatić, K. (2021). *Minority and Indigenous trends 2021. Lessons of the COVID-19 pandemic*. Minority Rights Group, International. minorityrights.org/ programmes/library/trends2021/australia/

Services Australia (n.d.). Services Australia. www.servicesaustralia.gov.au/

Soldatić, K. (2018). Disability poverty and ageing in regional Australia: The impact of disability income reforms for Indigenous Australians. *Australian Journal of Social Issues*, *53*(3), 223–238. doi.org/10.1002/ajs4.51

Soldatić, K. (2020). Disability's circularity: Presence, absence and erasure in Australian settler colonial biopolitical population regimes. *Studies in Social Justice*, *14*(2), 306–320. doi.org/10.26522/ssj.v14i2.2259

Soldatić, K., Bowman, D., Mupanemunda, M., & Magee, P. (2021). *Dead ends: How our social security system is failing people with partial capacity to work*. Brotherhood of St Laurence.

Sullivan, P. (2018). The tyranny of neoliberal public management and the challenge for Aboriginal community organisations. In D. Howard-Wagner, M. Bargh, & I. Altamirano-Jiménez (Eds), *The neoliberal state, recognition and Indigenous rights: New paternalism to new imaginings*. ANU Press. doi.org/10.22459/CAEPR40.07.2018.11

United Nations Department of Economic and Social Affairs (2015). *State of the world's Indigenous peoples: Indigenous peoples' access to health services*.

Wolfe, P. (2006). Settler colonialism and the elimination of the native. *Journal of Genocide Research*, 8(4), 387–409. www.tandfonline.com/doi/full/10.1080/14623520601056240

Wyndham, D. (2003). *Eugenics in Australia: Striving for national fitness*. The Galton Institute.

4

'Moving with the times' and uncertain futures: Butucarbin in the New Public Management era

Jennifer Beale, Jack Gibson,
and Deirdre Howard-Wagner

Introduction

> Over the years, our region has been neglected.
>
> —Jack Gibson

The chapter is a case study of Butucarbin Aboriginal Corporation, one of the longest-standing community-based not-for-profit First Nations organisations in the Western Sydney region, NSW, Australia. Butucarbin was founded in 1993, at the tail end of the era of self-determination and community development. Butucarbin is located in the suburb of Hebersham in Western Sydney, 47 km from Sydney's central business district. While Mount Druitt is the next suburb along, Beale and Gibson refer to the area, including Hebersham, as the Mount Druitt area. Butucarbin operates out of an old weatherboard housing commission home, which is set back on a large double block on one of Hebersham's main roads. It is a versatile community-based organisation that provides a range of services including TAFE-accredited training courses, skills training, cultural learning days, school holiday programs, support for local sports teams, and helping people without internet access find work. Butucarbin's establishment and operation is illustrative of what Bledsoe describes as 'a broader political drive to reassert Indigenous humanity and enact relations that respect a model of Indigenous self-determination grounded in kinship and community' (Bledsoe et al., 2019). At the turn of the 21st century, Butucarbin was one of 25 community-based First Nations organisations in the Western Sydney region.

This case study of Butucarbin's history makes visible the place of First Nations organisations as community infrastructure and as critical to building Aboriginal economies in urban contexts. The case study identifies how what Beale and Gibson refer to as the Mount Druitt area provided housing and employment opportunities for Aboriginal people in the 1970s and 1980s, which led to a rebuilding of Aboriginal communities and economies in the region and the formation of community-controlled First Nations organisations. Since the 1990s, the Western Sydney region has faced a wave of industrial change, a loss of community-controlled First Nations organisations, and a major social and economic decline in the living standards of Aboriginal people in the region. Instead of preserving community capacity and assets in order to maintain social and economic conditions, the government Indigenous service market has had a detrimental effect on First Nations community infrastructure in the region. Going forward, the Western Sydney region needs economic and social strategies that enable Aboriginal people to rebuild local First Nations community infrastructure and economies.

While Butucarbin has managed to navigate a constantly changing funding and policy environment, it is in a precarious and fragile organisational state, known elsewhere as organisational fragility (see Bendell, 2016). In this regard, Butucarbin is not alone. Twenty years ago, with 25 community-based First Nations organisations operating in the Western Sydney region, there was a solid base of First Nations community infrastructure that supported First Nations people. Today, Butucarbin is one of just five remaining community-based First Nations organisations in the Western Sydney region. This drastic reduction in the number of First Nations organisations suggests that the area's community-based First Nations infrastructure has been hard hit by policies passed by the federal and NSW governments in the NPM era.

The operation of the Indigenous service market, as described in Chapter One, has led to a systematic disinvestment – the sustained and systemic withdrawal of capital investment – from First Nations community infrastructure in the Western Sydney region. Similar to other contexts, the effects are evident in the shrinking of Indigenous-led services, investment in Indigenous community infrastructure, and democratic practices (see Pulido, 2016a). This economic abandonment of First Nations organisations in the region is a separate phenomenon from the numerous political and economic shifts that led to the economic downturn in the Western Sydney region at the turn of the 21st century.

Authors Beale and Gibson were co-researchers as well as informants to the case study, which meant that they had the opportunity to review their individual transcripts of evidence as well as participate in the interpretive analysis of all informant data, ensuring Indigenous data sovereignty principles were followed. Presenting Beale and Gibson's firsthand account of managing an urban First Nations organisation in the NPM era, this chapter gives an empirically grounded example of the effects of what Cedric Robinson called 'racial capitalism' at work (Robinson, 2000, p. 9; see also Bledsoe et al., 2019, p. 8). The chapter situates that firsthand account within the wider context of the loss of community-controlled First Nations organisations in the Western Sydney region. It is our contention that racial capitalism is constitutive – it is not only a way of hierarchically organising, but of configuring dispossession in the Mount Druitt area and wider Western Sydney region. It is also an example of what Byrd et al. refer to as a relationship of taking and violence that works to delimit Indigenous value, and thus operates as an economy of dispossession through expropriation and appropriation (Byrd et al., 2018, p. 3). In exploring this assertion, the chapter analyses Beale and Gibson's account of running Butucarbin to show the distinct way in which the Indigenous service market extracts and expropriates labour and resources from First Nations people and organisations while, at the same time, devaluing their contribution to Indigenous service delivery. By engaging closely with Beale and Gibson's accounts, this chapter reveals how systemic disinvestment, discrimination, and devaluing operate through the Indigenous service market. This systemic disinvestment impacts First Nations organisations but also has wider implications for the First Nations community in the Mount Druitt area. This chapter connects the functioning of neoliberalism, manifested as NPM and the Indigenous service market, to race and extant configurations of power.

This chapter goes beyond narrow descriptions of the Indigenous service market as an economic system, to understand it as an institutionalised social order. The chapter draws on a body of scholarship that explains how racial capitalism is achieved – first by producing social difference in order to extract value, and then by operationalising non-white devaluation (Jacobs, 2021; Pulido, 2016b). As Jacobs argues, whiteness, and by extension white people, are seen as having innate value, whereas nonwhiteness, and non-white people, are only valued if labour, or some other value, can be extracted from them by whiteness/white people (Leong, 2013; cited in Jacobs, 2021, p. 59). The scholarship also links the devaluation of First Nations people to colonisation (Dorries et al., 2019).

Aboriginal relocation and resettlement in Mount Druitt

In one of our long yarns, the founder of Butucarbin, Jennifer Beale, explained the history of Butucarbin. Beale situated Butucarbin's origins within the history of Aboriginal relocation to and resettlement in the Mount Druitt area, which dates back to the 1970s. She also refers to Aboriginal peoples now living in the Mount Druitt area as the Mount Druitt Aboriginal community. As Beale explains:

> My parents came down here, from the bush in the 1970s, under the government resettlement policy. They were resettled in the St Marys, Mount Druitt area, under the Housing for Aborigines (HFA) program. The Department of Housing had a policy then of only having one Aboriginal family in a street because they didn't want to create a 'ghetto,' but this began the establishment of the Mount Druitt Aboriginal community. Aboriginal people from all over NSW and even interstate came here. Lots of women worked in the textile industry as cutters but that went offshore.

> I started work in Mount Druitt as an Aboriginal health worker and later became an outreach adult educator, with Tranby Aboriginal College, Glebe. I was really concerned that there was nothing in adult education out in the Mount Druitt area, and said so to Kevin Cook, the CEO at the time. He said, 'Well, if you can go and find some funding, you can start something out there'.

Beale describes how the suburbs of the area she refers to as Mount Druitt were originally designed and planned in the 1960s to form a new government housing estate accommodating up to 70,000 people. In the 1960s and 1970s, the growth of the Mount Druitt area offered First Nations people from rural and regional NSW employment and independence, and a place to raise families free of government intervention. But ultimately, First Nations people would be let down. Industries withdrew from the area and high unemployment rates followed. Poor public transport meant that many other parts of Sydney were too far away for many to secure work.

Today, Mount Druitt area, known officially as the City of Blacktown, is believed to have the largest and most diverse First Nations population of any urban area in Australia. In the 2016 Census, 3.7 per cent of the population of Blacktown/Mount Druitt State Electoral Divisions 'identified' as Aboriginal and/or Torres Strait Islander, compared with an average of 2.9 per cent in NSW and 2.8 per cent nationally (ABS, 2016). Importantly, over 53 per cent of First Nations people in the area identified as being under 24 years of age. ABS Census data for 2016 indicates that 18.9 per cent of the Aboriginal and Torres Strait Islander population in the Mount Druitt area were unemployed (ABS, 2016). This unemployment rate highlights the importance of First Nations' community infrastructure for this region.

Butucarbin in the era of self-determination and community development

Butucarbin is a small nonprofit organisation with two full-time staff, two part-time staff, and six members on its management committee. All Butucarbin staff are First Nations people, and its governance body is wholly composed of local First Nations people. Butucarbin's work cuts across several social service sectors including community development, education, and early intervention. It engages in small-scale social enterprise activities and provides consultancy services, such as in cultural heritage protection. The organisation is part of the community, as Beale's account will show. Butucarbin is highly dependent upon state support, with almost all its running costs and revenue coming from NSW Government funding.

Butucarbin started out of the carboot of its CEO and founder, Jennifer Beale, who was working at Tranby College as an adult educator at the time and had previously worked as an Aboriginal health officer and trained nurse. Through the voluntary mobilisation and organisation of Beale and others with direct experience in adult education and community development, Butucarbin was founded. Its founder, board, and members did not see Butucarbin as a service provider, seeing it instead as a vehicle for local community development and self-determination.

Beale explains here how Butucarbin secured funding to achieve its objectives while still under the auspice of Tranby:

> So, we looked around for funding, and got it from the Western Sydney Area Assistance Scheme (WSAAS), Department of Urban Affairs and Planning, for a Community Adult Education Project

(CAEP). WSAAS was a really good scheme. A lot of Aboriginal organisations got their start from that funding. Back then, WSAAS had an Aboriginal panel who made funding decisions for Aboriginal organisations, and an Aboriginal community needs analysis was undertaken every year. The Aboriginal community identified their needs, and WSAAS provided the funding; typically, for a two-year [pilot] project, which was usually picked up by a government department. Our CAEP was actually picked up by the then Department Y.[1] WSAAS was really a great way to build the capacity of Aboriginal organisations and the community.

Beale goes on to explain what came out of that funding.

The WSAAS funding, through a two-year pilot program (1989–1990), employed a Community Adult Educator, who was responsible for the coordination of the CAEP. The project started by doing numeracy and literacy programs with the Aboriginal community. I started working out here [in Mount Druitt] with a whiteboard, out of the boot of my car. We then rented an office in another Aboriginal organisation, and Tranby paid the rental on that office. The Advisory Committee recommended we incorporate and then, framed within a self-determining, community-control understanding between Tranby and the Advisory Committee and negotiations with the Department Y, Tranby handed the Advisory Committee the reins; that is how Butucarbin came into being. When Department Y picked it up in 1990, they also picked up a lot of the infrastructure costs; telephone, rent … all those types of costs.

In October 1993, Butucarbin was incorporated, and, as Gibson explains, the management committee became the Advisory Committee for the Butucarbin Aboriginal Corporation.

In its early years of incorporation, Butucarbin felt valued and supported by public officials and government agencies who, through various forms of funding, enabled self-determination and supported their role in the community. As Beale explains, Butucarbin later secured ownership of the building it occupies and the surrounding land.

In 1995, the house and an adjoining vacant block was purchased with funding from the Aboriginal and Torre Strait Islander Commission (ATSIC).

---

1   Name of department withheld.

… there were two properties: the house on the small block was owned by the Department of Housing, and the vacant land was owned by Lancom. Negotiations for one property became re-negotiations for two properties, but with the support of a Lancom employee we were able to negotiate a very good price for the properties. I think we still had about $100,000 to $120,000 left from our ATSIC grant and were hoping to put that towards building our training room, the first stage of our buildings.

After securing a substantial block of land in Hebersham with a house on it (see Image 4.1), Butucarbin's staff and board agreed to extend its facilities to enable it to run adult education and community programs. Butucarbin engaged architectural students from the University of Sydney, who worked with the CEO, board, and members to design a facility that contained spaces for education, community programs, local artists, and a community amphitheatre. The vision was for Butucarbin to be a meeting place in the community.

Image 4.1. Butucarbin Aboriginal Corporation.
Source: Deirdre Howard-Wagner, 2022.

However, that vision did not come to fruition, as Beale explains:

> When I look back, over the years, and look at the plans the student architects had drawn up for this beautiful college, I know our vision wasn't realised because ATSIC wouldn't let us keep the money. So, for many years we just went without having that room. Later though, the NSW Department of Community Services gave us $100,000 but, by that time, it wasn't enough money to build the building. It was getting more and more expensive. So, we negotiated with Redfern Aboriginal Construction Company to build the training room. Unfortunately, they folded, and we lost $6000 of our money to them.
>
> DoCS [Department of Community Services] were pressuring us to spend the money. So, the only thing that we could get for that money was a demountable, which we ended up getting, and to which we contributed about one third of the costs. All that we've had to go through and all the work that we've had to do, we did ourselves.

Beale and Gibson also explain how Butucarbin developed the large block and site through government programs. As Beale explains:

> Most of our landscaping was done by women through a TAFE course. Through Work for the Dole programs the barbeque, pizza oven, and barbecue area were built. Painting was also done through a TAFE course.

While Butucarbin did not realise its aspirations for developing a community centre, it did create a safe space within the local First Nations community. Butucarbin was able to develop programs that were responsive to community needs and to ground its organisational practices and knowledge in ongoing community relationships of trust, respect, and dignity. In the policy and funding environment of the early 1990s, innovation came. Butucarbin went on to facilitate a range of community programs to strengthen First Nations community individuals, families, and communities. Butucarbin maintained an open-door policy, with First Nations people constantly walking in from the street for support, including, as Beale and Gibson say, 'Aboriginal public servants seeking respite from their racist managers and racist workplace cultures/environments'. Butucarbin did this through accredited and non-accredited programs, as well as support services tailored to meet the needs of individuals and families. Butucarbin's innovations, and the benefits it generated for local Aboriginal people, promoted high levels of community cooperation, motivation, and commitment to Butucarbin, and respect for community members working in the organisation.

Butucarbin went from strength to strength in the early 1990s, contributing to community development and the creation of a strong Indigenous social economy in the Mount Druitt area. As Gibson and Beale explain, Butucarbin has always been engaged in supporting community and advocacy. Beale elaborates:

> We assist local Aboriginal people with funeral transport support. We have women's groups, men's groups. We run TAFE courses. We're really doing community development, in that community identifies their need and then we do that. For the last five or six years we've been doing a youth football program. That was to keep the kids out of trouble. That was from community members coming to us and talking with us about what we can do together for these young kids?

As Beale goes on to explain, this led Butucarbin's team to win the under-12s Koori Knockout, which, she says, put Mount Druitt 'on the map':

> Our under-12s were the first Aboriginal team from Mount Druitt to ever make it into the Koori Knockout semi-final and then win the grand final. No other Mount Druitt men's team or women's team had ever got that far. So, our youth teams put Mount Druitt on the map.

Beale and Gibson reflect on how the Mount Druitt Aboriginal community's many strengths, including the close connections between families and community members and the strength of other community-based organisations, gave support to Butucarbin. The Mount Druitt Aboriginal community was quick to advocate, mobilise, and provide support where government and NGOs had failed. As Gibson notes,

> At that stage, we had something like 25 Aboriginal organisations. Community-controlled organisations in the Mount Druitt area – Mount Druitt, St Marys, Penrith area, and … they employed a lot of people.

Gibson then goes on to explain how the last 25 years have become increasingly difficult, not just for Butucarbin, but for the Aboriginal people in the Mount Druitt area. There are now higher numbers of Aboriginal people living in the area, higher rates of unemployment, fewer opportunities, and now only five community-based First Nations organisations. Two half-day yarning circles with senior position-holders from those five community-based First Nations organisations confirmed that their observations were similar to those of Beale and Gibson, as too were their experiences of the Indigenous service market. Today, as the rest of this chapter will show, the NPM policies that have been steadily introduced since the early 21st century have meant those organisations are engaged in a constant struggle to secure resources – even in late 2023, three years from the signing of the National Agreement on CTG.

Goodbye Indigenous self-determination, hello deficit mentality

> We've paid a high price, especially when we're being an advocate, the government then tends to not want to deal with us. We're making trouble. They see us as troublemakers.
>
> —Jack Gibson

Beale and Gibson identify the time when political will began to change as 1996, with the election of the federal Howard Coalition Government. They believe the writing was on the wall for Butucarbin by 1997, when the Howard Government announced its move to 'practical reconciliation' and substantially cut funding to the ATSIC and Indigenous affairs.

Beale and Gibson refer to how the Howard Government started to frame First Nations organisations as a policy problem, particularly in relation to their administration, accountability, and advocacy. A body of scholarship confirms this. For example, according to Moynihan and Pandey, the Howard Government's discourses about First Nations organisations relied on a theoretical explanation of cause and effect (2006, p. 120). The Howard Government framed First Nations organisations within a deficit mentality and as a policy problem that needed to be fixed (Howard-Wagner, 2016). The solution was to change the way Indigenous services were funded along the lines of the administrative doctrine of NPM (Howard-Wagner, 2016). Moynihan and Pandey argue that the purported aim was to embed the 'desirable organisational characteristics' of this administrative doctrine in First Nations organisations, to improve administrative performance and enhance accountability (2006, p. 120). The intended aim was to get First Nations organisations to focus on their governance, aligning governance practices with that of mainstream corporations, and develop businesslike, if not entrepreneurial cultures. Businesslike qualities were valued over the more networked, innovative ways in which First Nations organisations prefer to operate.

As outlined in Chapter One, community and not-for-profit organisations in general, and not just First Nations organisations, have been devalued in the NPM era. Many scholars have noted the negative effects that the marketisation of the social service sector and the new contractualism have had on civil society (Salamon, 1999; Williams et al., 2012). These negative effects include, but are not limited to, undermining the role that nonprofit organisations play in civil society, discouraging advocacy, devaluing democratic citizenship, and democratic ideals such as fairness and justice, eliminating distinct specialised services, diminishing social capital, and disempowering citizens (Eikenberry & Kluver, 2004).

For the Howard Government, applying the so-called logic of market rationality, First Nations organisations were meant to occupy a neutral third space between government and First Nations people, delivering services on behalf of government to individual First Nations people. The Howard Government's position or way of framing the societal function of community-controlled organisations was at odds with, and ignored, the fact that the community-controlled movement came out of not only a desire for self-determination but also the desire to sidestep the intrusion of governments and white charitable organisations in the lives of Aboriginal people (Howard-Wagner, 2016; Howard-Wagner et al., 2022).

Beale reflects on this moment, particularly on how the abolition of ATSIC and the subsequent loss of funding for community infrastructure led to a loss of capacity:

> First, they dismantled the ATSIC community programs by cutting the program funding. We lost quite a number of organisations. Following those cuts the ATSIC health portfolio was transferred to mainstream health and, in 2005, the Howard Liberal government abolished ATSIC altogether. As a consequence, there was no longer funding available for community infrastructure.

Beale explains how these changes led the local Western Sydney Aboriginal community-controlled health service to go into administration. A coalition was formed to take over the Western Sydney Aboriginal health service and maintain it as a local community-controlled organisation. Beale goes on to explain that this coalition comprised four local community-based organisations, supported by the National Aboriginal Community Controlled Health Organisation (NACCHO), and Sydney University. However, the health service was ultimately taken over by the Wellington Aboriginal Corporation Health Service (WACHS), located in central-west NSW. WACHS planned to manage the Aboriginal Health Service at Mount Druitt from Wellington, without any input from the Mount Druitt Aboriginal community. Beale explains that Mount Druitt Aboriginal people were unable to become members of WACHS because they were out of the area, as the organisation's administrative arm was located in Wellington. As non-members, local Mount Druitt Aboriginal peoples' voices were silenced, and they were disempowered because they could not have a say through formal membership at general meetings on how the Aboriginal health service in their area should function to meet their health needs. This was confirmed through workshops with senior position-holders from the other five First Nations community-controlled organisations in the Mount Druitt, St Marys, and Penrith areas.

Beale's point is that the coalition's locally based organisational, management, and health knowledge was blatantly disregarded in the decision to award the contract for who delivered Aboriginal health services in the area. Further, the vast amount of evidence of the success of community control predicated on Aboriginal self-determination was not even considered. It seems, Beale says, that the Mount Druitt Aboriginal community has suffered in imposed silence due to the dominant, racist view of Aboriginal deficiency held by the government.

Gibson explains how First Nations organisations in the Mount Druitt, St Marys, and Penrith areas were drastically diminished to a meagre handful. Over the last two decades, the number of First Nations community and health organisations has dropped from around 25 to just 5. It is this undermining of urban First Nations community development, community infrastructure, and longstanding community-based organisations in the Western Sydney region that Beale and Gibson reflect on as one of the most damaging structural effects of the last 25 years on Indigenous self-determination.

The era of NPM: 'They are always on our backs because they think we are in deficit'

> I think it's informed by this neoliberal idea, so what we're seeing as an organisation that's, what you would call it? We're not recognised as an organisation that's very successful. That success to me is informed by people's idea of what an Aboriginal organisation is. Yet, [with governments and government departments] we're always operating in this deficit model of Aboriginality.
>
> —Jack Gibson

Beale and Gibson explain how the deficit mentality of the Howard era has carried forward into the present. They explain that government agencies and departments are 'always on their back' because they perceive Butucarbin to be in deficit. Countering this image, Beale and Gibson explain that Butucarbin is a small-scale organisation that carries the burden of a government funding deficit. Staff are not only overworked and underpaid, but highly stressed. What governments fail to see, for Beale and Gibson, is the ways in which Butucarbin supports the community, providing social services and doing the heavy lifting that underwrites the work of governments in CTG. Beale and Gibson's work often requires a significant voluntary component, which they give as an example of this underwriting, while explaining how government-designed social services are not doing their job and are just not hitting the mark.[2]

Today, Butucarbin encounters significant difficulties obtaining funding to continue its work with the Mount Druitt Aboriginal community. Unlike large non-Indigenous organisations, Butucarbin remains resource-poor, both in terms of its number of staff and its ongoing financial status. As a First Nations community-controlled organisation, Butucarbin's staff and board of management contribute many hours of voluntary service to make up for the funding shortfalls for the services that they provide to the Mount Druitt Aboriginal community.

Funding precarity as disinvestment

Beale identifies competitive tendering as a significant feature of the NPM era, and explains how this has affected the capacity of community-based First Nations organisations to secure funding:

> The Howard government brought in competitive tendering. So, you have large faith-based organisations, with professional submission writers, and then you have small organisations who do not have the infrastructure to compete. With the abolition of ATSIC more Aboriginal organisations folded, and it was only those not funded by ATSIC that remained. It's sad to see, but competitive tendering put the nail in the coffin of Aboriginal organisations. The Targeted

---

2   This finding was reinforced in a Discussion Circle with Chief Executive Officers from five other community-controlled First Nations organisations in December 2023 and remains the case despite the 2020 National Agreement on Closing the Gap.

> Early Intervention reform (TEI) that we're all going through now, is just another nail in the coffin of smaller [Aboriginal] organisations. There are also ethical issues around TEI.

Butucarbin has found that it is impossible to get large block grants to expand its work. The CEO has spent a lot of her scarce time and resources competing with large 'white' non-profits and private corporations to apply for smaller grants. Butucarbin has become increasingly reliant on highly competitive, small, short-term grants of varied lengths targeted at explicit contracted outcomes. These grants provide only stopgap support for Butucarbin's activities and often have burdensome reporting requirements. As a result, Butucarbin runs on a very limited budget of around $294,000 annually. While Butucarbin generates a small income from the social enterprises it has created, such as its consultancy arm, the income it generates is insufficient to fully subsidise community programs or cover shortfalls in operational costs.

A significant change for Butucarbin under NPM is the nature of its funding arrangement with its main funder, which is a NSW government department. Butucarbin has continued to deliver services and remained funded by that department for 20 years. Beale explains: 'While we are funded by Department Y, we have not received an increase in infrastructure funding in more than two decades'. Beale further explains:

> We are only funded until June next year. They are going through reforms now. They did it with other areas of funding, and now, they're reducing programs in our areas from 12 programs down to 5.

While the infrastructure funding was highly beneficial in the 1990s, and Butucarbin still accesses that funding through Department Y, Beale advises that Department Y has:

> never actually increased Butucarbin's infrastructure funding over the years. So, the only increase in funding we got was the annual increase in wage indexation, and an increase in wages when the equal remuneration order came with the award, but that will happen over 12 years.

Here, Beale highlights a serious funding problem that has emerged for First Nations nonprofit organisations. While insurance, including public liability insurance, workers compensation insurance, and other costs, have risen as a result of the insurance crises in 2000, and utility costs are continuously increasing, government funding has not kept up. As Beale points out: 'You're looking at $5000 before you can even open the doors now.'

Beale and Gibson explain how Butucarbin has always operated on a small budget. In the beginning, it was possible for their organisation to keep simple ledgers. However, while Butucarbin has continued to operate as a charity, and to work flexibly and responsively with communities, its administrative systems have had to change. Upgrading Butucarbin's administrative systems to meet the Australian Tax Office, Office of the Registrar of Indigenous Corporations, and other government requirements is a cost to Butucarbin. Despite this added burden, Butucarbin has not received any support to update its administrative systems and still has the same number of staff it had when it first started operating. Beale puts this in perspective:

> When we first started the organisation, keeping financial records was quite simple, it was a simple ledger. Over time, computerised systems came in and software had to be purchased. I remember, we had to be supervised for two years, using the software, to do the books until the auditor was happy that we were okay with the system.

> We can't even afford a bookkeeper. So, you have to incorporate those tasks into your work, and still meet the demands of the agreement. We worked out, that two of us did five different roles. We've spoken to Department Y about what we actually do and the effort it takes, with a possible chance of more funding; it just didn't happen. They said, no, there's no more funding. But, if we didn't do those roles, then the organisation would collapse.

> And when you look at Aboriginal people in the community sector, they have had a lot have cerebrovascular CVAs [cardiovascular accidents], cerebrovascular clots on the brain, and have died with cardiac problems. It's the stress. You see that adult mortality rates are extremely high. Aboriginal people who have had cancer and died, or strokes and those sort of things; it's enormous. People just say, oh, isn't that sad? So, and so dropped dead, and blah, blah, blah. You go to the funeral. Then you just get on with it. There is immense pressure.

> That's the difference, I think, with the white organisations who get the funding. They have all the infrastructure, and they're able to sign off at five o'clock. We don't sign off at five o'clock. We have a workload burden and then supporting community is virtually a 24-hour day. People will get you out of bed at two or three o'clock in the morning. You will, at times, work seven days a week, because crises don't happen just on Monday to Friday, nine to five.

Beale and Gibson reflect on the devaluing of First Nations people working in community-based nonprofit First Nations organisations. Two themes underscore Beale and Gibson's narrative around Butucarbin's devaluation by government funders: firstly, the funders' presumption of organisational deficiency and secondly, government paternalism. These are discussed below.

Beale and Gibson explain that Butucarbin was once valued by Department Y, but that this relationship has changed. As Beale and Gibson note:

> We've been in favour sometimes – we had a very good relationship with Department Y way back. We did a lot of work with them. We helped them set up advisory bodies and helped them with organisations, get organisations out of trouble …

> But today they won't give us enough funding. We subsidise the program we run for [Department Y] through our room rental and doing some research consultancy work. We have been able to make money, which goes towards topping up the program. That's another area that [Department Y] is always on our backs about. They believe we're in deficit. But, Butucarbin is not in deficit, it is the Departmental program (purchased by the Department) that is in deficit. Butucarbin has picked up that deficit over many years. We have refused to not show the deficit because it shows them that they don't give us enough money.

> They didn't even want us to take a rental component; you pay rent, everybody pays rent. They could not get their head around the fact that Butucarbin was the landlord, and the project was the tenant. It took a three-hour meeting, with our auditor involved. I had to get rental market value of the property, which was about $1,200 a week five years ago. We were only charging them $400. At the same time, there was a white organisation, one of us sits on their committee, and we know they were being paid $58,000 a year towards their rent. Nothing was said to this white not-for-profit organisation. But, as a 'Black' organisation, you are always under that microscope. There is a presumption that you must be doing something wrong.

> Now two new milestones have been built into our funding agreement; that we have to collect client data on the DEX [Data Exchange] system and we can't be in deficit. So, they're really pushing back. The only way that we can avoid being in deficit is to drop the levels of our wages. Funding hasn't kept up with rising oncosts and utilities, which chew into our budget. So, we have no choice but to reduce our wages, but still meet the milestones. But, a reduction in salaries means Butucarbin will have to go through a restructure.

A restructure points to our termination. If we are terminated who then will be the CEO, or will it possible to have a CEO? Avoiding a deficit raises new problems that someone will have to deal with.

Butucarbin's so-called deficit played significantly into the department's decision to offer us the lowest contract of two-years, rather than a three, or five-year contract, like the white organisations. They've come back and said, well, because you've been in deficit for so many years, we're only offering you a two-year contract. Butucarbin has always been in surplus and never in deficit. That's another slap in the face for our committee: an organisation that's never been in trouble financially, for over twenty years, and has been treated this way.

The way that Butucarbin's funding is now structured means that the income from the funding it receives from Department Y is no longer enough to cover the salaries of Beale, the CEO, and Gibson, the long-standing Community Development Officer, who run the programs. Under the new funding structure, Butucarbin will be left without a CEO. New junior staff will have to come in to administer the programs. It is not a viable option for a functioning First Nations organisation to be operating this way.

The devaluing of First Nations organisations in the Indigenous service market

While Beale and Gibson attribute Department Y's underfunding of Butucarbin in part to the competitive undercutting of the cost of the services through the competitive efforts of large not-for-profit organisations now competing in the Indigenous service market, the reoccurring theme across their narrative is one of devaluation. The funding model undervalues the intensive time and work of Butucarbin, which has not received an increase in infrastructure funding in more than two decades. Butucarbin's salaries have been downgraded under its contract. It has battled to get its costs incorporated in the unit price for the services it delivers to ensure that the costs of delivering these services are properly covered. This program funding model is not well matched to the needs of a small-scale community-based First Nations organisation. Butucarbin raises small amounts of revenue from renting out rooms and engaging in research consultancies, which goes towards covering the shortfall in its service delivery contract. But Beale and Gibson note that Butucarbin can't run its heaters in the winter because it can't afford the bills. Importantly, it is funding bodies, and ultimately governments, who benefit in terms of cost savings – not First Nations people or the organisations who provide critical community infrastructure. Beale and Gibson's combined narrative reveals how this funding model is poorly matched to the needs of this small-scale, community-based First Nations organisation.

Devaluing is a key factor in the literature on racial capitalism. For example, Bledsoe illustrates how capitalism remains dependent on subjugation, in part, by the exploitation of First Nations peoples (Bledsoe et al., 2019, p. 3).

Who benefits from systemic devaluing?

Beale and Gibson identify two major aspects of racial capitalism's systemic presence in the Indigenous service market. First, this is an example of what Bledsloe et al. describe as a system that devalues First Nations organisations (Bledsoe et al., 2019, p. 3). Second, this is an example of what Bledsloe et al. refer to as the extractive and administrative nature of capitalism, which maintains a strong positive orientation towards a Western administrative doctrine and white organisations (Bledsoe et al., 2019, p. 3). Beale and Gibson give many examples of the ways in which the public officials who administer Indigenous service delivery through the Indigenous service market apply an administrative doctrine to assess 'desirable organisational characteristics' in their management of contracting relationships with Butucarbin and other local First Nations organisations. While Butucarbin has adapted its administrative practices to new requirements and is operating unambiguously in accordance with business sector tendencies, while trying to balance its commitment to the community, it is not in a position to compete in the market. Beale argues here that the Indigenous service market puts Butucarbin in competition with white organisations who are more likely to win contracts because of their greater administrative capacity:

> They have professional submission roles, so they have people who just do that job; they just write submissions. We can't compete with that, because we're doing so much – we've got to meet our targets. We've got to meet our numbers. We're working at the coalface. When do we get time to actually to sit down and write submissions that are at a quality to compete with the big organisations? We don't have the money to hire people at all, as well. This has come up over the years.

White organisations may have greater administrative capacity, which Beale attributes to their organisational infrastructure. Beale argues that, if they had the same infrastructure as larger organisations, she believes Butucarbin too would be able to function at this level. However, Beale explains this is not the point. Gibson, and Beale too, believe that the Indigenous service system privileges white organisations because of the perceived fit between their so-called administrative capacity and the doctrine of the system. Throughout our two long discussions, Beale and Gibson substantiated these claims many times.

Beale explains that her fundamental concern is that the Indigenous service system rewards organisations because of their white administrative capacity, as opposed to the capacity to engage with Indigenous communities. Beale has a fundamental problem with a system that allows those organisations to then go and build this capacity through engaging First Nations organisations without remuneration, as she explains here:

> So, the white organisations win the tender, and it may be 12 months or so, or getting close to the completion of the program and getting the numbers they need, that they come back to us and say, well, if you won't help us engage with the Aboriginal community the money will go back and the community will miss out. They pull on our heart strings, and so, although not getting paid for it, we engage with Aboriginal community. We did that for a long time. But we took a stance, now we say to them that when you tendered for that project, you said that you have had this history of engaging with the Aboriginal community. That's why you were selected. So, unless you're willing to pay us to help you engage with community, to get the people, then no, we will not help you. That has really stopped them coming to us now. Because we maintain that stance, they don't even bother to come near us. Occasionally, they might still ring and ask us to write a support letter for funding, or whatever?

Beale believes the Indigenous service system is orientated towards a model that values how white organisations operate and deliver services as opposed to one that values the way First Nations organisations operate and deliver services. For example, no value is placed on the organisation's longstanding success in relation to delivering services to First Nations people in the Mount Druitt community. As Beale goes on to explain:

> You're comparing oranges and apples. There should have been a matrix that said, you've got so many points already. There's no measurement of how long we've been going, what we've been doing in the community, our record of our financial management, or anything of that type.

> I suppose that's a lot to do with Howard but, basically, white's better. They know what is best for us. The idea that white is better takes you back to the protection era days. That's really frustrating and oppressive. All of our negative memories of childhood come back to haunt us, and that is detrimental to our mental health and our emotional wellbeing.

Another important point of contrast between white organisations and community-based First Nations organisations that emerge from Beale and Gibson's analysis is that the community-based First Nations organisations, such as Butucarbin, have knowledge of the diversity of First Nation peoples, communities, and cultures, and the skills and attitudes to work effectively with them. Butucarbin can and does assist what they refer to as 'white organisations' in connecting with the community because white organisations cannot replicate the skills and attitudes that enable First Nations organisations to work effectively with First Nations people throughout the service delivery process. Yet, Butucarbin acts as an unpaid cultural mediator and consultant to white organisations in the delivery of services to First Nations people. Gibson suggests that this is because white organisations simply do not have the capacity to recognise and accommodate the Indigenous knowledge, know-how, and skills that are required for effective and responsive Indigenous services in line with community expectations. By way of example, Gibson explains how Butucarbin has to manage the problems that are created in communities as a result of mainstream organisations delivering services to First Nations people:

> Mainstream organisations are out there delivering national programs, that are getting funding. Then, you've got people within community coming to you because of the problems with those programs and because of the structural problems that exist. So, you're playing a really significant role in community, while continuing to operate and maintain this community organisation. But there's no recognition of what you do?

Beale and Gibson argue that the Indigenous service system is not attuned to Indigenous expertise and knowledge. This expertise and knowledge are not remunerated within the Indigenous service market. For example, as longstanding community members and Elders, Beale and Gibson are able to act as cultural agents and mediators. They bring expertise and knowledge to the delivery of Indigenous services in the Mount Druitt area that cannot be replicated. So, devaluing operates at multiple levels.

Put simply, Beale and Gibson explain how the Indigenous service market's failure to accommodate Indigenous expertise and knowledge renders the system culturally unsafe. There is no shared respect, shared meaning, shared knowledge, deep listening, or learning together. There has been no strategic and institutional reform to remove barriers within the system. There is no power sharing in the Indigenous service market in terms of community decision-making around community needs and resourcing of Aboriginal communities. There is no engagement with the community or organisations around the design, delivery, and evaluation of services for First Nations people. Instead, the Indigenous service system has created new barriers. It is a system that perpetuates unconscious bias, racism, and discrimination, and fails to support self-determination.

Gibson describes the framework or model government departments impose on First Nations organisations as a mismatch and not a good cultural fit for the way the First Nations organisations work:

> There seems to be this mismatch with the framework that they impose upon our organisation, and the way we do work. There's this cultural fit, the way we work is much more organic, and takes a lot longer than this model suggests. This model to me, is a process line. We just have these little cookie cut-outs, and we produce those types of people.

Gibson points to a lack of alignment between the beliefs and values that are embedded in the Indigenous service market and those of First Nations people, organisations, and communities. He describes the cultural impact that the Indigenous service market and those administering it have on First Nations people, organisations, and communities. For Beale and Gibson, everything from the structures of the system to the way those administering it interact with First Nations organisations, shape the culture of the Indigenous service market as 'white'.

During our discussion, Gibson also explains how the relationships organisations form with the community should be an integral measure of the effectiveness of the services offered. Gibson and Beale return to this point on a number of occasions, explaining that one of the key distinctions between mainstream and First Nations organisations is in their relationship with First Nations communities and people. Gibson gives the following as an example:

It's about these relationships. To me, the government's imposed model doesn't account for the relationships that you develop over the years. What keeps an organisation operating is not these structures, policies and processes – it's relationships.

We've been here for so long because people know and trust us. We have this relationship with people, and I think that's the difference, compared to that of a non-Aboriginal relationship. There may be worker/client relationship, but they don't go home with the people. They can leave at five o'clock or whatever time they finish in the afternoon. They don't need to worry about anything else.

Beale draws attention to the disconnect between the value that the Mount Druitt First Nations community places on Butucarbin compared with its devaluing among public officials and bureaucrats. As Beale states:

The community value us because of the type of work we do. It doesn't happen overnight; it takes a long time. We've had people who require long-term support. For example, one of the women who came to us in a domestic violence situation, had young children, but had finished school, and nobody supported her. We asked, 'What do you want to do?' 'She said, I want to do teaching.' So, we were able to help her get enrolled into a block release program, and was able to give her a part-time job doing administration work for us.

We helped her transfer from Mount Druitt to the city. She finished her teaching, did a master's degree and she's now a lecturer. I was her referee when she applied for the job as a lecturer at one of the universities. We also wrote support letters to help get her children in some of the top schools in Sydney. We stayed with her throughout her journey. This has been over a 20-year period. How do you then, measure that; how and when do you measure that outcome?

Beale also explains how Butucarbin fills a lot of the gaps in mainstream service delivery:

It's all those little things. Say, for instance, a barrier to employment is transport, so having a licence is important. TAFE might have a learner driver program, the person goes there and gets their training, but how then do they get their hours up? Or how do they then go for their licence when they haven't got a car, or cannot afford to use a driving school? It's all those things, and over the years, that's been something that we've actually done. We've seen all ages get their licence. That's been the pathway for them, because once they've got their licence, they're able to compete for employment, which they hadn't been able to do before. So, I suppose because we're a small organisation, we have that flexibility. Yeah, we have policies and all that, because that's a requirement, but how many times do you really use them?

Gibson explains that supporting the community also means supporting Aboriginal public servants who are struggling with the culture in their work environments:

We also get a number of public servants that come here when they're having trouble at work. I've had a lot of workers come here, and they need that release, because they cannot talk to their bosses. We've got a public servant that comes to us now. He has a boss that's just – just unbelievably racist, so he comes to us for emotional support. He's the man that monitors and tries to support organisations, but he comes to us for support.

Beale provides additional context to Gibson's point:

That's why they're like – they've changed Aboriginal workers over the years, like changing underwear. They just come and they go, they come, and they go. They get no support, and then they're out. Yeah – it's really difficult, isn't it?

Gibson goes on to explain:

Yeah. I was an Aboriginal CPO [Community Project Officer] once. That was a long time ago, and I really didn't know what the job was about. I had a statement of duties, but it wasn't really clear who I was and what I was supposed to do, no one actually knew. That was back in '95, so over that time, they've always been trying to work out what Aboriginal people do. Affirmative action is well and good, but if you're going to tick a box and say, I've done my job, and just throw a person in the deep end without any support, plus you've got bosses that think one way (they're enclosed in this little box and cannot think outside of it), then it's just a recipe for disaster. That impacts on us as an organisation.

While the system devalues and underfunds Butucarbin, it continues to occupy an important space in the community. Butucarbin is strongly valued within the Mount Druitt Aboriginal community. Its identity is very much embedded in the Mount Druitt Aboriginal community. It has brought about significant social change for the Mount Druitt Aboriginal community. Its immense success is evident in many examples of individual success.

Beale gives the example of how Butucarbin put in a bid for funding against a white organisation to illustrate the importance of cultural fit and to explain how the system reinforces racialised structures. The white mainstream organisation was judged by a white bureaucrat as more 'culturally competent' than Butucarbin. It's not a perception of Beale's, but the verbal feedback that she was given by a public official as the basis for Butucarbin not being granted the contract. Beale describes this process as a box-ticking exercise, in which the white organisation was awarded the contract because it indicated the cultural competence measures that it has in place. It had indicated that it has a Sorry Day event and reconciliation events. As Beale explains, Butucarbin does Sorry Day and reconciliation just about every day. Butucarbin administers a local funeral transport fund and organises local National Aborigines' and Islanders' Day Observance Committee (NAIDOC) week events, but there was no box for that. That a white organisation was deemed to have more 'cultural competence' than Butucarbin is illustrative of the racial bias of whiteness in measures of cultural competence. This culture is rendered visible through whiteness, which is the standard by which culture is differentiated (Pon, 2009, p. 60).

The finding about racial bias in the measurement of cultural competence is not new. A body of scholarship is now showing how cultural competency measures are a flawed attempt to mitigate racial inequalities that have instead entrenched systemic racism (Ray & Davis, 2021). Others, such as Pon, go as far as arguing that 'cultural competency promotes an obsolete view of culture and is a form of new racism' (Pon, 2009, 59). As Pon explains:

> The term new racism refers to racial discrimination that involves a shift away from racial exclusionary practices based on biology to those based on culture (Goldberg, 1993). Cultural competency, like new racism, operates by essentialising culture …
>
> (Pon, 2009, p. 60)

The idea that a white organisation can achieve a higher standard of cultural competency is where decisions taken in the Indigenous service system operate to essentialise culture and reify it in what Pon describes as 'modernist and colonialist ways' (Pon, 2009, p. 65), rendering invisible the everyday cultural practices of a First Nations organisation.

Gibson further argues that the ubiquitous and uncritical use of cultural competency, through myriad workshops, documents, and policies since the 1990s, has reinforced the narrow view that culture is conceived of as a separate, coherent entity (see Couldry, 2000, p. 92). As such, it has enabled and privileged the dominant white gaze to mis/treat culture as a commodity. A commodity is then able to be manipulated by whomever wants to manipulate it to meet their own (usually) economic ends, and make them feel good about themselves, while maintaining their positionality. Consequently, the very structural inequities that are meant to be challenged and transformed are literally bolstered. Little wonder then, that white organisations are more culturally competent than First Nations organisations.

Beale and Gibson also explain how the way they are contractually required to deliver services to local First Nations people is poorly matched to their needs, and are not helping to meet CTG targets. They give many examples of poor matches, such as the Data Exchange (DEX) system. Gibson outlines three problems with the DEX system:

> It's a moral and ethical dilemma for us to put names into a system that you know is going to be detrimental to Aboriginal people in the long term. I'm just surprised that there's no other organisations jumping up and down about it. We certainly have, and I think that's why Department Y did what they did to us. We had three-year funding under the previous program and under the new TEI program we were only offered a two-year contract, and they've taken six months off because of the pandemic. Now it's only 18-months or so, we have left.

> The DEX system fails to understand the way community is embedded in our organisation. We are an organisation where people walk in for help. The DEX system will change this culture. People won't come in and we will lose community trust. It will be seen as 'white surveillance' in the long settler colonial history of white policy makers and bureaucrats' surveillance of First Nations peoples in Australia; surveillance on steroids. Such surveillance also plays into Aboriginal people's fear of the cashless debit card.

For Beale and Gibson, the introduction of the DEX system is symbolic of white surveillance and the whiteness of a system that harks back to the racialised systems of the pre-1970s.

What Beale and Gibson make visible is not only how white organisations benefit from the Indigenous service system, but how the system itself privileges whiteness. By positioning privilege as the analytical frame, Beale reveals how the whiteness of the system should be made to answer for the ways in which privilege plays out in the Indigenous service market. In making whiteness visible, Beale is not merely asking for public officials to acknowledge that the system privileges white organisations, but to seriously reconsider the racialised nature of the Indigenous service market system through the multiple ways that it devalues First Nations organisations.

Conclusion: Butucarbin and community-based First Nations organisations in Mount Druitt today

Beale and Gibson believe that self-determination and community development are nearly non-existent in the Mount Druitt region today. As Beale explains:

> What has happened is that we have dwindled over the years. For instance, there was a refuge for Aboriginal women which operated for over 30 years – that closed down around four or five years ago. Today, Butucarbin is one of only 5 of the 25 community-based organisations remaining from the era of self-determination and development.

Their account reveals how the Indigenous service system devalues the social, political, and economic contribution of First Nations organisations. The consequence is that a First Nations organisation like Butucarbin misses out on the economic opportunities available to First Nations organisations through participation in the delivery of services to First Nations peoples. Beale and Gibson's accounts reveal how community-based First Nations organisations are partitioned from participation in the Indigenous service market as a market economy by virtue of white organisations winning funding contracts. Their explanation of how the Indigenous service market operates in the Mount Druitt region exposes how urban First Nations organisations contend with a structure of white domination through the continued enactment of capital relations. They expose not only the enormous barriers to the participation of First Nations organisations in the Indigenous service market as a capitalist system but also how the system rewards white organisations, who, in turn, exploit community-based First Nations organisations to facilitate access to communities or to write a support letter for funding without remunerating the First Nations organisation. 'Racial capitalism', the term coined by Cedric J Robinson, is apt for describing how a white organisation extracts social and economic value from a First Nations organisation (Robinson, 2000).

Butucarbin's experiences illustrate the forms of systemic disinvestment, discrimination, and devaluing that occur through interactions between the Indigenous service market and a First Nations organisation. Beale and Gibson's accounts about their interactions over the last 15 years with a government department reveal not only the competing priorities of different white governance layers in the Indigenous services market but also multiple layers of systemic devaluing of Indigenous expertise and knowledge at work in the Indigenous service market.

Beale and Gibson illustrate how systemic devaluing includes the devaluing of an organisation's expertise in delivering services to First Nations people and the embedded expertise and knowledge that come from being longstanding community members and Elders. So, there is not only evidence of an economic abandonment of the Mount Druitt First Nation community but an intentional disinvestment in community-based First Nations organisations. The Indigenous service market continues to displace community-based First Nations organisations in Western Sydney.

After 20 years of struggling to keep going, it is clear that First Nations organisations are experiencing NPM fatigue. This is not only due to the volume of administrative and regulative changes that have occurred in the last 20 years, but the increasing scarcity of resources and the increasing demand on workload. First Nations organisations like Butucarbin are experiencing instability, and are in constant battle to maintain their place in the service delivery space. Butucarbin is having to deal with the chronic problems the NPM era has created for community-based First Nations organisations. It is an era in which Butucarbin has lacked self-determination and agency. It is an era that has whittled away its capacity to continue the longstanding, grassroots, community-centred programs that it initiated in innovative times. The Butucarbin organisation has reached burnout and passive resignation.

In response to an unsustainable situation, the CEO, staff, and board members are looking to ways to keep Butucarbin going for the next generation. Butucarbin has held its ground, continuing to deliver programs to local Aboriginal people. Today though, Butucarbin and other longstanding organisations are looking for ways out of their situation. Butucarbin has decided it will need to change its organisational direction. While Butucarbin will not close its doors, the changes it must make will likely mark its end as a community-based First Nations organisation engaged in service provision. The changes Butucarbin must make will likely mark a further moment in the whittling away of Indigenous community infrastructure in a locality in dire need of community-focused and driven initiatives. These changes will further mark the end of an era of self-determination and innovation that saw the creation of 25 community-based organisations. These organisations were trying to improve the life outcomes of one of the fastest-growing populations of First Nations peoples in Australia, who are also living in one of Australia's poverty hotspots.

Butucarbin has some tough decisions to make about its future direction. While its doors will remain open, it is highly unlikely that Butucarbin will remain operating as a social service organisation in the coming years.

References

Australian Bureau of Statistics (2016). *Mount Druitt 2016 census all persons QuickStats*. abs.gov.au/census/find-census-data/quickstats/2016/SSC12756

Bendell, T. (2016). *Building anti-fragile organisations: Risk, opportunity and governance in a turbulent world*. Routledge. doi.org/10.4324/9781315570426

Bledsoe, A., McCreary, T., & Wright, W. (2019). Theorizing diverse economies in the context of racial capitalism. *Geoforum*, *132*, 281–290. doi.org/10.1016/j.geoforum.2019.07.004

Byrd, J. A., Goldstein, A., Melamed, J., & Reddy, C. (2018). Predatory value: Economies of dispossession and disturbed relationalities. *Social Text*, *36*(2), 1–18. doi.org/10.1215/01642472-4362325

Couldry, N. (2000). *Inside culture: Re-imagining the method of cultural studies*. Sage Publications. doi.org/10.4135/9781849209267

Dorries, H., Hugill, D., & Tomiak, J. (2019). Racial capitalism and the production of settler colonial cities. *Geoforum*, *132*, 263–270. doi.org/10.1016/j.geoforum.2019.07.016

Eikenberry, A. M., & Kluver, J. D. (2004). The marketization of the nonprofit sector: Civil society at risk? *Public Administration Review*, *64*(2), 132–140. doi.org/10.1111/j.1540-6210.2004.00355.x

Howard-Wagner, D. (2016). Child wellbeing and protection as a regulatory system in the neoliberal age: Forms of Aboriginal agency and resistance engaged to confront the challenges for Aboriginal people and community-based Aboriginal organisations. *Australian Indigenous Law Review*, *19*(1), 88–102.

Howard-Wagner, D., Soldatić, K., Spurway, K., Hunt, J., Harrington, M., Riemer, J., Leha, J., Mason, C., Fogg, R., Goh, C., & Gibson, J. (2022). First Nations organisations and strategies of disruption and resistance to settler–colonial governance in Australia. In K. Soldatić & L. St Guillaume (Eds), *Social suffering in the neoliberal age: State power, logics and resistance*. Routledge. doi.org/10.4324/9781003131779-16

Jacobs, F. (2021). Beyond social vulnerability: COVID-19 as a disaster of racial capitalism. *Sociologica*, *15*(1), 55–65. doi.org/10.6092/issn.1971-8853/11659

Leong, N. (2013). Racial capitalism. *Harvard Law Review*, *126*(8), 2151–2226. doi.org/10.2139/ssrn.2009877

Moynihan, D. P., & Pandey, S. K. (2006). Creating desirable organizational characteristics: How organizations create a focus on results and managerial authority. *Public Management Review*, *8*(1), 119–140. doi.org/10.1080/14719030500518899

Pon, G. (2009). Cultural competency as new racism: An ontology of forgetting. *Journal of progressive human services*, *20*(1), 59–71. doi.org/10.1080/10428230902871173

Pulido, L. (2016a). Flint, environmental racism, and racial capitalism. *Capitalism Nature Socialism*, *27*(3), 1–16. doi.org/10.1080/10455752.2016.1213013

Pulido, L. (2016b). Geographies of race and ethnicity II: Environmental racism, racial capitalism and state-sanctioned violence. *Progress in Human Geography*, *41*(4), 524–533. doi.org/10.1177/0309132516646495

Ray, R., & Davis, G. (2021). Cultural competence as new racism: Working as intended? *American Journal of Bioethics*, *21*(9), 20–22. doi.org/10.1080/15265161.2021.1952338

Robinson, C. (2000). *Black Marxism: The making of the black radical tradition*. University of North Carolina Press.

Salamon, L. M. (1999). The nonprofit sector at a crossroads: The case of America. *Voluntas: International Journal of Voluntary and Nonprofit Organizations*, *10*(1), 5–23. doi.org/10.1023/A:1021435602742

Williams, M. (2014). On the use and abuse of recognition. In A. Eisenberg, J. Webber, G. Coulthard, & A. Boisselle (Eds), *Recognition versus self-determination: Dilemmas of emancipatory politics*. University of British Columbia Press.

5

'If I don't prioritise that accountability back to my community …': National Centre for Indigenous Excellence

John Leha, Clare McHugh, Kim Spurway, and Karen Soldatić

Introduction

The case study in this chapter draws out the unique contribution to the Indigenous sector of an Australian Indigenous not-for-profit social enterprise, the NCIE. The NCIE was established to 'build capability and create opportunities with and for Aboriginal and Torres Strait Islander peoples across Australia' (NCIE, 2021a), which gives it a national remit. This chapter was co-written by members of the NCIE leadership team who were involved in the project in 2020–21 but are no longer with the organisation due to fundamental changes (John Leha and Clare McHugh) and the Australian Research Council Chief Investigator (ARC CI) (Karen Soldatić) and Research Associate (Kim Spurway). Interviews with key NCIE staff and in-depth ethnographic fieldwork were held in late 2019 through to the early months of 2020 prior to COVID-19 lockdowns, facilitated by the NCIE General Manager at the time, Leha, and conducted by the ARC CI, Soldatić. Authors Leha and McHugh were co-researchers as well as informants to the case study, which meant that they had the opportunity to review their individual transcripts of evidence as well as participate in the interpretive analysis of all informant data, ensuring Indigenous data sovereignty principles were followed. The chapter thus presents Leha and McHugh's firsthand accounts of co-managing a First Nations organisation in the NPM era, as well as the views of core NCIE staff across the various programs that were in operation from late 2019 to mid-2020.

The NCIE is located on the former Redfern Public School site in Sydney, NSW, Australia. At the time of interviews and writing in 2019/20, it was an autonomous yet federally funded entity, governed by the Indigenous Land and Sea Corporation (ILSC). The ILSC was an Australian federal statutory corporation set up to acquire land and manage assets for Indigenous people. In 2021, a decision was taken to no longer fund the NCIE. Framed in neoliberal management terms as a process of disinvestment (see NCIE, 2021d), this decision led to extensive local community protests, sit-ins, and campaigns against its inevitable closure (see ILSC, 2022). The tides turned, however, with the election of the Albanese Labor Government. Indigenous Labor Minister, the Hon Linda Burney, made public declarations of support. Yet, it is unknown how this will progress in the future years ahead, where NPM principles of management are driven by profitability, rather than social and community impact.

In this chapter, we explore the Centre's unique role in working with, and for, First Nations communities across Australia. The chapter examines some of the challenges and successes of this unique First Nations organisation as it resists and overcomes the constraints imposed on it by the exigencies of surviving NPM prior to the disinvestment period. We argue that in the NPM era, even with ongoing funding, there remains a tension between the federal government's focus on commercialisation and market-driven development, and the Centre's objectives of developing and maintaining a community-centric social enterprise that listens to, and meets, community needs and aspirations. This is no clearer seen than in the 2021 process of disinvestment leading to the proposed closure announced in August 2022.

This chapter reflects the views of NCIE staff and management prior to the NPM disinvestment assault that began in 2021. Therefore, the views, quotes, and circumstances outlined are in relation to the organisation's community mandate long before the process of 'disinvestment' began. The chapter first reviews the publicly available information about the history of the NCIE prior to the disinvestment era to contextualise the qualitative in-depth interviews with staff.

Finally, the chapter illustrates the ways in which the NCIE resisted the contingent challenges of navigating neoliberal public management in Australia.

Funding and governance of the NCIE prior to disinvestment

The Centre's original mandate was national. It was first established to be a First Nations peoples' organisation for all Australian states and territories. The NCIE was first financed in 2006, through the ILSC, and was officially opened in 2010 after significant redevelopment (ILSC, 2019). The NCIE was set up as an 'independent subsidiary' of the ILSC, an Australian federal government statutory authority (NCIE, 2021a). The ILSC was a corporate government entity created under the federal *Aboriginal and Torres Strait Islander Act 2005* and operated within the Office of the Prime Minister and Cabinet. The ILSC was composed of various corporate entities, which included the NCIE. Their main purpose was 'to return land, fresh water and saltwater country to Indigenous people, and enable sustainable management of country for social, cultural, economic and environmental benefits' (ILSC, 2019, p. 9). The Corporation's role included:

> obtaining and divesting land and water rights to First Nations people in Australia ... supporting First Nations people to reconnect with country and conserve and protect their cultures; to build First Nations' capacity and capabilities so that they can sustainably manage and protect country; and to partner with First Nations people to promote and enable opportunities on country. (ILSC, 2019, p. 9)
>
> As a subsidiary of the ILSC, the NCIE operates within these mandates and its governance body, the board of directors, is directly appointed by the ILSC Board.
>
> (NCIE, 2018)

The ILSC and the NCIE were registered corporate entities under the federal *Corporations Act 2001* (Australian Government, 2021). Government corporations such as the NCIE and ILSC were required to operate within broader government-mandated regulations and frameworks. Technically part of the federal government, corporate Commonwealth entities were established to operate 'commercially or entrepreneurially' and with 'a degree of independence from the policies and direction of the Australian Government' (Department of Finance, 2020). Although this aim gave the NCIE a great deal of independence in its activities, the NCIE still had to operate within the parameters of government policy, including funding and governance structures, as well as the Corporation's mandates and overarching goals.

The long-term goal of the Australian federal government and the ILSC was for the NCIE to be owned by First Nations communities and run with minimal government financial support. The NCIE supported this general goal, stating in 2018 that:

> In accordance with the ILC [ILSC] Divestment Policy, NCIE remains focussed on building a sustainable business model capable of supporting divestment to enable the property to be handed back to local land holder groups and traditional owners.
>
> (NCIE, 2018, p. 2)

The Corporation's strategy for the NCIE was designed to eventually withdraw from funding and move its management to another First Nations organisation. The idea was that the NCIE would become a fully autonomous social enterprise run by and for Aboriginal and Torres Strait Islander peoples (ILSC, 2020a). Much of this strategy assumed that the Centre's different revenue streams would become commercially viable businesses, including the social services it provided through user-pay systems. This is no clearer than in the following quote from the ILSC 2019–20 Annual Report that stated that it was 'optimising and developing the NCIE as a high-performing organisation for social impact, financial viability, internal culture and partnerships' (ILSC, 2020a, p. 71).

In its 2018–20 Strategic Plan, the NCIE defined itself as a 'social enterprise' that used 'the power of the marketplace to solve the most pressing societal problems' (NCIE, 2018, p. 3). The NCIE defined social enterprises as 'commercially viable businesses existing to benefit the public and the community, rather than shareholders and owners' (NCIE, 2018, p. 3). The NCIE described itself as 'driven by a public or community cause'; obtained most of its funding from commercial operations, not from grants or donations; and used these funds 'to work towards their social mission'

(NCIE, 2018, p. 3). Prior to the 2021–22 disinvestment strategy, the NCIE was made up of six separate businesses, each with slightly different funding modalities (NCIE, 2021c).

In 2020, the NCIE also trialled two services, a children's program and a social enterprise pathways program, but these have since been discontinued. The NCIE site included a fitness and aquatics centre, sports field, basketball stadium, indoor and outdoor training areas, and an indoor swimming pool (ILSC, 2020a). The site also had conferencing and accommodation facilities, as well as offices for other First Nations organisations such as the National Aboriginal Sporting Chance Academy, Australian Indigenous Mentoring Experience, Tribal Warrior Aboriginal Corporation, Inner Sydney Empowered Communities, Redfern Youth Connect (ILSC, 2020a), and BlaQ Aboriginal Corporation. These services and programs, while popular with the local First Nations community, were resource-intensive to maintain. To ensure that these services remained attractive and available to their many local First Nations members, their subsidised entry was necessary.

At the time of writing, despite successfully operating these programs, services, and business from the Redfern site, the NCIE still relied on federal government funding. In the 2019–20 financial year, for example, the NCIE earned $5.2 million dollars from its four businesses and third-party sponsorships (ILSC, 2020a, p. 71). This was before any grant money was received from the federal government. The NCIE, however, still ran a deficit of $4.3 million that included the cost of leasing the Redfern site at a cost of $2 million per annum from the ILSC (ILSC, 2020a, p. 71). The ILSC contributed $4.9 million in the 2019–20 financial year to make up the Centre's funding shortfall (ILSC, 2020a).

The biggest challenge for NCIE has been to design and implement commercial, for-profit programs and services for First Nations communities, given the high levels of social and economic disadvantage experienced by First Nations community members. Educational attainment, for example, affects a person's ability to earn a livable income. In 2016, only 47 per cent of Indigenous Australians reported they had completed high school. Although this was an increase over the previous reporting period, Indigenous education is not keeping pace with non-Indigenous educational achievements, which increased from 73 per cent to 79 per cent over the same period (ABS, 2021). In 2016, less than half (47 per cent) of the First Nations population aged 15 to 64 years in Australia was employed, compared to 72 per cent of the non-Indigenous population (ABS, 2021). Employment equates with better living standards, financial independence, improved wellbeing, and the capacity to spend income on non-essential commercial services such as fitness and hospitality, which are core parts of the Centre's business model.

Despite the economic and social disadvantage of its clients, the NCIE still attempted to build the commercial viability of the organisation, trialling and testing several business models that also met the community's need for affordable services.

The Centre's 'point of difference'

The NCIE takes a strengths-based approach – that is, an approach with culture at the core – to deliver outcomes. The NCIE started from a place of excellence and built from a foundation of positives. The NCIE recognised and celebrated the existing and emerging strengths and assets in Aboriginal and Torres Strait Islander communities (NCIE, 2021a).

Balancing the requirement for commercial viability, the NCIE aimed, at all times, to maintain its community focus. As one survey respondent states:

> … the service is complementary to the aspirations of community. They are transparent, accountable and purposeful. These are the foundation for good governance and leadership that has seen to the achievement of significant outcomes such as increased health and educational attainment supported with tangible employment and skills to support economic independence.
>
> (NCIE Survey Response)

Another survey respondent said that 'NCIE structures its programs around First Nation principles, values and practices and relevant community members and Elders are involved in the design of programs' (NCIE Survey Response). And another stated that the Centre's 'governance structure embeds the principles of First Nation values, governance and societal obligations' where 'First Nation culture underpins our organisation's philosophy and aims with First Nations' way of life reflected in our programmes' (NCIE Survey Response).

This was a key point of difference to the dominant social enterprise models operating in non-Indigenous organisations. The NCIE embedded these principles in its everyday operations, both internally, by prioritising the employment and retention of First Nations staff, and externally, by prioritising the needs of First Nations communities in the types of services it offered. The NCIE viewed success as balancing New Public Management's market logic with community-centric values which was demonstrated by the Centre's substantive social impact – its achievements in First Nations employment, and its ability to meet the needs and aspirations of First Nations communities.

Building skills and providing opportunities

As part of its overall strategy and principles, the NCIE aimed to be predominantly staffed and managed by First Nations peoples. At the time of the interviews, focus groups, and writing, the NCIE employed Aboriginal and Torres Strait Islander staff and actively recruited and retained a strong First Nations workforce. The NCIE had a majority of First Nations people on its board of directors and executive team (NCIE, 2021b), and employed a majority of First Nations peoples in its business enterprises. The Centre's Strategic Plan for 2018–20 stated that the NCIE would 'build skills and provide training and employment opportunities' for First Nations peoples (NCIE, 2018, p. 13). The NCIE aimed to achieve this goal by maximising the number of First Nations people employed at the organisation, prioritising 'culturally appropriate skills development, training and pathways for all staff' and exploring ways to employ and train young First Nations people (NCIE, 2018, p. 13).

The Centre's commitment to First Nations employment and retention, as outlined above, was a key feature highlighted in the staff interviews. NCIE employees openly expressed satisfaction with the way the NCIE implemented its employment strategy. All of the staff interviewed, Indigenous and non-Indigenous, expressed strong feelings of belonging and support, and spoke of their positive experiences working with the organisation. Staff reported working in a supportive, positive work environment where they felt encouraged to pursue and achieve individual professional development. Another key contributor to staff wellbeing was the widespread sense of achievement that comes with contributing to an important First Nations-led initiative. The hospitality events coordinator, for example, explained that she loved working at the NCIE and that, 'there's nothing bad about this place that I can say'. She went on to give more detail about how the NCIE encouraged her professionally and how there was a clear line of progression for those who wished to pursue a career at the NCIE:

> Well, they encourage professional development, and they offer opportunities for you to do things and branch out, if you wanted to. For instance, I've been given the opportunity to do the leadership program, so I go away next week to do that. I've never been offered that before; I've heard so much about the program. Yeah, another worker did the same program last year, so people do get opportunities to do things. For example, you can start off as a kitchenhand and work your way up to duty manager, you don't have to be in the kitchen for the whole time that you're here. You could move around into another position if you wanted to, so there's opportunities like that. Or moving from a receptionist to a duty manager.
>
> (NCIE Hospitality Events Coordinator interview)

Another NCIE staff member said that the NCIE was a real change from her previous experiences working in the corporate sector. She agreed that the NCIE values interconnectedness among its staff and that this allowed for a strong congruence between personal and professional values. The NCIE made her feel valued as an individual, supported her career development in a creative way, provided emotional growth, and enabled her to contribute to the overarching values of social justice espoused by many First Nations people:

> I found the more I got into it, the more I just felt a connection to levelling the social justice of our First Nations People. I also felt that my particular skills are really useful in this sector. I also found it a huge learning opportunity to develop my creative thinking and my emotional intelligence and that side which, although I am quite creative and I think I'm quite perceptive and have a good EQ [emotional quotient], it's not necessarily the driving force in banking and corporate finance and that background. So, I found that my experience in the corporate world was very useful in Aboriginal organisations and the benefit for me was a huge learning opportunity to develop a part of me that had not really been developed through my previous career. So, it was a really mutually beneficial move and I like being useful. I like knowing that what I do is both useful to the organisation and useful to the organisation's outcomes. Not just a cog in a wheel.
>
> (NCIE Social Enterprise Pathways Lead interview)

Meeting the needs and aspirations of First Nations communities

The second way in which the Centre's point of difference as a First Nations social enterprise was demonstrated was in its provision of services that met the needs and aspirations of the communities it served. The NCIE applied strong principles of community service to all its business operations. Job Ready was a good example of a program that the NCIE operated that aimed to accommodate and respond to the aspirations of local communities. The NCIE Job Ready program was implemented in a community-centric way that recognised and accounted for longstanding First Nations disadvantage under settler colonialism and the complex needs that arise with intergenerational dispossession and deep racial vilification. The NCIE Job Ready program actively supported participants from highly disadvantaged backgrounds, thus balancing community and government objectives to streamline Indigenous employment market services. The program actively recruited its participants from the local area of Redfern, a community that has experienced intergenerational poverty, and labour market discrimination and exclusion. The Job Ready manager offered intensive mentoring and support to each of the participants who often had highly complex needs, so that they could successfully complete their courses and training. The ultimate goal was to enable First Nations people to find and retain employment in sectors in which they were interested in working. The NCIE also spent considerable time making sure that mainstream, non-Indigenous employers were genuinely interested in Aboriginal advancement, and were not just ticking boxes:

> So, that's part of the mentoring aspect, that we also do one-on-one mentoring for those students that are presenting with a few more complexities than other students, just to make sure that they're able. Because we've had students that have become homeless, that have been victims of DV [domestic violence] during the course of their education. We've had to be able to attend to those issues for them. So, ideally, it's a mentoring, education and employment pathway. So, once they've come through the mentoring and the education program we have partnerships with particular employers and employers of choice. So, employers that we've researched and that we've met with and that we've signed MOUs [memorandums of understanding] with that we know have a commitment to Aboriginal engagement and betterment of Aboriginal communities, and not

just organisations that are thinking, oh I need to tick a box to meet my RAP [Reconciliation Action Plan]. So, we sign on employers that are genuine and genuine with their outcomes.

(NCIE Job Ready Manager interview)

The Centre's approach to employment did not fit into the neoliberal public management's narrow definition of efficiency. The NCIE placed communities first, and this meant taking the time to listen, understand, engage, and offer support as and when required. Such an approach ensured that the Centre's mandate remained accountable to the community and that the programs offered were effective and in line with community values in the long term. Despite the challenges Job Ready participants faced, the NCIE attempted to maintain their engagement.

The NCIE Hospitality Manager gave an example of how she tried to support a young First Nations woman who had graduated from the Job Ready program as quoted below:

If I applied strict business ethics to – the way I would in a normal business out there then a lot of the employees wouldn't last probably as long as they would. We are more generous in trying to make them successful. But that comes with frustrations. If people don't show up on time, don't come in, give us late notice that they're not coming. So that is part of the frustration with – an example is that a young girl came through Job Ready program. She had a difficult background. She'd been in jail. She came in, did the program and came into the kitchen, she'd been doing really well. To the stage where we were starting to think maybe we can offer her a cook position and give her some more responsibility. She had a great smile, really good with customers. During that time, she'd got herself clean and sober and then she got into another relationship with a guy. That turned violent. That caused all sorts of concerns. So, she stopped coming to work and in the end she just disappeared … Yeah, and when we look at our figures for profit and loss point of view and we look at how much we spend on labour, we have to build in the fact that it costs us a bit more in labour to get the job done because some of the staff aren't as productive as you will get from other staff, because they don't have the experience and haven't done it and just can take a bit longer.

(NCIE Hospitality Manager interview)

Demands for economic sustainability and tensions in community mandates

Despite the Centre's commitment to First Nations communities, the focus on financial sustainability under the dominant NPM regime created tensions between the expectations of the government funding body – the ILSC – and the First Nations communities that the NCIE aimed to serve:

> We have this tension where we have a parent body that expects us to operate in a more commercially viable way, but yet community's expectation is that we should be here to deliver services to community which need to be affordable, and reflect their needs and circumstances, so there's that inherent challenge.
>
> (NCIE CEO interview)

The NCIE had a diverse strategy to balance the need for profitability with the needs of communities. NCIE businesses tried to operate on a fee-for-service model and applied mainstream industry standards for setting fees. The Centre's hospitality program does this by attracting corporate and mainstream non-Indigenous customers to the organisation through catering for events and corporate lunches. The program targeted businesses, government departments, and nonprofit, non-Indigenous organisations with the capacity to pay professional catering rates. The unique market positioning as an Indigenous trainee catering organisation, offering a corporate experience that is different from that available in other hospitality spaces, was the driving value of this service. Therefore, it combined market efficiency for commercial success with the unique experience of spending time in a First Nations organisation:

> So – once they're [customers] exposed to us, we can tell that story that we're a not-for-profit social enterprise. Besides giving a really good experience here at either your conference or your catering or your accommodation, we're a not-for-profit Aboriginal social enterprise and you, as our customer, are supporting us to become self-sufficient and provide employment opportunities. I think it's a [pretty good] story to tell. We have to perform to a high standard. There's an expectation by our clients that we're not cheap to come here and price wise we're probably at the top end of the market. We provide really good food and a non-traditional, non-corporate experience. So that's our point of difference – as well as the social enterprise with the employment part. Feedback from customers is NCIE has a really strong family feel about it. Even people that

come to conferences may be exposed to a bunch of kids staying here from remote communities. They're having breakfast and they walk in and say, 'Oh. It's not like going to a traditional hotel in the city'. There's kids show up to do school sport or there's Aboriginal kids over in fitness doing boxing. So, it's a different feeling for when you come here for a conference. However, we still have to provide a high standard because if we don't, and the client's not happy – it doesn't matter how strong the social impact is, if they don't feel as though they're getting value for money or satisfaction, they're not going to come back. It's as simple as that.

(NCIE Hospitality Manager interview)

Despite the push to be a fully commercial enterprise, the NCIE maintained its strong accountability to the community. The Centre's services, while popular with communities, were also resource-intensive to maintain. A focus on commercial viability alone was a challenge for the NCIE, given the levels of disadvantage and inequity within First Nations communities. To ensure that these services remained accessible to communities, the NCIE maintained its commitment to subsidised entry for many local First Nations people. Cost is acknowledged as a key barrier for Aboriginal and Torres Strait Islander people to use the Centre's services and venues. This was the case for so-called non-essential services, such as the former NCIE fitness program. NCIE applied a commercial rate to gym membership and had different types of membership and visitor fees depending upon one's background (NCIE, 2021b). To promote fitness and wellbeing in Aboriginal and Torres Strait Islander communities, Indigenous people pay 50 per cent of the non-Indigenous rate (NCIE CEO interview). This was in recognition of the many compounding factors that discourage First Nations people from using the Centre's fitness program:

If I was struggling financially, for whatever reason that might be, the last thing I'm going to fork money out for is a gym membership to look after my health.

(NCIE CEO interview)

The NCIE was, therefore, not simply a profit-making enterprise, nor did it seek to be. Balancing accountabilities with government, donors, and the Aboriginal communities it worked with was extremely challenging, much more so than for non-Indigenous social enterprises that were not accountable to local, regional, and national communities. The problem is that the place-based, deep insider knowledge of First Nations communities, cultures, and values that made NCIE work so effectively were not acknowledged nor rewarded by non-Indigenous outsiders, especially government and mainstream non-Indigenous organisations, donors and funders who pushed for self-sustainability:

> Getting them [government] to fully understand what we're doing, and the value add that we're bringing ... all of the subsidiaries are bringing, was super frustrating. But then it also dawned on me we were doing that for about a year, and I was still getting the same barriers and questions and lack of understanding, and I was super frustrated because it was clear no one was reading the information they were getting.
>
> (NCIE CEO interview)

The 'ripple effect'

The success of the Centre's strategies was demonstrated through its impressive social impact over its former years of operation. In 2017, to promote understanding of the Centre's social impact, the management team established a set of social impact measures (NCIE CEO interview). These measures enabled the NCIE to speak about its successes in the same language as federal politicians and public sector executives:

> From the get-go I understood that we were doing some really great stuff, but we couldn't articulate it. We weren't articulating it in a way that was meaningful to people. Everyone wants to understand the impact that you're having, and we're great at collecting data but we're not necessarily great at determining what's the right data and what we should use to tell our story. So, we spent a significant amount of time – not last year but I would say 2017, when I first started, probably about a year of building our internal capabilities around reporting our impact, and we developed up a social return on investment tool.
>
> (NCIE CEO interview)

The NCIE identified two to three drivers to allow each business area to demonstrate its success and the complexities of the Centre's approach:

> We went through every business area, all of our services, and we basically – he [impact tool designer] sat with them and he helped them identify what the two to three business drivers were for success for each of their areas. For accommodation, it's bed nights and it's bookings and such. For catering, it's obviously how many orders

and all the rest of it. For fitness it's member numbers. We worked through what the different business drivers were for each of our services and then there's a whole complex world behind how you can work out – TATU [the Talking About Tobacco Use program] is a good example. For them their business drivers are built into their – the dollar agreement. It's smoking cessation and smoking prevention; those sorts of drivers, and it's quite easy to find data, and it's based on global data, not Australian research. I'm talking to someone who understands all of this stuff. So, if we can prevent one person from taking up smoking, the impact that this is going to have in terms of the cost of the burden of poor health on government.

(NCIE CEO interview)

Since 2017, NCIE businesses had a demonstrable social impact among First Nations communities nationwide, most particularly within the Redfern area and the City of Sydney. This could be seen in the Centre's own social impact data. During 2018–19, the NCIE calculated a return of $3.10 in social value for every dollar of funding it received, representing approximately $13.9 million of social value creation (NCIE, 2021a). During the same period, the Centre's services were delivered to a total of 193,000 clients, Indigenous and non-Indigenous (NCIE, 2021a). In 2019–20, the NCIE successfully mentored and supported 33 First Nations people in training and/or jobs through its Job Ready program (ILSC, 2020a). NCIE Hospitality hosted 6,043 conference guests from corporations, community organisations, universities, and government agencies, including the NSW Department of Premier and Cabinet (ILSC, 2020a). Catering successfully delivered 518 orders, totalling 15,121 customers from diverse organisations including the NSW Government, the City of Sydney, and universities (ILSC, 2020a). The NCIE accommodation program hosted 1,251 people from schools, universities, and community groups over the same period (ILSC, 2020a).

The NCIE also successfully engaged and supported First Nations artists, businesses, and communities through other programs. Sixty-one per cent of customers using accommodation services in 2019–20, for example, identified as First Nations people (ILSC, 2020a). Another 49 First Nations artists and businesses were promoted, and their products were sold through NCIE retail and café businesses (ILSC, 2020a). Nineteen per cent of the NCIE fitness and aquatics program customers were First Nations people (ILSC, 2020a). The Centre's Redfern Youth Connect program also collaborated with The Homework Centre to deliver time management and tutoring sessions for 169 First Nations youth in Years 8–12 (ILSC, 2020a). Workshops were attended by 284 First Nations young people, 51 community-based organisations, and 15 regional and remote communities from across Australia (ILSC, 2020a). The NCIE had planned to further develop and expand its programs, despite the impact of the COVID-19 pandemic on its ability to run its businesses and meet the needs of communities (ILSC, 2020b). These figures demonstrated the Centre's successful engagement with the community, as well as its effectiveness in supporting community needs and aspirations.

As a First Nations social enterprise, the NCIE had to account for, remain part of, and act in the best interests of communities. Without a strong community voice and buy-in to the Centre's strategic direction, the NCIE risked becoming just another private, for-profit service provider that may no longer place the needs of First Nations communities first. The Centre's success story did not just rest with each individual First Nations person supported by the organisation. Rather, the NCIE had a collective impact that improved the lives of people's families and communities, so clearly demonstrated by the vast numbers who protested against its potential closure. As one interviewee argued: 'There's lots of ripple effect from this program that has massive social impact, not just for the individual but for extended family, friends and communities' (NCIE Job Ready Manager interview).

The 'ripple effect' was powerful language for the ways in which the NCIE met the criteria for successful engagement and positive change in First Nations communities – including through community ownership, Indigenous leadership, respect for Indigenous worldviews, and the critical importance of establishing and sustaining meaningful relationships and connections to the community (Hunt, 2016). Most importantly, like many First Nations organisations, the NCIE was extremely proud to be founded on First Nations' implicit understandings of Indigenous culture, history, and experiences, and to balance this understanding with financial accountability and commercial success (Hunt, 2016).

Over the decades since its establishment, the NCIE had a proven, sustained, and wide-reaching positive impact on communities. This impact could not be captured by measurements of cost efficiency that assumed achieving more with fewer resources, such as time and personnel, was always better (Taylor et al., 2001, p. 126). The NCIE did not want to be 'efficient' in a non-Indigenous sense. The NCIE placed a higher value on the efficacy of its programs – that is, making the programs work by ensuring they met the requirements of First Nations communities. If communities did not want a service, couldn't afford a service, and could not access a service, it would fail no matter how efficient it might appear. For the NCIE, this meant centring the work on Indigenous ways of doing and knowing when working with communities. The NCIE persevered and supported First Nations peoples in its programs to a degree not seen in non-Indigenous organisations. The NCIE took the time and invested in the considerable resources needed to work closely with the community in a culturally appropriate way. The NCIE had the natural advantage of being embedded in First Nations communities, which enabled it to respond to changing community needs and aspirations. The Centre's CEO, at the time, explained that this involved a different kind of accountability and engagement, requiring the investment of time and the blurring of personal and professional spaces, even within the constraints of neoliberal NPM structures of governance:

> I grew up in Redfern. Redfern is my community, it's the community I connect with. I'm a member of the local Land Council up the road. I have been a patient at the Aboriginal Medical Service since I was a kid, so I'm an active participant in all of the services from around this area and it is my community. When I leave the gates to go for lunch it doesn't mean I'm not going to get pulled up by 10 people on my way to lunch [laughs], whether it's a good thing or a bad thing, whatever it might be … Every time we go for a walk, we'll get interrupted or pulled up by community. So, it's difficult and it's challenging. I have to be – there is a level of accountability that I have to have back to community, and I will always have that. If I don't prioritise that accountability back to my community, I couldn't do this job.
>
> (NCIE CEO interview)

Concluding discussion

> Modern bureaucracy is ruthlessly efficient, but efficiently organising against it effectively risks reproducing and perpetuating it. Resistance is important but seeking out alternatives is also necessary. While a valid reaction to the totalising effect of bureaucracy is to subvert, undermine and resist, another is to reform, to humanise bureaucracy, so that it becomes adequate for the task of realising the values of citizens, not least Indigenous citizens holding values rooted in a society that long pre-dates their colonisation.
>
> (Sullivan, 2018, p. 212)

The NCIE operated within the Australian colonial-settler state. The key NPM concepts of marketisation and commercialisation, however, had been adapted and transformed by the Indigenous-led and managed NCIE in ways that enabled the NCIE to resist settler colonial dispossession and thrive. The dominant focus of commercialisation did not alter the core of the Centre's ongoing commitment to First Nations communities and Indigenous ways of doing business with and for communities. Despite the ongoing pressure to become more like a 'Western business', the NCIE continued to build skills and opportunities for its staff as well as continuing to recruit and retain First Nations people, from frontline service provision to management and the board of directors. The Centre's leadership worked to consistently maintain a relationship with the community that is unlike that of most non-Indigenous organisations. Its staff and management were First Nations people and were recognised by local community members as such.

Being embedded in the community means that the staff and management are accountable to the community. This embeddedness was reflected in the amount of time and resources the NCIE staff and management spent talking and listening to the community, even when they were off the clock, outside during their time with family and friends. With all the pressure being applied to the organisation through the deep infusion of neoliberal policies from their primary government funder, the ILSC, the NCIE maintained its focus on Indigenous values around community and culture. As illustrated throughout this chapter, a raft of strategies to respect and maintain Indigenous values have been consistently directed into all areas of organisational practice. These organisational practices were regularly reviewed in collaboration with community members to ensure that the organisation remains focused on its core values:

> We respect, honour and celebrate the unique and diverse cultures and heritage of Aboriginal and Torres Strait Islander peoples, and recognise the importance of embedding culture in all that we do.
>
> (NCIE, 2021a)

The NCIE had, in effect, successfully resisted the Australian tendency towards 'monoculturalism' in Indigenous policy and governance that Sullivan (2018) argues has contributed to the fragmentation of the Indigenous sector. This tendency towards homogeneity and an 'antagonism to diversity' means that First Nations organisations operate within a government environment that is 'deaf to cultural nuances, so that third-sector organisations' statements about their learning, governance and relation to others in the sector quite literally cannot be heard' (Sullivan, 2018, p. 206).

The success of the Centre's strategy was its focus on the community and its ability to engage with and meet community needs and aspirations. As one survey respondent put this:

> The [Centre]'s strategy is founded on a strengths-based approach – with culture at the core – to deliver outcomes. We start from a place of excellence and build from a foundation of positives. We recognise and celebrate the existing and emerging strengths and assets in Aboriginal and Torres Strait Islander communities.
>
> (NCIE survey response)

Despite the apparent success of the NCIE in building and sustaining a successful First Nations organisation, the future of the NCIE remains uncertain, given the ongoing dominance of NPM governance with a targeted focus on profitable social enterprises in Australian public administration and social service contracting across all tiers of government.

References

Australian Bureau of Statistics (2021). *2071.0 – Census of population and housing: Reflecting Australia – Stories from the Census, 2016.* www.abs.gov.au/ausstats/abs@.nsf/mf/2071.0

Australian Government (2021). *National Centre of Indigenous Excellence Ltd.* www.directory.gov.au/portfolios/prime-minister-and-cabinet/indigenous-land-and-sea-corporation/national-centre-indigenous-excellence-ltd

Department of Finance (2020). *Types of Australian Government bodies.* www.finance.gov.au/government/managing-commonwealth-resources/structure-australian-government-public-sector/types-australian-government-bodies

Hunt, J. (2016). *Let's talk about success: Exploring factors behind positive change in Aboriginal communities.* CAEPR Working Paper 109/2016. The Australian National University.

Indigenous Land and Sea Corporation (2019). *National Indigenous Land and Sea Strategy 2019–2022.*

Indigenous Land and Sea Corporation (2020a). *Annual report 2019–20.* www.ilsc.gov.au/wp-content/uploads/2020/12/ILSC-Annual-Report-2019%E2%80%932020.pdf

Indigenous Land and Sea Corporation (2020b). *Unlocking the Indigenous estate: Corporate plan 2020–2021 – Strategy to 2024.*

Indigenous Land and Sea Corporation (2022). *Closure of National Centre for Indigenous Excellence (NCIE) Ltd. announced*. www.ilsc.gov.au/home/news/closure-of-national-centre-for-indigenous-excellence-ncie-ltd-announced/

National Centre of Indigenous Excellence (2018). *Strategic plan 2018–2020*. NCIE.

National Centre of Indigenous Excellence (2021a). *About*. ncie.org.au/about/

National Centre of Indigenous Excellence (2021b). *About: Our team*. ncie.org.au/about/team/

National Centre of Indigenous Excellence (2021c). *NCIE Fitness is for everyone*. ncie.org.au/ncie-fitness-reopening/

National Centre of Indigenous Excellence (2021d). *Update from ILSC on the NCIE divestment*. ncie.org.au/update-from-ilsc-on-the-ncie-divestment/

Sullivan, P. (2018). The tyranny of neoliberal public management and the challenge for Aboriginal community organisations. In D. Howard-Wagner, M. Bargh, and I. Altamirano-Jiménez (Eds), *The neoliberal state, recognition and Indigenous rights: New paternalism to new imaginings*. ANU Press. doi.org/10.22459/CAEPR 40.07.2018.11

Taylor, J., Dollard, J., Weetra, C., & Wilkinson, D. (2001). Contemporary management issues for Aboriginal Community Controlled Health Services. *Australian Health Review*, *24*(3), 125–132. doi.org/10.1071/AH010125

6

Muru Mittigar: Country, culture, community, and contracts

Janet Hunt, Cheryl Goh, Ros Fogg, and Christopher Galloway[1]

Introduction

Muru Mittigar, which in the Dharug language means 'pathway to friends', is a Dharug-controlled social enterprise on Dharug Country. Dharug people are the traditional owners and custodians of much of Western Sydney, one of the first parts of Australia to be colonised, now the highly urbanised home for a very multicultural population. Dharug Country covers the Sydney Basin, from the Hawkesbury-Nepean in the north to the Georges River in the south, and west to the Blue Mountains.

The chapter begins by reviewing the literature about Indigenous social enterprises and outlining the socio-economic context of Western Sydney; it then gives a brief history of Muru Mittigar, which had an unusual beginning for an Aboriginal organisation, has been through a major disruptive transition, and is now trying to consolidate itself as a sustainable,

---

1   Fieldwork for this chapter commenced with one field visit in 2019 but was suspended for most of 2020 due to COVID-19 restrictions; the research resumed in late 2020 via Zoom and telephone and was completed with one face-to-face meeting in Rouse Hill and further Zoom sessions in 2021, when COVID-19 restrictions impacted again. During 2020, quite a lot changed at Muru Mittigar, including the CEO. Quotes throughout derive from this fieldwork, unless otherwise indicated.

community-focused, and independent business. The next section outlines Muru Mittigar's current programs and discusses the critical issues it faces as an urban Aboriginal social enterprise. The chapter ends by discussing the challenges facing Muru Mittigar as it tries to achieve its cultural and social goals in a competitive market environment. Muru Mittigar says its goals are:

> to create a better understanding of Aboriginal culture in the wider community; create new jobs; develop workplace skills training and increase sustained employment opportunities for Indigenous Australians. The organisation achieves this by providing quality contracting and consulting services to government and business, in land management, education and tourism and through investing in well-being and financial counselling services for the Aboriginal community.[2]

Such contracting is a key element of NPM which places the market at the centre of government services, so that governing involves managing the competitive process among private sector providers to achieve the most efficient outcomes (O'Flynn, 2007). However, the public value that social enterprises bring to their economic initiatives entails achieving multiple public goals simultaneously (O'Flynn, 2007). The regulatory aspect of NPM may involve incentivising certain social goals, such as through social or Indigenous-specific procurement, but these are subordinate to the overall market competitiveness of NPM. While social enterprises may find opportunities in NPM approaches to government, they may also struggle to meet social objectives through contracting and market discipline. Stanković (2020) suggests that social entrepreneurship has emerged in response to the shortcomings of NPM, particularly its narrow definition of efficiency and the fact that the main goal of the state, as well as of people, is not always profit maximisation – there are social goals to achieve. Yet Muru Mittigar operates within this NPM environment and must negotiate its way through these limitations.

Indigenous social enterprise

Muru Mittigar describes itself as a 'Dharug social enterprise'. While there is significant literature on social enterprises generally, there is only a little on Indigenous social enterprise in Australia. Some of this is focused on

---

2   See: www.murumittigar.com.au/.

individual social entrepreneurs (Foley, 2003), and more often on remote areas rather than urban centres (Banerjee & Tedmanson, 2010; Jones et al., 2019; Kerins, 2013; Pearson & Helms, 2013; Spencer et al., 2017). What is clear from the literature is that Indigenous social enterprises are viewed as suitable vehicles in the current market-driven environment for Indigenous people and organisations to achieve their social and economic goals, including their right to self-determination (Anderson et al., 2006; Giovannini, 2012). Yet there are often tensions between the economic or business goals of financial sustainability and the social, cultural, and environmental values and objectives such organisations pursue (Barr et al., 2018; Sengupta et al., 2015; Spencer et al., 2015; Vázquez-Maguirre & Portales, 2018). These multiple, communally based objectives are inseparable (Corntassel, 2008; Sengupta et al., 2015) but sometimes conflicting in these types of organisations (Douglas, 2015; Douglas et al., 2018; Vázquez-Maguirre & Portales, 2018).

For many Indigenous social enterprises, success involves the reduction of poverty, marginalisation, and related social problems that their communities experience (Lee & Nowell, 2014; Pearson & Helms, 2013). However, unless they can sustain themselves financially, they cannot achieve their social goals (Loban et al., 2013). As Spencer et al. (2015, 2017) pointed out, profit-making is a means to social ends such as creating employment for Indigenous people that reflects their interests, capacities, and ways of life. An Indigenous social enterprise may prefer to expend resources on creating employment, rather than reducing salary expenditure as a profit-maximising company may do, as this reflects the social outcome sought.

However, there are barriers to success noted in the literature, often related to access to or ownership of land, as well as access to capital and finance (Ketilson, 2014), the levels of staff skills and capacity, perception of value in the work (Denny-Smith & Loosemore, 2018), and, occasionally, overcoming addictions some people experience (Anderson et al., 2006; Rebutin, 2009). Research on Indigenous participation in the construction industry in Australia found other barriers to success which may apply equally to the land management industry, including,

> adjusting to unique construction industry cultures and practices, breaking into existing business networks and building social capital and being under-cut by industry incumbents and competitors when tendering for projects.
>
> (Denny-Smith & Loosemore, 2017, p. 788)

Spencer et al. (2015) discuss the need for a more supportive policy environment, following increased pressures for accountability through strict performance measurement since the IAS of 2014. This strategy, which is managed by the National Indigenous Australians Agency, brought most Indigenous funding under the Department of the Prime Minister and Cabinet, with contracts and performance measurements typical of NPM, such as specifying and reporting against Key Performance Indicators and complying with various risk management requirements. Aligned with the IAS, the federal government (Australian Government, 2015) and the NSW state government (NSW Government, 2021) have instituted Indigenous procurement policies (IPPs). These are designed to promote Indigenous businesses to win government contracts and participate in contracts government awards to private enterprises. While increasing the number of contracts awarded to Indigenous businesses, these policies are not always as effective as expected. An audit of the Australian Government's IPP revealed ineffective implementation and monitoring, and insufficient compliance, with concern that companies were 'black cladding'[3] to gain preference for contracts (Jenkins, 2020).

Other literature on Indigenous enterprises highlights that policies such as equal opportunity or Indigenous procurement are 'rhetorical devices' used to deny sovereignty to First Nations (Banerjee & Tedmanson, 2010). The broader literature on non-profits recognises the colonisation of everyday life by the market (Eikenberry, 2009), with market-based solutions to social problems becoming the norm, rather than community development and social movement mobilisation to transform society. In contrast, Anderson et al. (2006), writing about Canadian land-based organisations, suggest that Indigenous people can engage with the global market economy on their own terms through social enterprise. The question is: how does a landless urban Indigenous social enterprise engage with the market to solve longstanding socio-economic problems like unemployment, poverty, and cultural suppression flowing from the consequences of colonial settlement?

---

3   Supply Nation considers 'black cladding' the practice of a non-Indigenous business entity or individual taking unfair advantage of an Indigenous business entity or individual for the purpose of gaining access to otherwise inaccessible Indigenous procurement policies or contracts. See: supplynation. org.au/about-us/black-cladding/.

Context

The Western Sydney region presents both challenges and opportunities for Muru Mittigar. The organisation is based in Penrith, which has an Aboriginal or Torres Strait Islander population of 7,745 people (9 per cent of the total population), only 255 of them aged 65 or above, and over 34 per cent under 15 years (Penrith City Council, 2018). While Dharug people are the traditional custodians, Dharug culture has been suppressed by colonialism, though a resurgence is underway now. The area has also attracted very many Aboriginal and Torres Strait Islander people from across the nation, often in search of work – with Wiradjuri, Kamilaroi, and Bundjalung people common among them. Of the 2,728 Aboriginal and Torres Strait Islander people who were employed at the time of the 2016 Census, over 60 per cent were in full-time work, and the rest were employed part-time. The overall unemployment rate in Penrith was 11.8 per cent and many Aboriginal and other people struggle with low incomes (ABS, 2016).

Western Sydney is undergoing an economic transformation. The Greater Sydney Commission is planning a three-city model, which will include the Western Parklands City, in which Muru Mittigar is located. The population of this new Western Sydney Parklands metropolis is projected to double in the next 30 years, with economic development and major transport routes centred on the planned Badgery's Creek airport (Greater Sydney Commission, 2018).

The timing of such economic expansion is good for Aboriginal employment and promises many opportunities for Muru Mittigar and the entire community. In addition to Indigenous procurement incentives, many of the country's major corporations have adopted Reconciliation Action Plans (RAPs) (Reconciliation Australia, n.d.) with commitments to Indigenous employment, to contribute to a national reconciliation effort led by Reconciliation Australia. There is a growing demand for Aboriginal employees and Aboriginal contractors to fulfil these policies and aspirations.

The challenge for Muru Mittigar is to juggle the potential demand for Aboriginal participation with the capacities and aspirations of available workers, promote the Dharug culture, and sustain a financially viable business model in a competitive, commercial environment.

The early years

Muru Mittigar began operating in the mid- to late 1990s, as a cultural education, land restoration, and bush regeneration organisation for Penrith Lakes Development Corporation (PLDC), a body formed by three companies that previously quarried a 2,000-hectare site[4] in Penrith. The company aimed to rehabilitate the former mining site into residential land with a parkland and lakes for recreational use. Muru Mittigar was formed to enable local Aboriginal people to take advantage of this opportunity since the Deerubbin Local Aboriginal Land Council had declined PLDC's invitation to participate.

The objectives of Muru Mittigar were both educational and economic. The cultural education centre focused largely on school groups and tourists; the jobs, training, and economic aspects were met by the cultural education centre as well as the nursery, and most employment was provided by the extensive regeneration and rehabilitation of Penrith Lakes' former quarry site.

While Muru Mittigar was independently incorporated, the board was chaired by the CEO from PLDC, who also provided two board members, thus controlling it. Over 90 per cent of Muru Mittigar's revenue came from PLDC until 2010. As the regeneration work neared its completion, Muru Mittigar tried to diversify its operations to secure its future, but PLDC actively prevented it from doing so, as it had no vision for Muru Mittigar to sustain itself once the rehabilitation was completed. When PLDC resumed control of the land on which Muru Mittigar had been operating, Muru Mittigar was forced to relocate, and as PLDC cut ties, had to rapidly find land and new income sources to survive.

As a Muru Mittigar board member and co-author, Aunty Cheryl Goh, explained,

> In hindsight we were established as a convenience for Penrith Lakes, not really for any other purpose than for servicing their needs and that became really apparent in our last couple of years when we

---

4   'Under an agreement signed with the New South Wales Government in 1987, quarry operator Penrith Lakes Development Corporation (PLDC) – a consortium between building materials suppliers Boral, Holcim and Hanson is required to progressively rehabilitate the site as extraction is completed and to transfer some of the land to the state government for use as a major parkland and lakes system for the western Sydney community.' (*Quarry,* 2014).

were being told we were moving off, being dumped, and there was
nothing they were putting in place to give us any salvation, in fact
I think it was more the other thing and eventually locking us out.

However, Muru Mittigar owns no land, so it had nowhere to move to.
In NSW, land claims are made by Local Aboriginal Land Councils (LALCs),
whose membership should be open to any Aboriginal or Torres Strait
Islander people living within its boundaries. But the Local Aboriginal Land
Council for Penrith, Deerubbin (LALC) does not recognise the Dharug
as traditional owners, which prevents their participation. There are other
LALCs active in Dharug Country, notably the quite large Gandangara
LALC at Liverpool. Neither LALC has Dharug board members, and the
conflicts between the land rights system and the native title system in NSW
are creating community rifts and tensions (Norman, 2018). The Dharug-
controlled Muru Mittigar has had no opportunity to obtain secure land
tenure in its Country, on which to base its social enterprise.

The local Aboriginal community wanted Muru Mittigar to survive the
move from PLDC, but the transition from Penrith Lakes was difficult.
Over the previous 12 years, the organisation had developed a native plant
nursery to nurture local seeds for the native plants it used, and an important
cultural education centre with a small café and shop to complement the land
regeneration work it was doing. It had a total of 18–20 staff and things were
going well. But when the time came to move, shifting its operations to a
single alternative site was not possible, so it now operates from three separate
sites: an office in Penrith, a native plant nursery in Llandilo (also the base
for Muru Mittigar's rangers), and the cultural education centre at Rouse
Hill, on the Sydney Living Museum's historic site, several kilometres away.
Eleven years on, it has diversified funding, manages various contracts with
private and public sector clients, and provides employment opportunities
for Aboriginal people from Western Sydney and beyond.

Becoming an entirely independent organisation brought other challenges,
including the need for senior staff and middle management who could win
and manage contracts with a range of commercial clients, and manage a
more complex budget, due to the number of clients needed to sustain Muru
Mittigar's operations. Perhaps because the CEO[5] did not have the required
experience, for a period after its separation from PLDC, Muru Mittigar

---

5   Both the former and current CEOs are non-Indigenous men, but there is now an Indigenous
Deputy CEO at Muru Mittigar.

inadvertently failed to pay the correct amount of tax and subsequently had to clear a significant debt with the Australian Taxation Office. This reduced its available operating funds until 2020. It has run as a very lean organisation for several years.

When Muru Mittigar became entirely independent, the two Dharug board members, who had been engaged by PLDC to advise on culture, were also somewhat surprised to learn what their directors' legal and financial responsibilities and liabilities encompassed. The Westpac Foundation and law firm Minter Ellison have provided pro bono governance, financial, and legal advice for these board members to ensure they understand their responsibilities and have the necessary knowledge to carry them out. While the support is highly valued, it has been time-consuming for senior Aboriginal women with multiple obligations. As board members of what is now a complex multi-sectoral and multi-million-dollar business, they needed to ensure they maintained compliance and met all their accountabilities. Since 2020, the three-person board, all of whom are volunteers, has been supported by an independent financial adviser. Two of the three board members are now Dharug people, who remain crucial to the direction the organisation takes.

By 2019, when this research began, Muru Mittigar's major focus remained to educate the public about Dharug culture, especially through cultural awareness and education programs for NSW students and teachers;[6] to support the Aboriginal and Torres Strait Islander community, particularly in relation to secure, long-term employment; and provide financial advice.

To reach these goals Muru Mittigar must win and manage sufficient contracts. Finding contract work and winning contracts is time-consuming. Major contracts it was managing in 2019 included bushfire mitigation for the NSW Department of Education; land management for residential developments; and bush regeneration, land management, and native plant supply for Western Sydney Parklands and Parramatta Parks Trust. It also ran a financially self-reliant native plant provenance nursery.

Over its many years, Muru Mittigar has notched up considerable achievements, having created over 1,000 jobs for Indigenous people. In some respects, Muru Mittigar exemplifies what governments want to see:

6   During 2021 almost all this cultural education work ceased due to COVID-19 impacts.

a self-reliant Aboriginal organisation successfully competing in the market. However, this case study shows that combining culture, community, and contracts is not easy.

Muru Mittigar today

Muru Mittigar has now diversified its revenue sources, including earnings from cultural education work, contracts for land management and bushfire mitigation, and grants supporting the Community Finance Hub. But unlike many other Aboriginal organisations, Muru Mittigar's income in 2019 from government grants amounted to less than 5 per cent of its revenue (for services by the Finance Hub), with the remaining 95 per cent earned through its contract and education work. Thus, Muru Mittigar is self-determining in the sense that it earns its own income. Over 55 per cent of its $4.3 million expenditure in 2019 was staff salaries. Muru Mittigar employed twice as many people as 10 years earlier – around 40 full-time equivalent positions (shared between about 60 people, 70 per cent being Aboriginal). Any surplus from its contracting earnings subsidises its cultural education and community work.

While cultural and other community work (e.g., the Community Financial Hub to help low-income people) are very important, the imperative is to maintain contract income and related employment opportunities. In recent years, the bush regeneration work has expanded into broader land management programs and bushfire mitigation and the geographical scope of Muru Mittigar's work has widened so that it now works across the lands of many different First Nations. This reflects the fact that the geographic scope of many tender opportunities is broader than the Country of a single First Nation group.

Contracts

As indicated earlier, at the heart of NPM is the role of contracts in a privatised market. Contracts are at the core of Muru Mittigar's ability to financially sustain its social role. But for an Aboriginal social enterprise with limited capital, contracts can present risks, as the following example reveals.

Managing contracts and risks

One example of its geographically expanded role involved Muru Mittigar providing bush regeneration services to an international property developer off Dharug Country, in the Illawarra region of NSW. By late 2020 this contract had been terminated by mutual agreement. While Muru Mittigar valued its partnership with this developer, there were complexities and costs for an Aboriginal social enterprise working with a large global development corporation. Unfortunately, Muru Mittigar was pressured to sign a contract that placed much of the risk on itself, with significant consequences; the arrangements that Muru Mittigar had to undertake to work on the land, coupled with Muru Mittigar's social goals, also added to the costs. Ultimately, weaknesses in contracting and management sealed the fate of this project. 'Partnerships' don't always work out.

The most significant problem related to the contracts signed with the developer, and the risks that Muru Mittigar carried. For example, the developer required the site compound, with an office and training room where Muru Mittigar kept all its equipment, to be relocated three times, all at Muru Mittigar's expense; the compound was also broken into on several occasions and essential tools and equipment stolen, with replacement at Muru Mittigar's cost; such losses also meant work was delayed until replacements were purchased. Adverse weather and other delays sometimes meant that weeding or rehabilitation work had to be repeated, all adding to costs. For example, following a change of CEO at Muru Mittigar, in early 2020, a flood in the river corridor where the rehabilitation work was being undertaken caused major damage. The rehabilitation work was washed away, and replanting was required. Unfortunately, the contract held Muru Mittigar responsible for recovery in a *force majeure* event, which amounted to a large extra cost (over $100,000). A close examination of the contract also revealed that Muru Mittigar had quoted badly, omitting the costs of the plants required, only quoting for their installation; it had also been wrongly advised and purchased mulch that did not meet the contracted specifications, so that had to be re-purchased; and it was employing more people than it had charged for in the contract; so its weak management along with poor budgeting and contracting had contributed to a situation which was financially unsustainable.

Furthermore, there are Aboriginal protocols about working on another peoples' Country which a Dharug organisation must observe, but which may be disregarded by a non-Indigenous land management contractor.

Overall, Muru Mittigar had to work with multiple different partners and stakeholders, among them a local Aboriginal employment service intending to take over the environmental maintenance when Muru Mittigar had built their capacity to do so. Muru Mittigar also engaged a local university staff member who helped its ranger team with daily reporting on progress and preparing graphs that the developer required to monitor whether the rangers had met their allocated work target and to project the work plan for the coming months, including quoting for future contracts. Contracts were only three months long, so had to be constantly renewed. Other partners included an Aboriginal company that provided mentors to the rangers, and a civil engineering company that supported them with the office and training base at the site.

While any land management company might have to deal with some of these partners, Muru Mittigar faced many extra obligations. It had to negotiate its presence on land where the custodianship is contested;[7] it was building the capacity of the local Aboriginal employment corporation so that it could take over maintenance of the site and perhaps develop its own native nursery; it had to train, equip, and develop the rangers while it delivered on the contracts, and built their capacity, both as individuals and as a team. Availability of suitable training was an issue, as the local TAFE did not offer a course in Indigenous conservation and land management; Muru Mittigar carried the training costs, including the provision of work clothes and boots for trainees. Then it had to mentor and support its team in monitoring and reporting; yet contracts were only short-term, which could make staffing unstable. Clearly, Muru Mittigar had to manage considerably more complexities and carry more costs than a non-Indigenous contractor would, and yet provide a service at like quality and a competitive price.

As the new CEO explained, compared to a mainstream contracting organisation, Muru Mittigar puts a lot of effort into training people:

> We spend more time training people that I would see in normal practice [i.e., in a mainstream contracting organisation]. I wouldn't put people through degrees or courses. I'd hire them after they finish them. I wouldn't take school leavers and put them through literacy programs … I expect that's the Department of Education's job. That's not what Muru does, we help them through the process.

---

7   Groups variously call it Dharawal, Yuin, Wadi Wadi, or Wodi Wodi land.

The new CEO estimated that 'we were donating $25,000 per month' to the developer through all the uncosted aspects of the contract. As he said, 'We're a charity, but we're not a charity to [the developer]!' After the flood incident, he wanted to extract Muru Mittigar from the contract. Fortunately, the developer obliged, and the CEO acknowledged that the company was forgiving, and they parted on good terms.

This experience illustrates how an Aboriginal social enterprise, which may struggle to attract highly skilled and experienced management, could be ruined by failure to attend to the terms of contracts and business management, while trying to support more Aboriginal employment than its budget enabled. The social part of the social enterprise, coupled with weak management, may mean that the enterprise cannot be sustained as it cannot manage or carry the risks entailed. And clearly, with little capital in the bank, Muru Mittigar is not able to risk losses.

This also raises questions about how companies 'at the big end of town' with RAPs see their contribution to reconciliation. They may procure business from Aboriginal enterprises, but this does not mean that the Aboriginal businesses' interests and capacity are enhanced. The market route to reconciliation may not necessarily strengthen the Aboriginal enterprise. Global companies may not see this as their responsibility. Muru Mittigar has certainly learned from this experience and will not sign such high-risk contracts again. In fact, the board members are being extremely cautious now.

For example, subsequently, an opportunity arose for Muru Mittigar to provide landscaping works as well as cultural education for a new enterprise in Western Sydney. Muru Mittigar did not take up this opportunity because it did not have sufficient senior staff to manage the program, and because the contract risks were too great. The enterprise wanted Muru Mittigar to employ educational staff to work *as required* at the enterprise. This meant Muru Mittigar had to have a certain number of capable education staff available for the enterprise at any time. For Muru Mittigar, this arrangement would have meant retaining and covering the costs of the maximum number of staff the enterprise might require, without any guarantees about how often they would be required. The model was not sustainable for Muru Mittigar.

This illustrates an issue Muru Mittigar is often faced with. Managers must match their supply of suitably trained Aboriginal workers with demand from contractors. This demand can fluctuate significantly, even day-to-day, and this makes it hard for Muru Mittigar to manage the flow of work for those it trains and prepares. Contracting can also require fast-paced responses, and Muru Mittigar can't always move fast enough (e.g., to quickly get a bank loan to purchase equipment for a new contract or find the required number of appropriately skilled workers).

While the organisation tries to minimise its risk profile with every project it takes on, as its former CEO said, 'nothing is ever risk free'. Muru Mittigar is now trying to move away from these types of contracts. The organisation wants to be an employer of choice for Aboriginal people in Western Sydney, but to do that it needs to be able to provide them with a greater level of job security than it sometimes can in this contracting environment.

Changing contracts

A second area of Muru Mittigar's work involves the reduction of bushfire risk at NSW public schools (Cormack, 2020). This project began small and grew through ad hoc engagements with Schools Infrastructure NSW. The work now extends to many parts of NSW and employs around 25 people. As the new CEO explained, the schools where they work provide key community safety infrastructure in the case of fires:

> Muru Mittigar establishes and maintains Asset Protection Zones to the specification of the Department's Bushfire consultant. The specification provided to Muru Mittigar has been developed off the Rural Fire Services Asset Protection Zone standard and the Australian Standard AS 3959 Construction in Bush Fire Prone Areas. The program was established to mitigate the risk and impact of bushfires on schools in bushfire prone areas. It is a crucial program as often the school is the local emergency point for the community and some of the schools have been designated as a Bushfire neighbourhood safe place (a place of last resort for local residents in a bushfire).

The Muru Mittigar rangers spend up to a week in each location carrying out this important fire mitigation work. In 2020 responsibility for bushfire mitigation work at schools shifted to the NSW Department of Works, with which Muru Mittigar had no relationship. As the new CEO explained:

> The procurement process has changed significantly. The previous engagements were by purchase order and now they are by competitive tender, this has seen a reduction in revenue of 30 per cent.

By late 2020, Muru Mittigar had undertaken less work in this area, in part because they did such a good job in 2019 and less bushfire mitigation was required by the Department, but also because they now shared the remaining work with new competitors:

> We appreciate the risk mitigation process of having more than one supplier to deliver such a crucial program, but the current engagement of tranches of three months to deliver a program that would normally take two teams of four six months to deliver has forced us to increase casualisation of our workforce and the use of subcontractors to cover the inevitable peaks and troughs of this delivery model.

This is pushing Muru Mittigar to consider how they can create new business, based on the skills they have:

> CEO: To improve the sustainability of Muru we have diversified our offering and are developing an Arboriculture and Landscaping service. We have chosen these services as these are highly valued services and often the engagement is for three years.

> These new services share skills with our current offering in Bush regeneration and APZ [Asset Protection Zone] works. These new services will also allow us to offer greater career opportunities to our team.

While Muru Mittigar finds that gaining, managing, and reporting on the government's bushfire mitigation work is straightforward compared to working with the private sector, there is increased uncertainty about the amount of work Muru Mittigar will obtain through the Department of Works' competitive tender process in future years. This more recent short-term and reduced-scope market environment makes funding insecure and jeopardises Muru Mittigar's goal of providing secure employment for rangers.

Contract and staffing costs

Another challenge is that in a competitive market environment, skilled senior Aboriginal staff in Sydney are snapped up by government departments and major companies as part of their commitment to Aboriginal employment in their RAPs. They can offer attractive employment conditions and relatively secure jobs; Aboriginal social enterprises with insecure funding streams struggle to compete.

Muru Mittigar tries to employ Aboriginal people wherever it can, but as the former CEO explained in 2019:

> The operations manager role – which is technically vacant at the moment – needs to look after 25 to 30 staff on the ground across half of New South Wales. There's contracting experience, operations experience, a trade or a particular level of expertise that obviously suits what we do as a contracting outfit. All the HR and human elements around managing staff, face to face and remotely. … Strong client relationship negotiation skills, so you're really talking a senior project manager type person.

Given the demand for senior Aboriginal staff, Muru Mittigar is in a highly competitive market and the consequences of inexperienced senior staff at Muru Mittigar dealing with major contractors has already been explained. This also occurred when such senior staff were non-Indigenous and did not have the required experience, or accepted risks the Dharug board members were uncomfortable with.

However, the majority of Muru Mittigar's staff are those undertaking land management of some sort. A major cost that Muru Mittigar carries is the cost of developing the skills and capacities of the people available for these roles. This can include motivating some to work and helping them attain the necessary literacy, numeracy, information technology, and other work skills for the jobs, as well as assisting them with non-work-related challenges. Developing a strong work ethic and a commercial mindset is an ongoing issue.

In providing employment for community members, the issue is how Muru Mittigar can create and maintain jobs for a long enough period, with adequate support to the people they appoint, for these individuals to succeed and achieve long-term employment outcomes. As the former CEO said:

> I think the six month model nationally is about 45 per cent success rate with full time employment after two years whereas the employment – consistent employment for 18 months to two years in a row – our success rate jumps up to something like 80 – mid-80s – 80 to 85 per cent … It's almost double just by keeping – hanging onto these people for longer … Surprise, surprise. The longer you support someone the longer they become employable and resilient and can deal with all the – life's challenges that come along.

For Muru Mittigar to succeed in their goal of long-term employment for Aboriginal people, they need to sustain people in jobs for around two years and provide considerable support and mentoring to them throughout. This is what makes the difference to their success rate, but it has a cost which Muru Mittigar carries.

As one staff member said,

> That's what Muru Mittigar is about is bringing in people and upskilling them. Yeah. So – and that's challenging too, because in lots of other places when you're going against other organisations for tender, they've got fully trained, they've got all their certificates, whereas we've got staff that are, they're in the training phase and they're still being trained and – yeah, it's hard to compete against these ones that employees are already skilled.

As an example of how Muru Mittigar works to attract and develop Aboriginal employees, one staff member explained how they recruited local Aboriginal staff,

> So initially it was [name] and me and the three – the Senior Aboriginal Ranger and two Aboriginal Rangers, which started on the project, and that went for about six weeks. In the background during this time, part of the process for recruitment of trainees we had arranged with [Aboriginal employment service] to run a pre-traineeship training period, which was Cert Two. Some of the modules from Cert Two. We had about 20 people between the ages of 16 and 26 that undertook that training. We ended up with about eight or nine completing that pre-traineeship period.

> From those, we interviewed all those people that remained, and we selected the first four trainees from that group, who are still on board and one of those trainees is now, well, halfway through Cert Three in conservation and land management. That person, which is [name], we've deemed that he has the capacity and the willingness to step up to an Aboriginal Ranger position. At some point, the remaining trainees, they continue with the training, will also be bumped up.

One of the senior staff explained that Aboriginal staff get opportunities at Muru Mittigar that they are less likely to get in mainstream organisations:

> We have two rangers now, head rangers, that started off as rangers. They're taking the leadership role out there with four blokes each … It's a pyramid effect. [Name]'s now moved up in the project … So, what it does is it actually trains them specifically in each field

… and there's a chance for growth. There's a chance for – to climb the chain of command. Which, outside of this, that's hard to get, and hard to do because you're in mainstream. Here it's kept within the Indigenous community, and everyone's approved. Everyone's happy. Most of all, these young people have a future. Long term work.

As Muru Mittigar trains staff and provides them with development opportunities, they may then be attracted to better-paid or more secure work with companies seeking Aboriginal staff to meet their own RAP requirements. While this may have an overall benefit for Aboriginal employment, and it counts as success for Muru Mittigar, the organisation itself does not always reap the returns on its investment in training costs.[8] And though it can win contracts, such funding fails to recognise and pay Muru Mittigar for the cost and the value of the cultural expertise it brings to attract and develop Aboriginal people who may have never been employed in land management before.

Culture and community

The contracting work sustains the organisation and enables it to provide much-needed jobs for Aboriginal people, but cultural educational work and engagement with the Dharug community are core to Muru Mittigar's purpose. Here, Muru Mittigar's multiple objectives meet that tension evident in the literature: its cultural education work is at the heart of its purpose, but this must be subsidised by other parts of the business. Surpluses earned from the land management work, bushfire mitigation contracts, and any other earnings, including from the native plant nursery, underpin this work. It has no core funding to help fulfil the social, CTG objectives it meets.[9] As an Aboriginal social enterprise, Muru Mittigar also has various community obligations and expectations to meet. There are two broad expectations from the Dharug and wider Aboriginal community: providing suitable employment, and ensuring that cultural education occurs and other cultural expectations are met. For example, it has recently supported an

---

8   For example, two experienced cultural education staff left for higher paid jobs at the new enterprise mentioned earlier.

9   Its employment generation work contributes to Closing the Gap targets 7, 8, 15, and 16 and possibly others. See: www.closingthegap.gov.au/national-agreement/targets.

emerging network of Dharug people to meet under its auspices. In doing all this it has to navigate its way through the complex social dynamics within the Aboriginal and wider community of Penrith and surrounds.

While contracting provides most of the jobs that Muru Mittigar creates, the staff and board emphasise the importance of their Dharug cultural awareness and education work at Rouse Hill. The cultural education centre sits in a rural area on the outskirts of Western Sydney, in a corrugated iron building with a large meeting room with audiovisual technology, and other smaller spaces for meetings, painting, or other activities. Outdoor areas allow space to learn how to throw a boomerang, and much else. Elders are engaged along with the centre's coordinator to run cultural education programs for primary and older students.

While the cultural education centre attracts many school groups for cultural workshops and activities, the income earned does not currently fully cover costs:

> … all the advisors that the board have got [that] just want to shut culture down because on the balance sheet it just looks like a hole – a money hole, but it doesn't have to be … If you lose your culture activity you're really – Muru Mittigar will lose a big part of its identity … Not that we don't do cultural immersion with everything we do, in contracting for example, but people – it's our core business. It's like General Electric not making light bulbs anymore, it's kind of – you know, it's – this is really – people are still really seeking this. This type of program and product.

Before COVID-19 forced Muru Mittigar to suspend the cultural education program, Muru Mittigar saw an opportunity to strengthen its financial viability[10] by developing adult cultural education programs for companies and institutions. But this requires Aboriginal staff with higher levels of skill and confidence to deliver programs to these clients, and to manage the bookings, catering, and to have better systems for the organisational and administrative aspects of the work, an issue the new CEO has been working on during this COVID-19 time. As one staff member said,

10   The Cultural Education Centre also has venues that it hires out for community use, to bring in supplementary income.

Particular audiences for those programmes can be quite demanding. They can really challenge the competency of some people if they're not experienced or prepared, and we don't want to set people up to fail in that way.

So, while Muru Mittigar has identified a new market in adult cultural education and gained accreditation with the NSW Education Standards Authority as a provider, it struggled with the organisational and capacity issues needed. It remains to be seen whether this market will return when COVID-19 concerns are reduced.

The nursery, on the other hand, is financially viable, as the new CEO reported:

> We've made some investments in there, automated as much as possible. Pursuing wholesale sales to large construction infrastructure programs. It'll make a profit this year, about 12%, which is pretty good. We'll reinvest those profits into the sector.

But efforts by one major company to use the nursery to meet its Indigenous requirements to win a large contract were rebuffed as simply 'black cladding' by Muru Mittigar. Judging whether companies are serious about mutually beneficial partnership arrangements, or just using an Aboriginal corporation for their own purposes, is necessary in the current contracting environment.

The Community Finance Hub is another important service Muru Mittigar offers to the whole community. This is grant-funded but also subsidised by the contracting business. Initially, the program was funded by the National Australia Bank (NAB) to promote Aboriginal financial literacy, but the Hub is now funded by the NSW Department of Fair Trading (a three-year contract) and Good Shepherd Microfinance. As one of the staff explained:

> … and that's used for our No Interest Loans Scheme (NILS) program, the Good Shepherd funding, and the Office of Fair Trading funding is used for our financial counsellors and also has a NILS admin component as well for their funding … That's for the NILS program and providing loans to very low-income people and … it's only $1500 – up to $1500 and they can only purchase essential items … fridges, things like that.

The Hub works from the Penrith office, with weekly outreach to six or seven other locations in the region each fortnight.[11] And while the service is open to anyone in need, not just Aboriginal people, the fact that Muru Mittigar is an Aboriginal organisation makes it easier for Aboriginal people to access help. One of the Hub team commented,

> They probably don't feel as judged, like you should be managing your life better. They feel that they can come and openly say, I'm in trouble here. Yeah. I'm having difficulties, yeah.

This is an important service to the very low-income members of the Western Sydney community that Muru Mittigar serves. Among other things, it tries to counter the predatory loan sharks and constant pressure from advertising that suggests people need consumer items that they cannot afford. Staff keep detailed records of the people they help, and the NILS loans granted, and report regularly, but funding is not always ongoing, as the ending of the NAB funds demonstrates.

Another aspect of Muru Mittigar's relationship with the community is its network of linkages with other Aboriginal businesses that both compete with and complement each other. And Muru Mittigar must also navigate the social dynamics of the community and the perception of fairness in who gets employed. Muru Mittigar insists that people who apply for jobs are selected on merit, but in the Aboriginal community some hold the view that jobs must be shared fairly around the different families, so this is a difficult balance for Muru Mittigar. It needs to retain its legitimacy with the community, but it also wants to take the best people for each job. Muru also increasingly recruits through the Aboriginal Employment Strategies and Aboriginal Education Units to enable them to verify Aboriginal identity for positions which must be Aboriginal-identified.

The other aspect of Muru Mittigar's engagement with the community is the expectation that Muru Mittigar will host or participate in important cultural events like the NAIDOC week celebrations and other community occasions. Muru Mittigar must balance these demands on its time and limited resources with its need to retain community legitimacy in how it responds to such expectations. NPM's tender processes do not allow

---

11   These services have been provided by phone and teleconference during COVID.

resourcing for such important cultural activities, which are fundamental to Muru Mittigar's relationship with its community and its ability to maintain their trust and work with them successfully.

Conclusion

So, can an urban Indigenous social enterprise turn market engagement to its advantage towards solving longstanding socio-economic problems of poverty and unemployment and educating about Dharug culture? Muru Mittigar is demonstrating that Aboriginal social enterprise can use the market to create jobs and thereby turn some lives around. But it does not operate on a level playing field and has to overcome many challenges:

- The complex nature of its goals as an Aboriginal social enterprise and the fact that some parts of the business are highly valued but must be subsidised by earned income from other parts.

- The short-term and increasingly uncertain contracting environment that makes sustaining ongoing employment for Aboriginal people transitioning from unemployment to stable employment difficult.

- The risk of being a subcontractor for major corporations, as market arrangements of this type leave no room for mistakes; nor are they designed for capacity building of a relatively small social enterprise.

- The growing competition from other Indigenous organisations or 'black cladding' from non-Indigenous ones competing in a weakly defined social procurement environment.

- The extra support needed to bring unemployed Aboriginal people into the workforce, help them adjust to regular work routines while managing the social and economic challenges of their lives, while still delivering cost-competitive contracts. Success in doing this depends on the unrecognised and largely unremunerated cultural skills and knowledge embedded in the organisation.

- Managing and resourcing the additional cultural responsibilities of an Aboriginal enterprise when it works on the land of other First Nations.

- Having the required skill levels in business, finance, and management on the governance board and in senior management while remaining Aboriginal-led and controlled.

In summary, while Muru Mittigar is providing a training and development role for rangers and other staff who get opportunities through Muru Mittigar that they would not have received in mainstream organisations, it must achieve this while maintaining cost-competitive contracts that also support the cultural and community programs. The cross-subsidisation of that cultural and community work in fact facilitates the success of Muru Mittigar in supporting and developing previously unemployed people into reliable and capable workers.

Expanding genuine social and Indigenous procurement, including at the local government level, with tighter rules to reduce 'black cladding', could strengthen Muru Mittigar's market position. Governments recognising that organisations like Muru Mittigar are stepping in where the market is failing to meet significant community needs, and resourcing that work through social procurement, would provide more opportunities for the organisation, and help it attain the employment and other goals it strives for. IPPs assume that the market can build Indigenous enterprises, but these policies embrace both Indigenous for-profit businesses and those operating as *social* enterprises whose goals include broader community benefit, with the associated costs. NPM's focus on competitive market efficiencies fails to acknowledge the hidden subsidy that an Aboriginal organisation provides to enable the social goals of closing gaps to succeed.

There is also a vast inequality of power in a procurement arrangement between major corporations and a subcontracted nonprofit Aboriginal organisation like Muru Mittigar. IPPs assume that an Aboriginal organisation can deal as an equal, but subcontracting in a competitive market is fraught with risk. The goals of a corporation, or even a government department, are not to support a social enterprise to develop; they simply contract it to complete a task. Procurement from Aboriginal organisations may look good in an RAP, but procurement alone may not strengthen an Aboriginal enterprise towards its own self-determined agenda. On the other hand, long-term pro bono support geared to its needs, such as the governance and financial advice Muru Mittigar has received from a bank and a legal firm, may be more significant in helping it achieve its goals. But ultimately, if Aboriginal organisations are to be self-determining, market arrangements must support *their* social goals and approaches directly through more fully costed social procurement.

References

Anderson R. B., Dana, L. P., & Dana T. E. (2006). Indigenous land rights, entrepreneurship, and economic development in Canada: 'Opting-in' to the global economy. *Journal of World Business*, *41*(1), 45–55. doi.org/10.1016/j.jwb.2005.10.005

Australian Bureau of Statistics (2016). *2016 QuickStats: Penrith.* www.abs.gov.au/census/find-census-data/quickstats/2016/IQSLGA16350

Australian Government (2015). *Commonwealth Indigenous procurement policy.* www.niaa.gov.au/our-work/employment-and-economic-development/indigenous-procurement-policy-ipp

Banerjee, S. B., & Tedmanson, D. (2010). Grass burning under our feet: Indigenous enterprise development in a political economy of whiteness. *Management Learning, 41*(2), 147–165. doi.org/10.1177/1350507609357391

Barr, T. L., Reid, J., Catska, P., Varona, G., & Rout, M. (2018). Development of indigenous enterprise in a contemporary business environment – the Ngāi Tahu Ahikā approach. *Journal of Enterprising Communities: People and Places in the Global Economy*, *12*(4), 454–471. doi.org/10.1108/JEC-05-2016-0014

Cormack, L. (2020, 23 November). 'We thought the fire would skirt around the town': 175 NSW schools at high risk during bushfires'. *Sydney Morning Herald.* www.smh.com.au/national/nsw/we-thought-the-fire-would-skirt-around-the-town-175-nsw-schools-at-high-risk-during-bushfires-20201122-p56gs2.html

Corntassel, J. (2008). Toward sustainable self-determination: Rethinking the contemporary Indigenous-rights discourse, *Alternatives:Global, Local, Political*, *33*(1), 105–132. doi.org/10.1177/030437540803300106

Denny-Smith, G., & Loosemore, M. (2017). Integrating Indigenous enterprises into the Australian construction industry, *Engineering, Construction and Architectural Management, 24*(5), 788–808. doi.org/10.1108/ECAM-01-2016-0001

Denny-Smith, G., & Loosemore, M. (2018). Cultural counterfactuals: Assessing the impact of Indigenous social procurement in Australia. In C. Gorse & C. J. Neilson (Eds), *Proceedings of the 34th Annual ARCOM Conference, 3–5 September 2018*. Association of Researchers in Construction Management.

Douglas, H. (2015). Embracing hybridity: A review of social entrepreneurship and enterprise in Australia and New Zealand [online]. *Third Sector Review*, *21*(1), 5–30.

Douglas, H., Eti-Tofinga, B., & Singh, G. (2018). Hybrid organisations contributing to wellbeing in Small Pacific Island countries. *Sustainability Accounting, Management and Policy Journal, 9*(4), 490–514. doi.org/10.1108/SAMPJ-08-2017-0081

Eikenberry, A. M. (2009). Refusing the market: A democratic discourse for voluntary and nonprofit organizations. *Nonprofit and Voluntary Sector Quarterly, 38*(4) 582–596. doi.org/10.1177%2F0899764009333686

Foley, D. (2003). An examination of Indigenous entrepreneurs. *Journal of Developmental Entrepreneurship, 8*(2), 133–151.

Giovannini, M. (2012). Social enterprises for development as *buen vivir. Journal of Enterprising Communities: People and Places in the Global Economy, 6*(3), 284–299. doi.org/10.1108/17506201211258432

Greater Sydney Commission (2018). *Greater Sydney region plan. A metropolis of three cities—connecting people.* www.planning.nsw.gov.au/plans-for-your-area/a-metropolis-of-three-cities

Jenkins, S. (2020, 21 February). Indigenous procurement targets undermined by implementation and compliance issues, audit finds. *The Mandarin.* www.themandarin.com.au/125752-indigenous-procurement-targets-undermined-by-implementation-and-compliance-issues-audit-finds/

Jones, J., Pi-Shen, S., Acker, T., & Whittle, M. (2019). Barriers to grassroots innovation: The phenomenon of social–commercial–cultural trilemmas in remote indigenous art centres. *Technological Forecasting & Social Change, 164*(March). doi.org/10.1016/j.techfore.2019.02.003

Kerins, S. (2013). *Social enterprise as a model for developing Aboriginal lands.* CAEPR Topical Issue No. 4/2013. The Australian National University. caepr.cass.anu.edu.au/sites/default/files/docs/TI2013_05_Kerins_social_enterprise_0.pdf

Ketilson, L. H. (2014). Partnering to finance enterprise development in the Aboriginal social economy. *Canadian Public Policy, 40*(1), 39–49. doi.org/10.3138/cpp.2012-098

Lee, C., & Nowell, B. (2014). A framework for assessing the performance of nonprofit organizations. *American Journal of Evaluation, 36*(3). doi.org/10.1177/1098214014545828

Loban, H., Ciccotosto, S., & Boulot, P. (2013). Indigenous corporate governance and social enterprise [online]. *Indigenous Law Bulletin, 8*(8). classic.austlii.edu.au/au/journals/IndigLawB/2013/38.pdf

New South Wales Government Treasury (2021). Aboriginal procurement policy. buy.nsw.gov.au/__data/assets/pdf_file/0007/949174/app_policy_jan_2021.pdf

Norman, H. (2018, 18 November). Land rights and native title aren't the same – and the two systems could spark Indigenous conflict. *ABC News Online*. www.abc.net.au/news/2018-11-16/heidi-norman-ticking-timebomb-for-indigenous-conflict-in-nsw/10376778

O'Flynn, J. (2007). From New Public Management to public value: Paradigmatic change and managerial implications. *Australian Journal of Public Administration*, *66*(3), 353–366. doi.org/10.1111/j.1467-8500.2007.00545.x

Pearson, C. A. L., & Helms, K. (2013). Indigenous social entrepreneurship: The Gumatj Clan Enterprise in East Arnhem Land. *Journal of Entrepreneurship, 22*(1), 43–70. doi.org/10.1177%2F0971355712469185

Penrith City Council (2018). *Community profile*. www.penrithcity.nsw.gov.au/resources-documents/community-info/community-profile

Quarry (2014, December). State government releases vision for quarry rehabilitation. *Quarry*. www.quarrymagazine.com/?s=State+government+releases+vision+for+quarry+rehabilitation

Rebutin, J. A. (2009). *Social enterprise and tourism, the key to a better integration of indigenous populations* [unpublished Masters thesis]. Université de Toulon. dumas.ccsd.cnrs.fr/view/index/identifiant/dumas-00418823

Reconciliation Australia (n.d.). *Reconciliation Action Plans*. www.reconciliation.org.au/reconciliation-action-plans/

Sengupta, U., Vieta, M., & McMurtry, J. J. (2015). Indigenous communities and social enterprise in Canada: Incorporating culture as an essential ingredient of entrepreneurship. *Canadian Journal of Nonprofit and Social Economy Research*, *6*(1) 104–123. doi.org/10.22230/cjnser.2015v6n1a196

Spencer, R. Brueckner, M., Wise, G., & Marika, B. (2015). *Measuring performance: A story of 'Closing The Gap' through Indigenous social enterprise.* Working Paper 2015–1. Centre for Responsible Citizenship and Sustainability, Murdoch University.

Spencer, R., Brueckner, M., Wise, G., & Marika, B. (2017). Capacity development and Indigenous social enterprise: The case of the Rirratjingu clan in northeast Arnhem Land. *Journal of Management & Organization*, *23*(6), 839–856. doi.org/10.1017/jmo.2017.74

Stanković, M. (2020). Demystifying the relationship between New Public Management and social entrepreneurship: A conceptual framework. *Sociologija, 62*(3), 438–454. doi.org/10.2298/SOC2003438S

Vázquez-Maguirre, M., & Portales, L. (2018). Profits and purpose: Organizational tensions in indigenous social enterprises. *Intangible Capital, 14*(4), 604–618. doi.org/10.3926/ic.1208

7

The Glen Centre: A strength-based culturally immersive model of care hidden in plain sight

Deirdre Howard-Wagner and Chris Mason

The yarning circle is the heartbeat of The Glen.

—Chris Mason, The Glen

Introduction

Located on the edge of a state forest, and metres from Chittaway Bay, the campus is surrounded by wide open spaces and trees.[1] The Glen is an Aboriginal community-controlled and self-determining 37-bed residential

---

1   In early October 2019, Deirdre Howard-Wagner arrived at The Glen Drug and Alcohol Rehabilitation Centre for a week-long fieldwork visit. The objective of the field research was to observe the day-to-day interactions within a First Nations community-controlled drug and alcohol rehabilitation centre. Howard-Wagner observed and discussed with Chris Mason The Glen's governance and leadership style, organisational dynamics, and how its program works. Howard-Wagner observed and discussed with Mason how the objectives of the organisation are realised in its day-to-day operation, and how the men in the program come to experience and benefit from this distinctive Aboriginal therapeutic community, including the cultural and communal aspects of the program. Howard-Wagner observed and discussed with Mason The Glen community itself: the dynamic between the staff, between the staff and men in the program, and between The Glen and the wider community. Howard-Wagner relied on several field visits to The Glen along with important insights from Mason. Field visits included two

Aboriginal drug and alcohol rehabilitation centre for men. It accepts Indigenous and non-Indigenous clients from all over Australia. The Glen has been described as a 'triumph of the Koori spirit' since proud Aboriginal man Cyril Hennessy started it in 1994 (Interview, The Glen Chief Executive Officer). The Glen was named after Hennessy's son, who lost his life through dependency. It is run by the Ngaimpe Aboriginal Corporation, which is registered under the *Corporations (Aboriginal and Torres Strait Islander) Act 2006* (Cth), and has a board of five Aboriginal female directors, and a chief executive officer. While not part of the justice system per se, the board, the CEO, and The Glen's staff are focused on trying to support men coming out of the criminal justice system and into treatment for their drug or alcohol dependency. They not only hope to reduce the rate of recidivism among Aboriginal men but also to reintegrate them into society.

The central focus of the chapter is how The Glen navigated its organisational fragility in the NPM era, making visible its model of care and building its social networks and administrative support system, moving from a fragile to antifragile organisation in terms of securing government funding. The chapter is co-authored by Deirdre Howard-Wagner, a non-Indigenous academic researcher, and Chris Mason, a proud Ngemba man whose family is from Brewarrina in the far north-west of NSW. Mason is a co-researcher with Howard-Wagner as well as an informant of the case study.

First Nations organisational fragility/ antifragility in the NPM era

The Glen is a relative latecomer as a community-controlled Aboriginal drug and alcohol residential rehabilitation centre. Other Aboriginal drug and alcohol rehabilitation centres have been operating in NSW since the early 1970s. The Glen has gone on to become not only an Aboriginal sector leader but a national leader in drug and alcohol rehabilitation. The CEO, Alex Lee, is a member of the National Alcohol and Drug Data and Research Advisory Group, and Joe Coyte, Executive Director and former CEO,

week-long observations of The Glen's environment, programs, and operations, activities organised by The Glen in the local community, as well as interviews with 13 staff members and a research yarning circle with 23 men who were in The Glen program at the time of the second field visit. Howard-Wagner also made shorter field visits to The Glen a third, fourth, and fifth time to verify and develop the findings of the research with Mason and The Glen's CEO Alex Lee, and continue the conversation about its ongoing journey navigating the era of New Public Management.

is a member of the Australian National Advisory Council on Alcohol and Other Drugs. The Counsellor and Community Engagement Officer, Chris Mason, also co-author of this chapter, is a board member of the Aboriginal Drug and Alcohol Residential Rehab Network. The Glen has adopted a community-of-practice approach for developing its model of care, which has led to the standardisation of client admission and outcome data for the sector, along with the development of a quality improvement framework with the best evidence and routine data collection and analysis process.

A decade ago, while maintaining a steady state of existence, The Glen was experiencing what Tony Bendell (2016) refers to as organisational fragility. Bendell draws on the work of Nassim Taleb, who considers fragility and antifragility not only to be two different ends of a spectrum, but states that exist within political and other states of order and disorder, with antifragility growing from those states of disorder (Taleb, 2012).

With the introduction of a new, Indigenous service delivery market, arguably a political state of disorder for community-controlled First Nations organisations in NSW, The Glen struggled to get recognition for its expertise. The NPM era had seen Indigenous sector organisations in critical service areas – drug and alcohol residential rehabilitation, health, and community housing, for example – come under significant scrutiny. A number of researchers have pointed to what they considered deficits in the Indigenous drug and alcohol rehabilitation sector (Brady, 1995; Chenhall, 2007; Chenhall and Senior, 2013). Key among them is Brady, who has argued that the governance, training and networking, and program content within the sector were wanting (Brady, 2002, p. v). The Glen did not simply adapt, adjust, or work around the New Public Management's threat to its existence, but strategically tailored its response to correct the misconceptions and deficit mentality that prevailed in government and academic discourses about the sector. What existed then exists now. The Glen's successful, strength-based, culturally immersive model of care appeared to have been hidden in plain sight, with researchers and public officials failing to see the important contribution it was making to the lives of Indigenous and non-Indigenous men dealing with drug and alcohol dependence.

The Glen's heartbeat

Deirdre's field visit to The Glen in October 2019 was her third. Chris Mason, the Counsellor and Community Engagement Officer, met her at the campfire, which is located in the north-eastern corner of The Glen's large expanse of land.[2] The campfire sits in a large open space on the corner between two of The Glen's main buildings – the oversized farm shed, about the size of a three-bedroom home, which houses the music and art studio and the gym, and another building that houses the meeting room and secondary offices. The campfire is the focal point of the residential rehabilitation program. It is where the yarning circles take place. As Chris explained to Deirdre: 'The yarning circle is the heartbeat of The Glen.' Chris is referring to the significance of the yarning circle that takes place around the permanent campfire several times a week. Deirdre observed the significance of the yarning circle, but also the campfire, to The Glen's residential rehabilitation program on each separate field visit. On her first visit, Deirdre observed a group of new arrivals go through a smoking ceremony. On her second visit, Deirdre observed the morning yarning circle at the campfire. On her third visit, Deirdre observed a group of men in the residential rehabilitation program perform an Aboriginal dance at the campfire. On her fourth visit, Deirdre joined the current intake of men in the residential rehabilitation program at the campfire for a music session with songwriters and musicians Kasey Chambers, Alan Pigram, and Brandon Dodd. Prominent Yawuru man Pigram shares some of his journey as a musician with the men and speaks to the men in Yawuru. Chambers, Pigram, Dodd, and the men then write a song together as part of The Glen's music therapy program.

The prominent place of the campfire yarning circle is a physical reminder that its program is based on Indigenous values and spirituality. Chris explained the campfire's significance to the program: 'culture and community are an important part of how we look at ways we can combat trauma and engage in trauma-informed care with the clients'.

---

2   At this time, Deirdre Howard-Wagner had known Chris Mason for 18 months. The Glen is one of six First Nations organisations that have partnered in a three-year Australian Research Council–funded research project, and Chris Mason is The Glen's representative on the ARC research project committee. The committee has met every three months or so and has done intensive work around the research co-design, including the development of the data management plan, organisation case study design, and survey. Chris Mason is co-chair of the ARC research project committee.

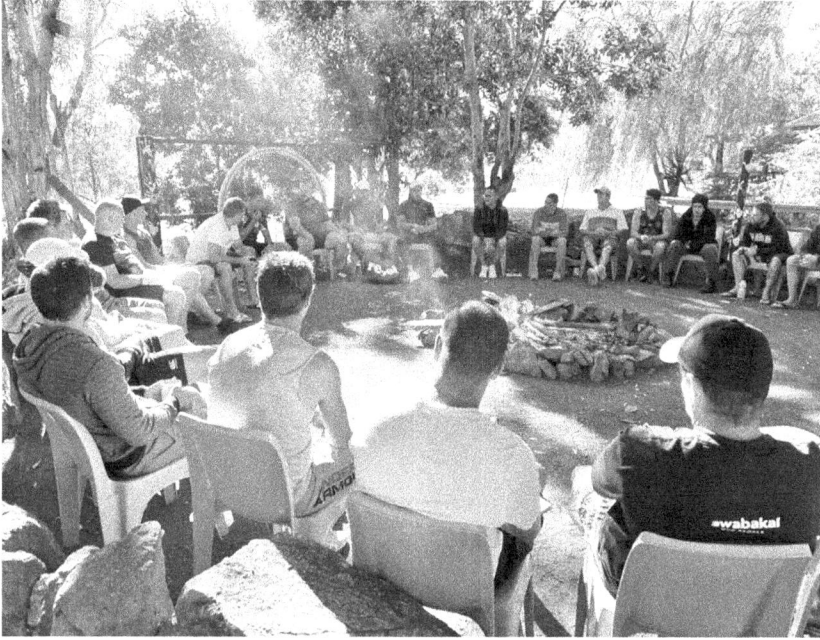

Image 7.1. Yarning around the campfire.
Copyright: The Glen.

Chris handed Deirdre a T-shirt. As he explained:

> So we've done a shirt that encapsulates everything that we stand for at The Glen. We've got the emu on the front, and we've got all the stars. We've got the Aboriginal flag and the official Australian flag there. The philosophy of our program is culturally based, and so the emu it can go forwards, but it can't go backwards. So, when the men at The Glen join the Running Program, the men go forward and not backwards.

Deirdre now understood why the program Chris manages is called the Running Program.

Chris then explained to Deirdre how The Glen operates as a residential Aboriginal Therapeutic Community for men. By treating the person as a whole (spiritually, mentally, and physically), The Glen helps the men on their road to recovery so that they can eventually return to their families and community as active members. Indigenous values are adopted throughout The Glen's program, in line with its strength-based approach. Chris explained The Glen's cohesive, culturally specific and responsive model of care for Aboriginal residential rehabilitation, and how its distinctive culturally immersive therapeutic approach contributes to the success of its program.

He went on to describe aspects of cultural immersion: 'We do a smoking ceremony when they just start the program, and we actually use story – so we use story to engage the men, so we use cultural concepts to explain pretty complex situations', Chris explained. 'We take the men to sites too and tell them a bit about the story of the sites, especially around the local area and down Warrimer Road or even up at Mount Yengo and Wollombi National Park', he added. 'There's blokes who come through here that have a lot of more cultural knowledge than I ever will', Chris laughed, 'but we learn from each other – that motivates the men's journey at The Glen'.

Image 7.2. The Glen T-shirt.
Source: Photograph by Deirdre Howard-Wagner.

Chris elaborated:

> The thing is that they're connecting culturally – they are connecting to all these people in the community and through their culture – Elders come in and they might talk about creation stories and spirituality, and so then they can sort of make a decision based on what they want to believe. So, if they want more help [with it], and so one of the counsellors tells them how he prays to Baiame and his two grandmothers – he prays to them every night, and so they understand – the ancestors and Baiame and Mother and Father and Mother Earth. And, so, they're learning things along the way in what they do.

Over Deirdre's many field visits to The Glen and interviews with staff and men in The Glen program, and through ongoing conversations with Chris, she comes to understand the significance of The Glen's model of care to the outcomes of rehabilitating men that come through its program, reintegrating them into their families, communities, and society.

The Glen's model of care: Beyond the clinical approach to drug and alcohol rehabilitation

> If we didn't have the rehabs or The Glen, then I don't believe that it would be doing the community any justice out there. I really don't. I think what we've got here is pretty amazing and we do it differently, but we do it well. It's not clinical. We're not just sitting in a room all day, every day talking about just addictions and things. It's not clinical.
>
> (Interview, The Glen case worker)

> Like for me, I come from a Yamatji-speaking group in Western Australia and when I come out of my community and I went looking for help for recovery, people spoke a language I couldn't understand. So, when I went into other rehabs outside of an Indigenous one, the way that they spoke, I didn't understand them. But then I had to go – because I was Aboriginal and I walked in my own world, I had to go and learn how to walk in a whitefellas' world to fit in. Then the worlds that I have to walk in, I have to go and learn how to walk in their world. So, I'm forced to walk in two different worlds. Coming to an Indigenous organisation has made it better for me. I've had to come from a whole different state to get rehab.
>
> (Yarning circle, The Glen program participant male #1)

Yarning circle facilitator: *Has it made a difference?*

A hundred and twenty per cent. It changed my life. It changed my thinking, my perspective, everything. It changed the direction of my life. I don't want to go back ever again.

(Yarning circle, The Glen program participant male #1)

The Glen's approach aims to move men out of the criminal justice system and reintegrate them back into their families, communities, and society. They are not just passing through a program. The Glen's model of care works on the men's dependency but also reconnects them with their culture, families, communities, and society. As Chris explains:

Yeah, they can go back out and not only go back to their families but go back to work, go back and are able to support their family how they want to support it. A lot of these boys want it. It's just they don't know how to get to it. They feel that they have lost all their chances, and no one is prepared to give them a shot at rebuilding their life and getting well and getting clean and sober. So, I think our program here, we are a holistic rehab, and it is, it's so important that we do what we do here and how we do it.

I think we do things a lot differently because they're learning everyday living skills again to be able to go back out there; make appointments to go to doctors, be able to go to the shops and buy their things and whatever, be able to cook. We have cooking classes here. We do a small group each time they come, and they get to learn how to cook good, healthy meals. They get back into the gym and they train. We have a fully equipped gym. So, it's good for their mental health.

It is not only about living skills, employment, and housing and being able to make a doctor's appointment. It is also about the men's self-esteem in society and creating positive encounters with society so that the men feel safe re-engaging with it.

We're getting involved in society; so, it might be a Bunning's barbecue, it might be doing a scout hall, it might be doing Aboriginal dancing in the community, it might be doing smoking ceremonies, it might be attending Aboriginal events like the Koori Knockout or the Indigenous Marathon running for Father's Day.

So, we do all that as an aim to introduce them back into the community and society, but then on the whole, while we're here we give them employment, so they save money, they can buy a car, they go into private housing. So that gets them back into society and they become taxpaying [full] citizens of society, you know what I mean? So, it's working backwards from that stuff – does that make sense?

(Formal interview, Chris Mason)

Over seven years, Deirdre observed how what Chris explains is evident. The Glen has developed strong connections with other services to assist the men in removing barriers that can affect their capacity to move forward. For example, The Glen works closely with the Aboriginal Client Advisory Officer from the NSW Office of State Debt to assist the men in resolving longstanding debts that are affecting their lives, such as when debts result in licence suspension.

Chris explained how immersion in the culture is central to The Glen's model of care. Respect for Aboriginal culture and pride play a key role in its healing process. Chris is not alone in pointing to the significant role that cultural immersion plays in The Glen's program: the current and former CEOs agree. The former CEO of The Glen provided one of many examples during his interview:

> The boys really enjoy the Elders coming in and sharing some of the history of themselves. Everyone has got a story. It is also important to a lot of the guys that come in to make sure that we're not doing anything wrong, and they've got permission to be here.
>
> (Interview, Executive Officer and former CEO Joe Coyte)

The men who participate in The Glen's program also appreciate its cultural aspects. During a research yarning circle, many of the men – both Aboriginal and non-Aboriginal – want to speak about the importance of Aboriginal culture to the program. They describe it 'as the best thing about this place and what it does' (Yarning circle, The Glen program participant male #4). Many of the participants in the research yarning circle went on to explain its significance to the program. Here are examples:

> The boys that come in here, some of them know about the culture and some don't know about the Aboriginal culture. You know, [you get] the boy that hasn't danced before, they'll want to get up and dance. For me, I could dance when I was 15/16. I've lost all that. Culture, pride, dignity, spirit. Coming here, you get all that back. You know, I have six kids, they've never been a part of that side. So, for me, you get all that back. I can leave here, which I do tomorrow, but I can go back to my kids and show them what I've learnt in here and how to respect the culture and continue on with it. But for me, I'm just glad to be just add my culture back in my life … This place here has given me it all back.
>
> (Yarning circle, The Glen program participant male #4)

The importance of culture. It's like that's our identity. We lose our culture and like government and that, they've been trying to kill our culture for – since they got here. So, going to a church-run thing, the church-run thing has massacred our people all over this land. You know? Us getting our culture back, we get our identity back. We can restore like brothers that never grew up in that. Their stories. They get their identity, and they get stronger, and you have more pride in yourself. Then you want to see good in people. Then you can walk around with your head held high in your community.

(Yarning circle, The Glen program participant male #7)

So, like as an Aboriginal Torres Strait coming into a place that's run by Aboriginal and Torres Strait Islander people that values our culture, that's important. Like you know, that really is something that – like as Aboriginal and Torres Strait Islander, you look at that straight away. Jails and all that stuff, that's run by a thing, and it doesn't work for our people. Like our community, we get to heal our community, but we also get to show people that aren't from our community that there's good in it. We get to see the good in us and in our people and we get to build on that and get our pride back.

(Yarning circle, The Glen program participant male #10)

I've heard non-Aboriginal people say that they've actually got their spirit back through our culture. That's amazing. That's crazy when you hear that. When you hear that non-Aboriginal people can identify with Indigenous culture and it shows how much power that Aboriginal culture really does have. When they say stuff like that, that really makes you feel good that this place is actually doing something right. It's not about [culture], it's not about that, it's about saving the next person's life. This is just a platform made by Indigenous people to help every Australian and that's great. Do you know what I mean?

(Yarning circle, The Glen program participant male #5)

Cultural immersion has multiple dimensions. Chris explained that the men in the program engage in local cultural events:

like it might be the Warrior Room on Father's Day, or the Walk a Mile Koori Style, or any of the suicide preventions, the Are you Okay days and all that, where we do the dancing or the walk or both. If it's dancing, the blokes paint up and everything. They dance to kick start a lot of these events off.

So, while the campfire yarning circle is the heartbeat of The Glen's model of care, the culturally immersive therapeutic program is the heart of The Glen. As the current CEO explains, 'culture and knowing who they are and pride' (Interview, CEO Alex Lee) and a holistic case management approach are central to The Glen's model of care.

Deirdre comes to understand the importance of community engagement activities, such as running a fundraiser barbeque in the carpark at one of the Bunnings hardware outlets. As one case worker explained:

> By being able to go out and be on the barbeques and being able to talk to the community and they're not afraid or ashamed to tell people that they're from The Glen and when people say, what's The Glen that don't know they will say to them, it's a drug and alcohol rehabilitation and they will come back and they will say, we've had people say, good on you, that's great, you're trying to do something about your addiction and things.
>
> So, it builds their self-esteem and their self-confidence back and their self-worth, and they don't have that when they come in here. They're just so broken. They walk in with their heads down. They don't look you in the eye. They're embarrassed and ashamed. They feel guilty. But as time goes on and they're in here you see the changes. They start to stand tall. They hold their head high. They're looking at you when they talk. They're smiling. I think it's because of what we do and how we do it here, and that's why The Glen is important.
>
> (Interview, The Glen case worker)

Deirdre comes to understand the powerful effect it has on the men. The program not only gets the men back out into society but builds their self-esteem:

> You don't see it when you first come in because you're still sick, you come out off the street and your mind is foggy with all this stuff. You don't realise a lot of stuff. But as you get towards the end of your 12 week period, you look at the stuff that The Glen does in the community. Like painting under the bridge, doing the waterway clean ups, going on recovery walks, yeah, clean up the oval down here.
>
> … The Glen is a fantastic place to be at. So not only does it heal you doing things for the community, but I also remember we did a cancer walk for the little kids that died from cancer. Now, as an addict in myself, I used to think – I had this huge, big problem but all these little problems were bigger than my biggest problem because I didn't want to deal with that stuff.

> But then all of a sudden, The Glen gives me an opportunity to go down and do a cancer walk for kids who have cancer, who are dying, who die every year, for a cause. So, it gives us boys more understanding in our hearts for us to do that stuff in the community. So, that way it makes The Glen … It's got so much heart and spirit and soul in this place.
>
> (Yarning circle, The Glen program participant male #6)

Deirdre observed too how a program that includes sports and community events is critical to the men's recovery. She observes this while watching the men proudly participate in NAIDOC Kikupa Cup at Woongarrah Oval in July 2019. The men not only participate in the event, but The Glen organises it. The Glen boys compete in a touch football match against teams from the local council, the local WIN News, and other major organisations. Deirdre witnessed the men's pride when they danced in 2019 at Western Sydney 7's as the Indigenous team played.

Running a marathon gives the men pride and purpose too. On 1 November 2020, Gurindji man Ethan Mulholland ran the Indigenous Marathon in Alice Springs. On 21 November 2020, Ethan conquered an ultramarathon through the hills of Mount Stromlo. Three years earlier, he was in a freefall of drugs and alcohol. Today, Ethan is a highly regarded counsellor at The Glen.

Deirdre also observed firsthand how the delivery of the program is made possible through The Glen's local and wider social networks. The Glen's connections with Bunnings, Jawun, and even local musicians like Kasey Chambers, strengthen its capacity. Chambers has been an enthusiastic supporter and helper since coming across The Glen with her 'mum' hat on in 2015 (Barnes, 2016, p. 1). Her then 13-year-old son Talon, a talented Australian Football League player and member of the Central Coast Academy of Sport, attended an educational session at The Glen (Barnes, 2016, p. 1). Chambers drove her son and some of his other teammates to a session at The Glen where the guys got up and told their stories (Barnes, 2016, p. 1). This is part of the men's community engagement, as the men educate young people through telling their stories.

Deirdre observed The Glen as a culturally safe community in which the men in the program are respectful of each other, and the staff are respectful of the men and each other. She could see why staff and the men in the program refer to 'The Glen family'. She sat with the staff to eat lunch together on an open verandah on three occasions while doing field research. She ate a healthy lunch cooked by the men as part of their cooking class.

Deirdre observed, for example, how The Glen treats the men's complex social problems in a therapeutic and culturally embedded way that helps the men deal with their complex childhood and continuing intergenerational trauma and grief. She observed the case worker adopting a holistic and therapeutic approach which, the case worker went on to explain, addresses the men's underlying grief and trauma:

> It's not just their alcohol and drug dependency that they're coming in with. They're coming in with so much more, their grief. Grief is another massive one for them. So, we address their grief with X, our grief counsellor.[3] So, we have specific people come in and help us out from different services for whatever is going on with them.
>
> So, we take that holistic approach, which is really important, because unless we address the underlying issues it's probably not going to help them with their dependency because a lot of them I find when I'm working with them it comes out – they will disclose to me that a lot of it is because of their past, whether they've come from broken families themselves or family/domestic violence, sexual abuse and it has never been addressed, being with their partners and domestic violence is a big one.
>
> So, gambling, loss of jobs, it all ties in, it sort of marries in and goes hand in hand, with their mental health. So, usually a lot of that leads to their dependency. That's where it takes them because they feel that they've got no other way out and that's the only way they can cope with some situations. So, if we can address a lot of the underlying issues. Hopefully, then that will help them with their dependency when they go back out that they don't feel they need to go back out and drink or take drugs and use to cope.
>
> We give them different coping strategies and the skills and tools I guess to be able to go out there, and that's why to sit and talk to them is really important because a lot of them feel that they have never been listened to before and to have somebody – and that's where the staff come in. Everybody is here to support them and do the best we all can and just to sit and listen sometimes. Sometimes you don't even have to say anything. It's just they're talking and getting things off their chest. They know that they are safe here and I will often say to them, this is a safe – these four walls are a safe place for you to deal with the hard things that you haven't been able to deal with out there unless you've picked up a drink or a drug.
>
> (Interview, The Glen case worker)

---

3   Name withheld.

Other staff also explained the multifaceted aspects of the counselling program.

Chris elaborated to Deirdre how a 'stress management and anxiety' group forms part of The Glen's program:

> What I talk about there is the effects of generational trauma and its symptoms. It's a coping strategy; when your stress levels are that high you need something and that's what we reach for – that's what affects a lot of the individuals with substance abuse issues. So, in the stress management and anxiety, we look at how we can reduce some stress levels so they'll lower the walls, so then we can get the professionals who can deal with it.
>
> But then we do it the other way; we work on the individual distress to strengthen them and then we introduce them back to their families, and we invite the families in and show them what we do and everything like that, so they feel part of it.
>
> (Formal interview, Chris Mason)

Deirdre observed a program that aims to enable and support individual recovery journeys through counselling, while creating a social environment that encourages recovery through immersion in culture, supportive recovery groups and recovery journeys. There are no gates at The Glen. There are no surveillance cameras at The Glen.

Chris explained that the men engage in group work, individual counselling, case management, and mental health programs, as well as various specialised counselling services on issues including grief and trauma, financial management, gambling, parenting, and anger management. Counselling approaches – for example, cognitive behavioural therapy, psychodynamic approaches, narrative therapy, solution-focused counselling, motivational interviewing, and mindfulness – are core components of The Glen's program. The Glen's recovery approach involves participation in peer support groups and activities, immersion in culture, and active engagement in the community. Chris also explained that the men engage in educational programs, acupuncture, work programs, legal programs, financial programs, physical programs, and sporting activities. Deirdre learned that, after the first 12 weeks, in the transition program, clients are supported to obtain qualifications, build work skills, reconnect with their families, and find suitable employment and housing.

The Glen in the NPM era: From organisational fragility to antifragility

> The heart of the program has not really changed; it's been pretty similar, but we're trying to get it better and better every year.
>
> (Interview, CEO Alex Lee)

At the time of Deirdre's first research visit in 2014, The Glen was at a point of what Bendell terms organisational fragility. The Glen's organisational fragility was not due to what Bendell refers to as internal weaknesses or inevitable organisational failure (Bendell, 2016, p. 3), but because of an external shock to the organisation (Bendell, 2016; Taleb, 2012). Deirdre observed that there were two sources of this external shock: (1) funding precarity and (2) sector precarity.

In 2012, The Glen used a continuous quality improvement approach, not only to improve the efficiency of its operational systems, but to obtain accreditation, for the first time, against the Quality Improvement Council of Australia's Health and Community Services Standards. While successfully accredited, The Glen's formal accreditation made little difference in its next quest, to secure funding. In 2012, The Glen's funding from the NSW Government was cut by 15 per cent, despite supporting more than 170 men in 2011 and winning a statewide Aboriginal Drug and Alcohol Network award for Program of the Year. By 2014, The Glen was struggling to secure Commonwealth funding. It had recently found out it had been unsuccessful in its bid for funding under the new IAS. Then, as current CEO Alex Lee explains, 'we also lost the Aboriginal Hostels funding'. The Glen was re-accredited in 2015, setting a national record for exceeded accreditation standards. The independent assessors have continuously remarked on The Glen's 'amazing governance structure' and the passion of its directors, according to Lee. As Lee further explains, The Glen's achievement has provided a highly successful service and product by forefronting Indigenous culture.

One possible explanation for the disconnect between The Glen's achievements and its funding security is that the government has misconceived The Glen's governance capacity as a First Nations organisation and that this misconception has shaped the conduct of government business with The Glen.

In reality, The Glen demonstrated remarkable governance capacity. While running on a shoestring budget, The Glen's programs were growing and prospering. The new transition program, which assisted clients to reintegrate into the community, had created additional demand from clients in its 12-week program, who were eager to also apply for housing and arrange work experience. This increase in demand put a greater burden on The Glen's day-to-day operations. So, as CEO Alex Lee explains, 'we realised it was better to consolidate' and to concentrate on its program in Chittaway Bay. Concerned with keeping pace with its rapid growth by increasing its operating efficiency, The Glen closed down its annexe site in the Hunter Valley. The CEO, board, and staff, 'which was always reviewing and one thing it does really well at', according to former CEO and current Executive Director Joe Coyte, took a hard look at what The Glen needed to do to survive. The Glen had to find other funding sources.

As current CEO Alex Lee explained, the integrity of The Glen's governance was strong. It was not facing an internal governance crisis or a failure of governance, but external pressure. However, The Glen's board did decide to strengthen its expertise, as Lee explained:

> At a governance level, we'd always had, and we have the same board. In 2014, a big change was we started inviting mentors and advisors to come and join the board. So, the board were very honest and said getting through that period was going to be very difficult.
>
> Given their limited understanding on financial risks and long-term sustainability, and a few things like that, the board wanted to bring in that expertise. So, we had people from Bunnings join, KPMG and a few law firms came in over the next 12 to18 months back then. By having some corporate support, that's how we got those new buildings. Bunnings donated those because they saw that we were shutting beds down there, but the demand was still huge, so we had to fill that gap. So, there was a few little governance changes there. Otherwise, the board has stayed the same.

The Glen focused on strengthening its administrative expertise and building its organisational social capital. It built on its existing knowledge and relationships to improve its capacity to innovate and strengthen its administrative expertise. This strategy allowed The Glen the opportunity to share its knowledge and educate the wider community about the realities of drug and alcohol rehabilitation. While the board and CEO brought in expertise to assist this process in an advisory capacity, The Glen did strengthen its governance structure. Outside expertise assisted the board and CEO in ensuring a strategy that focused on finances, quality assurance, property management, marketing, information technology, and workforce capability.

The Glen's board, CEO and staff also made the decision to become 'transparent', as the CEO explained:

> In 2015, there was also a big – a bit of a decision by Joe and all of us to be very transparent. So, we can start changing that narrative of what drug and alcohol rehabilitation is. Especially residential rehab.
>
> We can't overhaul the sector, but what we can do is lead by example. That's why our Facebook and YouTube channels all got set up in around 2014/2015 when we did a lot of videos, a lot of interviews, we shared lots of client stories to start showing the positive side of rehabilitation. That's gained a lot of traction and I think we're at the point now where we have so many followers on Facebook. We get a lot of media coverage. We're quite – we're very well known in the sector now which we weren't – so that's put us in a really strong position.

Throughout this time, The Glen resisted changing its program. Instead, it focused on being recognised as a sector leader for its Indigenous-led model of care. The board and CEO were determined to protect The Glen's historical institutional context, its unique organisational culture, and its professional values. It believed that The Glen's program content and model of care was its organisational strength, and the reason why it was a successful Aboriginal drug and alcohol residential rehabilitation program. The Glen set out to work with others in the sector to develop an Indigenous model of care, rather than having one imposed by outsiders. The Glen enhanced its program through relationship-building. In an accreditation report by Quality Innovation Performance Ltd (an industry accreditor), The Glen was described as the 'fabric of the Central Coast community', working with over 40 local organisations to deliver its program.

Today, The Glen fits Bendell's definition of an antifragile organisation. Its flat management style and inclusive leadership create a culture of developing the capability of its staff; it is a people-orientated organisation that meets the men's needs; and it has strong networks, technology, and administrative systems (Bendell, 2016, pp. 60, 73). The Glen is today recognised as an exemplar of a strengths-based approach informing Indigenous policy. However, the most significant shift is in terms of funding precarity. The Glen is no longer financially precarious. In 2018, the then prime minister Malcolm Turnbull visited, took off his tie, sat around the fire, and talked with the men. Three years after that, the federal government allocated $9 million dollars for a centre to help women suffering from alcohol and drug dependency. The board chair, Coral Hennessy, Cyril's sister, has continued his legacy after his passing in 2008. Coral brought to the role a 20-year dream to establish the first women's rehabilitation centre in the state, which had finally come to fruition.

Like many First Nations organisations, The Glen has accomplished extraordinary things in the NPM era despite chronic underfunding and considerable regulatory scrutiny. Like most urban First Nations organisations, NPM reforms to government Indigenous service delivery presented new challenges to The Glen. The NPM has increased the fragility of urban First Nations organisations, trapping them in a government service market that hinders their capacity to act in a way that fulfils their core mission of transforming the lives of First Nations people, their communities and Indigenous society in a deliberate, conscious way (Howard-Wagner et al., 2023). According to the survey of urban First Nations organisations in NSW discussed in Chapter One, many report being either more or somewhat more fragile or precarious in the NPM era, while still maintaining a misleadingly 'steady' state of existence (Howard-Wagner et al., 2023). There are multiple causes of this fragility, including the way external funding is structured, and the administrative pressures placed on urban First Nations organisations because of contractual requirements for compliance. Perhaps more importantly, this fragility relates to the lack of capacity to operate as autonomous First Nations organisations in terms of being responsive to the needs of First Nations people and communities in urban localities (Howard-Wagner et al., 2023).

As an antifragile organisation, The Glen is among the less than 10 per cent of urban First Nations organisations in NSW surveyed that report having become stronger in the NPM era (Howard-Wagner et al., 2023). The Glen's outstanding efforts in mobilising its story, and its significant contribution to addressing drug and alcohol dependency, are widely recognised. This contribution to drug and alcohol services comes from The Glen's holistic approach to rehabilitation and its focus on cultural strength. The heartbeat of The Glen – its model of care – has not changed much in the last decade. Its expertise in addressing drug and alcohol dependence among First Nations men illustrates how Indigenous practices can benefit others from non-Indigenous backgrounds, and it has become a leader in developing a model of care for its sector. Over the last decade, The Glen has become a leading community-controlled First Nations enterprise.

The Glen has focused on its many stories of success and has developed a unique brand around those stories. The Glen's stories are about its overcoming Indigenous disadvantage, its relating to the broader Central Coast community, including the business and professional communities, and its survival in the NPM era. The Glen's business story of the adaptation of its managerial style and administrative systems is the surface story. Staff also tell the story about how The Glen has attracted support from the business sector, developing relationships and partnerships with industry and professionals who have gone on to support The Glen. The Glen 'reached out in every direction and every way for opportunities: grants and donations, employment partnerships and other forms of in-kind support' (Interview, Executive Officer and former CEO Joe Coyte).

The story of how The Glen has navigated the complex NPM system illustrates that there are cases of how organisations can interact with a government Indigenous market system without compromising their own values and systems, but those cases are the exception. The Glen did not simply adapt and adjust to work around the threat to its existence but strategically tailored its response.

Conclusion

> We're in kind of – we're in a really strong position where our voice is quite important. So, when we get consulted, I think people – like anytime there's an industry consultation process, The Glen has got to be part of it. We give them – yeah, we give them really honest opinions about things. Yeah, I think sometimes like – yeah, funding bodies can still do – so sometimes they'll do the consultation and go off and still do their own things, but they come to us for advice now.
>
> (Interview, CEO Alex Lee)

The Glen has always been a leading drug and alcohol rehabilitation service. The Glen's success comes from building relationships with the wider community at the same time as maintaining the cultural integrity of its model of care. It is those relationships that have allowed The Glen to thrive and forefront the social and economic value of Indigenous practices in the treatment of drug and alcohol dependence among Aboriginal and Torres Strait Islander men, and to extend that quality of service to non-Indigenous men.

Over the last 10 years, Deirdre has observed The Glen's strategy to make its residential drug and alcohol rehabilitation program transparent and visible. She has observed too that the heart of The Glen's program has not changed since she first visited. It has organically strengthened. What has changed is that The Glen has become highly effective at communicating the story of how its distinctive approach has contributed to the success of its program. The Glen is innovatively leading the way in community-controlled Aboriginal drug and alcohol residential rehabilitation.

Deirdre has observed how The Glen has built its relationship with industry and business to strengthen its capacity and its administrative practices, and to diversify its funding sources. She has also observed how this strategy has assisted The Glen, as an organisation, to move from what Taleb (2012) identifies as a precarious or fragile state to an antifragile state, or what Bendell (2016), applying this theory to organisations, calls an antifragile organisational state.

Today, The Glen is no longer solely dependent on Commonwealth funding. The Glen has diversified its funding sources, and only 20 per cent of its funding comes from the Australian Government's IAS. The Glen is funded from a mix of state and federal sources, including Indigenous-specific and mainstream health funding. The Glen now receives funding from all levels of government and has multiple funding agreements. The Glen has also developed business arms that generate 10–15 per cent of its income with a commercial lawnmowing business and a consulting arm. All profits from the two businesses are being reinvested into The Glen to support its programs. Funding bodies are now coming to The Glen for advice.

The Glen is among a minority of antifragile First Nations organisations (Howard-Wagner et al., 2023). Antifragile organisations are organisations that can offer a government-subsidised fee-for-service model at a market rate, by covering the cost of fees for services while generating a small income from social enterprises (Howard-Wagner et al., 2023). But other factors have also contributed to The Glen moving from a state of precarity to a state of antifragility, including reforms in the alcohol and drug treatment sector. Some of those changes come from within the sector, but there have also been changes to the IAS and the CTG Implementation Plan. For example, under the CTG Implementation Plan, the NIAA is strengthening the First Nations Alcohol and Drug Treatment Services initiative to support expanded First Nations Alcohol and Drug Treatment Services, including improvements to infrastructure and employment and training opportunities for First Nations alcohol and drug workers (NIAA, 2023). The Glen has also played a lead role in developing a standardised assessment tool for the sector, defining core treatment and its organisational components, and developing an evaluation framework that can be used to evaluate individual treatment components, such as follow-up care, and to estimate the total net benefits and costs of services (Shakeshaft et al., 2018).

As this chapter explains, The Glen's slow and steady progression is a far cry from its experiences in 2013 and 2014. The Glen struggled within the government's Indigenous service system in the initial 10 years of the NPM era. The Glen is among a small percentage of community-controlled organisations that have developed a capacity to generate income from a fee-for-service model (Howard-Wagner et al., 2023).

The story of how The Glen has navigated a complex NPM system that initially took a deficit approach to First Nations community-controlled organisations shows how a small percentage of First Nations organisations are in a position to interact with it without compromising their own systems. Some First Nations organisations can reconcile the NPM and its systems with their community-controlled ways of doing business. While not all First Nations organisations are in a position to do this, The Glen, to its credit, did not simply adapt and adjust to work around the threat to its existence, but strategically made the success of its strength-based culturally immersive model of care visible.

References

Barnes, D. (2016, 10 March). Coast country music stars happy to lend a hand for new sound studio at The Glen rehabilitation centre. *The Daily Telegraph*. www.dailytelegraph.com.au/newslocal/central-coast/coast-country-music-stars-happy-to-lend-a-hand-for-new-sound-studio-at-the-glend-rehabilitation-centre/news-story/8bda44ae1920ed69513768fd1be4c8e1

Bendell, T. (2016). *Building anti-fragile organisations: Risk, opportunity and governance in a turbulent world*. Routledge. doi.org/10.4324/9781315570426

Brady, M. (1995). Culture in treatment, culture as treatment: A critical appraisal of developments in addictions programs for Indigenous North Americans and Australians. *Social Science and Medicine*, *41*(11), 1487–1498. doi.org/10.1016/0277-9536(95)00055-C

Brady, M. (2002). *Indigenous residential treatment programs for drug and alcohol problems: Current status and options for improvement.* CAEPR Discussion Paper 236/2002. The Australian National University.

Chenhall, R. (2007). *Benelong's Haven: Abstinence from alcohol and drug use within an Aboriginal Australian residential treatment centre.* Melbourne University Publishing Ltd.

Chenhall, R. D., & Senior, K. (2013). 'The concepts are universal, it is the picture you paint that is different': Key issues for Indigenous Australian alcohol and drug residential treatment centres. *Therapeutic Communities: The International Journal of Therapeutic Communities*, *34*(2/3), 83–95. doi.org/10.1108/TC-05-2013-0011

Hennessy, C. (1981). Running an alcohol rehab centre: Some problems. *Aboriginal Health Worker*, *5*(3), 47–50.

Howard-Wagner, D., Soldatić, K., Riemer, J., Leha, J., Mason, C., Hunt, J., & Gibson, J. (2023). Organisational fragility among urban FNOs in the era of New Public Management. *Australian Journal of Social Issues*, *58*(3), 523–549. doi.org/10.1002/ajs4.243

National Indigenous Australians Agency. (2023). *Strengthening Aboriginal and Torres Strait Islander alcohol and other drugs treatment services.*

Shakeshaft, A., Clifford, A., James, D., Doran, C., Munro, A., Patrao, T., Bennett, A., Binge, C., Bloxsome, T., Coyte, J., Edwards, D., Henderson, N., & Jeffries, D. (2018). *Understanding clients, treatment models and evaluation options for the NSW Aboriginal Residential Healing Drug and Alcohol Network (NARHDAN): A community-based participatory research approach.* Prepared by the National Drug and Alcohol Research Centre (UNSW Sydney) for the Department of the Prime Minister and Cabinet, Canberra, Australia. www.niaa.gov.au/resource-centre/understanding-clients-treatment-models-and-evaluation-options-nsw-aboriginal-residential-healing

Taleb, N. (2012). *Antifragile: Things that gain from disorder* (3rd edition). Random House.

8

Decolonising the Indigenous service market

Deirdre Howard-Wagner

> Governments *necessarily* design markets, including social service markets. They bring these markets into being with actions that support and/or constitute market actors, define the products to be exchanged, construct social arenas and rules for market exchange, promote for-profit service provision and encourage consumer choice and competition …
>
> … By recognising markets as social institutions, we see existing markets as social arenas of exchange that, as noted above, use competitive mechanisms to allocate goods, services and information … Market exchanges involve the complex interplay of businesses, organisations, suppliers, workers, consumers and the state … and it is the governance of these exchanges through legislation, regulation, practices and norms that shape the capacities and opportunities of the actors engaged in them …
>
> (Meagher et al., 2022, p. 20)

In 2005, the marketisation of Indigenous service delivery brought about significant institutional change; a new Indigenous service system was created. The way Indigenous services were designed and delivered fundamentally shifted. The chapters in this volume do not treat the design of the Indigenous service market as a neutral endeavour. They adopt a more expansive and critical palette to problematise the issue of market design, the system that has been created, and the tools used by public officials to operate that system (Meagher et al., 2022, p. 21). The chapters confirm that

Australian governments purposively designed the Indigenous service market as a social institution and social arena of exchange using competition. The chapters illustrate the many instances of organisations trying to make an economically focused system serve social ends. The chapters capture how and for whom the marketisation of Indigenous services works in the interests of. The chapters in this volume reveal that, whether we choose to acknowledge it or not, Indigenous service delivery and design policymaking is fundamentally raced.

The reasons for system change go to the important strategic as well as operational function of the Indigenous service market system in achieving multiple outcomes, not least its function of closing the gap. Retrospectively, as this volume shows, the imperative for policy change is unmistakable, and there is much work to be done. The key concern of this chapter is not how to build the community-controlled sector and transform service delivery arrangements in NSW to close the gap, but how to decolonise the system. While the chapter returns to an analysis of the overarching effects of funding arrangements and explains what needs to change, it returns to the proposition that a purely NPM approach was never suitable for government Indigenous service delivery in Australia. It reflects more deeply on what it is about the system that needs to be transformed. In doing so, it focuses on the institutional practices that operate as extractive and exploitative, explaining why the system needs to be not only reconfigured but decolonised. To make such a contribution, this concluding chapter considers the key findings across the volume, which illustrate how what is valued, and by what measure, has been a point of tension in the way governments and others do business with First Nations organisations in the NPM era. It revisits the findings in the chapters about the economising, exploitative, and racialised effects of the existing government Indigenous service delivery market, particularly the function of funding arrangements in this regard. Ultimately, this concluding chapter argues that fundamental change needs to be made to the way governments fund Indigenous service delivery, which is the objective of Priority Reform Two under the National Agreement on CTG (2020), but empirically points to important practical changes needed to achieve this end.

To begin with, the chapters in this volume illustrate how urban First Nations organisations became and remain important expressions of Indigenous agency, empowerment, autonomy, and self-determination (Howard-Wagner, 2021; Howard-Wagner, Riemer et al., 2022). Our case studies illustrate, and associated field observations confirm, that all organisations have sound, strong governance arrangements in place that comply with both Western legislative and Indigenous community governance arrangements. The case studies have also shown that obligation to the community is a core organisational value and a principle that dictates organisational behaviour. The case studies reveal that self-determination is expressed not only as organisational autonomy, but the autonomy of urban First Nations people to pursue collective, community-orientated visions and agendas through community-controlled First Nations organisations. In the context of the communities that they serve, self-determination means that First Nations organisations create enabling conditions for First Nations people living in urban localities to solve their own problems. This was confirmed via a statewide survey of community-controlled First Nations organisations in SUAs in NSW (Howard-Wagner et al., 2022).

The case studies also reveal the ways in which diverging funding arrangements impact organisations. They can enable First Nations organisations to flourish, such as The Glen, or radically diminish the capacity of First Nations organisations to achieve their commitments to their communities, such as the FPDN and Butucarbin. The case studies also reveal that one of the most consistent and hindering effects of the NPM Indigenous service market is the way the value of First Nations organisations is reduced to their utility as service providers, funded to deliver government services. A further failing of the system is that, within the logic of the market, there is a widely held perception that non-Indigenous organisations could do the same work as First Nations organisations just as effectively, albeit with cultural competency training. The architects of the Australian Government's IAS held this view at the federal level (Page, 2018), and it is clear the state government agency funding Butucarbin holds this view. Competition with larger mainstream organisations has had the effect of pushing First Nations organisations out of the market entirely, as the Butucarbin case study has shown.

So, as this volume has shown, these few assumptions alone undermine the goals of autonomy and self-determination that are intrinsic to First Nations organisations. This undermining creates difficulties for First Nations organisations as they try to hold their ground as autonomous expert community-controlled organisations, maintaining their governance, identity, and purpose, and their legitimacy as agents of community, pursuing adaptive strategies in the NPM era. Butucarbin's vision to be a hub for the

Western Sydney First Nations community has never been realised. Muru Mittigar can deliver contracts, but these do not fund its aspirations for broader community engagement and social change.

Reflecting on the governance problems in Indigenous service delivery then, the gaps in the public sector are evident when explained from the perspective of community-controlled First Nations organisations. The system is failing to close the gap. There is extensive evidence presented over the last 14 years in CTG reports (2009–2023) that government-designed and funded services are not achieving their goals.[1] While government agencies aim to provide a socially optimal level of government service delivery by equating marginal social benefit with marginal social cost, those social services need to do their job. Those services are just not hitting the mark. First Nations people often cannot afford to replace deficient government services with the costlier alternatives the private sector provides, so they are presently stuck with any government-designed and funded services that do not adequately meet their needs. Also, First Nations people and the wider Australian society judge the quality of governance by First Nations peoples' experience in receiving essential government services. They infer that the public sector is poorly governed if First Nations people cannot access adequate services targeted to their needs and close the gap. So, the quality of governance is reflected in the capacity of the state and federal government agencies to design, formulate, and implement appropriate Indigenous policies, programs, and services that close the gaps in socio-economic circumstances between Indigenous and non-Indigenous Australians. All of the chapters in this volume indicate that the governance arrangements for Indigenous service delivery in federal and state governments vary considerably, even within government agencies, in terms of the ways in which federal and state agencies finance, allocate, and deliver Indigenous services on the ground in NSW.

This concluding chapter does not treat the correction of the Indigenous service market as a matter of pragmatic problem-solving (Meagher et al., 2022, p. 21). Nor does it argue for a reconfiguring of the Indigenous service system. It argues instead that effective public policy reform requires a decolonisation of the government's Indigenous service system. Without decolonisation, the government's Indigenous service system will fail to close the gap.

---

1   See Closing the Gap Reports 2009–2021 – www.closingthegap.gov.au/resources/reports.

It argues that decolonising the system requires Aboriginal and Torres Strait Islander people to be in the driver's seat of decision-making, and for those operating the system to value First Nations knowledge and community expertise.

Decolonisation necessitates systems functioning in the interests of local and collective needs. This does not mean that the needs of individuals are not met, but that those needs are better understood in terms of the wider experience of the collective and in terms of collective needs, care, and wellbeing. Indigenous services should be considered complex and as requiring innovative service delivery solutions in which a more interactive, multi-staged process is used. Relatedly, the commissioning process, procurement lifecycle, and purchasing strategies need to be designed in a way that place a social, and even potentially economic, value on Indigenous knowledge, ways of doing business, and the important knowledge and expertise that First Nations people and organisations bring to the service delivery space. The commissioning process, procurement lifecycle, and purchasing strategies should entail a full co-production process in which service design is developed in collaboration with community-controlled organisations and their communities. The system must work in the Indigenous interest and have indirect and direct socio-economic benefits for First Nations people and communities. Community-controlled organisations and the communities they represent must be closely engaged in determining what services are needed and the methodology for the source phase. The commissioning process, procurement lifecycle, and purchasing strategies need to shape longer-term social and economic outcomes for First Nations people and communities.

Without such reforms, the government's Indigenous service system will be just another system formed through the lens of colonisation (Cooms, 2022, p. 115).

System failure

This volume offers the expertise of community-controlled First Nations organisations operating in urban settings in NSW, which variously operate as social enterprises, businesses, community development organisations, social service providers, and advocacy organisations. The chapters in this volume build on the existing literature on the failings of NPM. They confirm the public sector's role in the government Indigenous service market, which is as the purchaser, market shaper, and definer of procurement and purchasing strategies. The chapters confirm that public sector procurement is driven by cost-effectiveness and efficiency, or the best value for money and minimising risk, and is preoccupied with transparency of the process, competitive neutrality, and the lowest cost. They confirm that purchasing strategies control low-level outputs and are caught up in the minutiae. They also confirm that NPM-style procurement policies, systems, and tools have failed to be used for improving outcomes for First Nations people beyond the individual client receiving the service. The chapters confirm that even improvements for the individual client are not always guaranteed. Hence, the system's inability to close the gap.

While in a true market economy, service delivery procurement has the potential to provide significant employment, capacity building, economic opportunities, and even wealth creation, Indigenous service delivery procurement and contracts are presently limited in this regard. Read together, the chapters in this volume expose how the marketisation of Indigenous service delivery has exacerbated economic inequalities and produced economic precarity in the sector. The chapters lay bare how marketisation has enabled governments to capitalise on Aboriginal volunteerism and exploit the economic value of community-controlled First Nations organisations, Indigenous labour processes, and Indigenous expertise across the board. The chapters also reveal how the Indigenous service system has operated to colonise and subjugate community-controlled First Nations organisations and is extractive.

The chapters not only expose the disempowering role that the public sector plays in this market as purchaser and as market shaper, but also the disempowering role it plays as the commissioner and procurer of Indigenous services. Governments rely heavily on under-resourced and disempowered First Nations organisations to do the job of government, without their input into the design of programs and services. The Indigenous service market is a market in which Indigenous expertise and knowledge are devalued. The chapters illustrate the fundamental problems with the ways in which government buys and funds services.

Layered on top of this, the chapters in this volume expose the effects of designing a system in a way that has individualised Indigenous service delivery and ignored the wider societal functions and benefits of that system. The chapters reveal how the system has been unresponsive to the needs of local communities, and that any collective value that the system can produce around closing the gap has been well and truly beyond its purview. The epistemic framework of doing *for* individual service recipients rather than *with* First Nations communities and organisations has privileged white epistemic sites of power, knowledge, and expertise while decentring Indigenous ways of knowing, being and doing. This is an institutionally racist system.

This volume reveals that the marketisation of government Indigenous services sustains injustice and disadvantage, with the loss of First Nations organisations in Western Sydney as a poignant case in point. Chapter Four illustrates how the marketisation of government Indigenous services has led to a systematic disinvestment – the sustained and systemic withdrawal of capital investment – from First Nations community infrastructure in the Mount Druitt region. The effects are evident in the shrinking of Indigenous-led services, investment in Indigenous community infrastructure, and democratic practices (Pulido, 2016, p. 2). This economic abandonment of First Nations organisations in the region is a separate phenomenon from the numerous political and economic shifts that led to the economic downturn in the Mount Druitt region at the turn of the 21st century. Chapter Four gives a concrete or empirically grounded example of the effects of what Cedric Robinson called 'racial capitalism' at work (Robinson, 2000).

The way government agencies do business with Butucarbin works not only as systemic barriers but also signifies the presence of institutional racism. Delgado defines institutional racism as 'how a society's institutions operate systematically, both directly and indirectly, to favor some groups over others regarding access to opportunities and valued resources' (Delgado, 2015, para 1). Like Delgado, the chapters in the edited volume at hand point to the ways in which oppressive funding relationships can be a form of institutional racism. The academic literature confirms this. Griffith et al. explain how government agencies function as tools of oppression, reproducing, and reinforcing the very marginalisation that some are committed to undoing (Griffith et al., 2007, p. 287). They can do this as conduits to resources, decision-makers, and designers of services, and through governments impeding a community's power, agency, and ability to access resources and services (Griffith et al., 2007, p. 287). As Griffith et al. explain, oppression is interconnected with 'sociopolitical contexts through funding streams, government mandates, and individual staff members' (2007, p. 288). As this volume has shown, these assumptions alone, which constitute institutional racism, undermine the goals of autonomy and self-determination intrinsic to First Nations organisations. Having to operate in a system where these assumptions prevail has created major difficulties for First Nations organisations.

Together, the chapters illustrate how the very act of designing a system *for* First Nations people, rather than *with* First Nations people, has a colonising and racialising effect. They all serve to show that it is a system that colonises the actions and processes of Indigenous service delivery. Over the last 20 years, First Nations organisations have increasingly been on the receiving end of the Indigenous service system and have been largely passive within it. While the system directly affects them and the communities they serve, they have been excluded from shaping the design of the system and the design or delivery of the services it provides to First Nations people.

It is thus a premise of this volume that those who designed the system wilfully ignored Indigenous ways of knowing, being, and doing and the ways in which community-controlled organisations and societies customarily functioned. Even today, there are those who are charged with operating the Indigenous service system on a day-to-day basis who continue this practice of wilful ignorance, perpetuating the Indigenous service system's individualistic foundations and its dominant individualistic models of care *for* individual service recipients rather than *with* community-controlled organisations and communities. This service system model not only remains deeply problematic in Indigenous contexts, but also its insidious exploitative and racialised effects are troubling. Colonisation is both an ongoing lived experience and a political reality that continues to inform the experiences of community-controlled First Nations organisation of the government Indigenous service system (Puska et al., 2022, p. 5)

One important aspect of decolonisation is to disentangle the power relationships and assumptions that are currently embedded within the Indigenous service system. Understanding the Indigenous service system that First Nations organisations and public officials inhabit together, but often within different power relations, can be a useful starting point for decolonising practice. Decolonising the government Indigenous service system therefore requires public officials working with First Nations organisations to rethink the concept and practice of Indigenous service provision and reconceptualise relationships between community-controlled First Nations organisations and governments (Puska et al., 2022, p. 5). Rethinking and reconceptualising not only requires privileging a strength-based approach, centred around the value of community-controlled First

Nations organisations in the government Indigenous service system, but also recognising the important societal function of those organisations, including, but not limited to, closing the gap. Rethinking and reconceptualising necessitate system change.

Rethinking and reconceptualising adopting a decolonising lens inspires the disruption of hierarchical power structures through empowering marginalised First Nations communities and organisations, recognising them as part of the whole and welcoming them as agents of Indigenous service system transformation. This requires First Nations perspectives, lived experiences, expertise, and knowledge systems to come first and inform all areas of the Indigenous service system.

Rethinking and reconceptualising require not only a valuing of Indigenous labour and expertise but also recognition of the unique value that community-controlled First Nations organisations bring to the Indigenous service market with their knowledge and expertise. Rethinking and reconceptualising require that funding and infrastructural support be provided to First Nations organisations and communities to bring about the necessary change to ensure that the system works in their interest. First Nations organisations and communities must inform what success looks like, including the development of success metrics.

At present, community-controlled organisations may seek and attract a mix of NSW and federal government funding, combine income from social enterprises and philanthropy, and have input from volunteering – but that is not enough (Howard-Wagner et al., 2023). While all our case study organisations have had to become community enterprises in the new Indigenous service market, their enterprising activities have generally not generated enough funds to subsidise the shortfalls in government funding for services. The specific resource mix shapes their cost structures and their ability to subsidise their operations. The FPDN, and other organisational case studies, indicate that there is less than full-cost recovery funding for government services (Howard-Wagner, Soldatić, et al., 2022). While costing models are used, governments dictate the prices for those services and First Nations organisations are not recompensed with the full costs associated with service/program delivery. The reality and bottom line are that the market does not pay the true price for services. Organisations subsidise the costs of delivering government services to First Nations people and their bottom line does not cover these costs. Undervalued and unpaid work in service delivery is rife among First Nations people working in First Nations organisations, and that is layered on top of the many hours of volunteer work those working in organisations do for the community. There are high levels of volunteerism among First Nations organisations in SUAs in NSW (Howard-Wagner, Soldatić, et al., 2022).

The survey discussed in Chapter One revealed that 90 per cent of participant First Nations organisations self-identify as being in a fragile state (Howard-Wagner et al., 2023, p. 543). Those same fragile organisations have a decreased capacity to address the adversity of First Nations people and operate at the frontline of their communities (Howard-Wagner et al., 2023, p. 543). If not addressed, that fragility will have long-lasting effects on not only government service delivery but also on the resilience and recovery of First Nations people, hindering Australian government agendas around closing the gap (Howard-Wagner et al., 2023, p. 546). Strengthening those findings is our discovery of a significant relationship between organisational strength and income (antifragility) and the transformative capacity of organisations,

> ... particularly their ability to act autonomously and to be self-determining in a way that transforms the lives of First Nations people, their communities, and Indigenous society in a deliberate, conscious way.
>
> (Howard-Wagner et al., 2023, p. 544)

To move from reactive adaptation and fragility to antifragility, a transformation of funding processes for autonomous and self-determining organisations is needed (Howard-Wagner et al., 2023, p. 544). As Howard-Wagner et al. note, 'This is an important public policy finding of our research' (2023, p. 544).

Federal and state funding under most forms of contracts does not even cover the cost of the time it takes organisations like FPDN and Butucarbin to engage with community members properly. It does not cover the extra costs borne by the NCIE necessary to employ staff participating in the Job Ready program. It does not cover Muru Mittigar's efforts to support the First Nations community, particularly in securing long-term employment. A common experience is that the cost that a First Nations organisation incurs to deliver a service is not fully covered by the funding that governments provide. First Nations organisations are co-contributing to the cost of Indigenous service delivery. Knowledge and expertise are not remunerated appropriately. The cost of services does not allow time for community engagement and collaboration. In a decolonised system, those costs would be considered integral components of any project or service. This is because market-based funding mechanisms externalise costs onto First Nations organisations.

Thus, the chapters reveal the many ways in which the market fails to pay the true cost incurred by First Nations organisations for Indigenous service delivery. This is illustrated in the cases of FPDN, Butucarbin, and Muru Mittigar, whereby the Indigenous service market does not appear to even put a price on the social and economic value of Indigenous expertise. It is expected to come free rather than being sold based on knowledge and experience borne out of unique capacities.

The failure to pay for Indigenous expertise and knowledge is one way. The lack of economic or public value attributed to what a genuine connection to the community provides is but another. As their respective studies show, FPDN and Butucarbin are expected to provide their cultural expertise to large, mainstream service providers at no cost. These non-Indigenous organisations rely on FPDN and Butucarbin to implement their programs, but the value FPDN and Butucarbin provide is not costed into the contract or factored into the Indigenous service market. This approach puts First Nations organisations in a double bind, as they want to see their communities get access to appropriate services and care, yet the provision of their expertise for free undermines their own organisation's viability.

There is no demonstrated understanding of the public value of Indigenous knowledge and expertise. Such knowledge requires engagement with First Nations organisations and communities, which should also involve translating the public value of Indigenous knowledge and expertise to service delivery applications in a way that creates tangible measurable benefits. This work of translation must be undertaken, as Indigenous organisations and communities contribute valuable expertise and knowledge. This is the intellectual property of First Nations organisations. Likewise, non-Indigenous organisations exploit Indigenous knowledge and expertise. For example, we have seen that some organisations used Muru Mittigar's services as a form of 'black cladding' to gain contracts and appear to be working with the community at the expense of genuine, mutually beneficial partnership arrangements.

The chapters unmask how the government Indigenous service system has relied upon the unique value that First Nations organisations bring to the market. Further, First Nations organisations have been expected to share time-honoured and deeply respectful relationships, or rapidly develop new partnerships with mainstream organisations that have little understanding or commitment to the foundational principles of Indigenous values, ethics, and protocols. That same system obscures the diverse approaches of Indigenous-driven agendas and suppresses the agency and agendas of community-controlled First Nations organisations (Howard-Wagner, Riemer et al., 2022).

As discussed in Chapter One, the cumulative effect of these kinds of cost-externalisations and devaluing is already immense (see Cross, 2021, p. 1). The grassroots realities of this inequity are evident in the presented case studies. The unreliability of IAS funding, for example, and its incompatibility with the goals of their organisations, has led Muru Mittigar and The Glen to diversify their funding sources, which means they are diversifying the funding risk. Government contracts make up less than 5 per cent of Muru Mittigar's revenue and only 20 per cent of The Glen's funding comes from the IAS. Butucarbin refuses even to apply for funding under the IAS.

While IPPs may provide contracts for particular services, this funding model cannot be relied upon to provide the stability necessary for First Nations organisations to pursue more socially orientated goals. The experiences of NCIE and Muru Mittigar show this. NCIE and Muru Mittigar prioritise the employment of First Nations people and are prepared to contribute the extra money and time necessary to train them. Yet, because these employment programs, which are priorities for these organisations, fall outside the scope of IPP contracts, these organisations must find funding for them elsewhere.

Government IPPs and programs exist to assist Indigenous small businesses, enterprises, and industries. Government IPPs include statements about creating jobs. Yet, they have failed to extend this to the financing of government Indigenous service delivery and job creation in this sector.

Chapter Five goes as far as to explain how the Indigenous service market both extracts and expropriates labour and resources from First Nations people and organisations while, at the same time, devaluing their contribution to Indigenous service delivery. Butucarbin's experience illustrates how this devaluing or diminishing of Indigenous expertise and knowledge in the Indigenous service market is an example of Leong's (2013) description of racial capitalism, or 'the process of deriving social and economic value from racial identity' (Leong, 2013, p. 2152). In this way, as Melamed states, racial capitalism results in the 'unequal differentiation of human value' (Melamed,

2015, p. 77). Leong focuses on a particular process in which 'white individuals and predominantly white institutions use non-white people to acquire social and economic value' (Leong, 2013, p. 2154). As Leong states:

> … in a society preoccupied with diversity, nonwhiteness is a valued commodity. And where that society is founded on capitalism, it is unsurprising that the commodity of nonwhiteness is exploited for its market value.
>
> (Leong, 2013, p. 2154)

Governments need to remedy the high rates of Indigenous volunteerism in the Indigenous service system and come up with concrete ideas about policies and programs that achieve this end. Governments need to expand strategies to the First Nations sector that support and ensure growth within local Indigenous economies and build local Indigenous assets.

Ways forward

So, what are the ways forward? Organisations could commodify the Indigenous knowledge and expertise that are embedded in the routines of their organisations. If you ask First Nations organisations to operate like market-driven organisations, then you must pay for all they deliver, abandoning the assumption that their knowledge is a gift. It is a contentious solution, but there is growing acceptance of the public value of Indigenous knowledge to Australian society as a whole. This is manifest in many ways (the arts, broadcasting), and in the case of this volume, it is manifest in wide acceptance by governments that Indigenous community knowledge is an asset to the formation and implementation of government programs dedicated to closing the various gaps. The more contentious idea is that, if Indigenous knowledge is an asset not only to First Nations people (an obvious idea) but to governments, its public value should be recognised by assigning a monetary value to that knowledge. It should be fully paid for rather than extracted from First Nations people (which some chapters in this volume have called 'racial capitalism').

Transparent work could identify the cost burden of First Nations organisations under current funding arrangements. This would need to consider the unnecessary burdens associated with operating within the government's Indigenous service market. These burdens include unnecessary regulatory requirements and governance arrangements, and the fact that many organisations have to meet multiple regulatory requirements. It would also need to consider how to simplify the overly burdensome contractual and reporting arrangements that NPM-style approaches place on First Nations organisations.

There is also the issue of the actual cost of Indigenous service delivery. The cost that a First Nations organisation incurs to deliver a service should be covered by the funding that governments provide. That is, First Nations organisations should not co-contribute the cost of the service delivery. Knowledge and expertise should be remunerated appropriately. The cost of services should also allow time for community engagement and collaboration. It should remunerate organisations for administration, management, insurance, and information technology costs. Those costs should be considered integral components of any project or service. The contracts offered should be long-term – at least three, but mostly five years, while also providing greater certainty around the longevity of that service beyond the life of that contract. Governments could also be looking to strategically invest in broader community development goals around building community infrastructure.

The fiscal fragmentation identified by the Australian National Audit Office (2012) is a major impediment to community-controlled organisations achieving their objectives. In terms of the funding system itself, the funding arrangements that currently exist were never intended. In 2001, the CGC Inquiry into Aboriginal and Torres Strait Islander funding recommended that Aboriginal and Torres Strait Islander people should have authority to make decisions about the services they receive, be involved in decision-making for mainstream services, and ideally, control the funds to provide the services (CGC, 2001, p. xiii). The intent was for funding arrangements to change to 'enable community control of service provision as far as practicable' (CGC, 2001, pp. xv–vi). Again, in 2007, under the COAG National Framework for Government Service Delivery to Indigenous Australians, it was identified that effective collaboration between Australian government departments around service delivery to Indigenous communities and regions required the 'flexible use of funds which may involve pooling them from cross-agency projects or transferring them between programs' (Australian Government, 2004, p. 14). This would necessitate a 'moving away from treating program guidelines as rigid rules – [program guidelines would] be revised if they prevent innovation or fail to meet local needs' (Australian Government, 2004, p. 14). Ideally, funding arrangements need to be developed regionally, with communities, across governments – federal and state – and across government agencies to allow for funding to be responsive to the needs and priorities of communities. Ultimately, governments should be looking for ways to transfer power and resources to communities.

Governments also need to be moving beyond an individualised service delivery mentality and rethinking Indigenous service delivery as reinvestment in First Nations organisations, community development, and community infrastructure in urban settings. This includes thinking about how service delivery investment provides a community platform for communities to do the work of closing the gap. Through investment, governments could improve the economic and social performance of First Nations organisations around their capacity to close the gap.

Importantly, this volume shows that the application of NPM in its so-called market form in the area of Indigenous service delivery has proved incapable of providing solutions and responses to closing the gap. It exposes the New Public Management's economising, exploitative, colonising, and racialising effects. As this volume illustrates, the governance and budgetary arrangements for Indigenous service delivery since 2004 have been top-down, paternalistic, inconsistent, and detrimental to First Nations peoples. The move to put service delivery back in the hands of community-controlled organisations through the National Agreement on CTG (2020) is a welcome shift in Indigenous policy among community-controlled First Nations organisations. Three years on, it is not being achieved (Howard-Wagner & Markham, 2023; Productivity Commission, 2023). Indigenous service system decolonisation is not a solution in itself to a highly complex issue, but it does offer an important conceptual position from which to transform the system and the way that government does business, which is a very important step in the right direction.

The challenge is to create an environment in which calls for decolonisation are understood and accepted. Decolonisation takes as its starting point the belief that colonialism is an ongoing act that exists as oppressive mechanisms in systems, organisations and practices, which creates a situation in which First Nations people are marginalised, their agency is diminished and their knowledge devalued, and unequal and repressive relationships exist. Tuck and Yang explain that:

> … decolonisation can be defined as the tools, processes, and lived experiences of identifying, evaluating, rethinking, and intentionally changing parts of ourselves and society where privileged and oppressed identities hinder our progress toward an inclusive, sustainable and relational way of being.
>
> (2012, p. 36)

Decolonising systems and practices are a commitment to make marginalised First Nations people, organisations and communities unmarginalised by:

- acknowledging the strengths, culture, and knowledge of Aboriginal and Torres Strait Islander peoples,

- empowering First Nations peoples as agents of change,

- treating First Nations knowledge as expertise,

- providing a strong financial and economic base to allow First Nations people to flourish,

- ensuring that solutions are shaped and created by First Nations people,

- establishing reflective spaces for inclusive processes, in which non-Indigenous people become aware of and interrogate their privilege and how they can use it to make change that disrupts inequalities, and

- checking and challenging policies and practices that discriminate and continue to uphold oppressive systems (Taylor & Tremblay, 2023, p. 1).

Sanders provides a simple example of decolonisation in terms of moving from a deficit-based to a strength-based approach as part of that process of government transformation, pointing to tensions around seeing Indigenous people as 'populations' (disadvantaged groups) and 'peoples' (socially and politically organised groups). As Sanders explains:

> the language of political communities, peoples and First Nations opens a whole other terrain in Indigenous affairs, as too does the language of colonisation and decolonisation. Without these languages, Indigenous affairs conducted solely in the population's idiom is severely lacking.
>
> (Sanders, 2018, pp. 123, 125).

While some may wince at the term decolonise (Begum & Saini, 2019, p. 198), governments are starting to ask what a decolonised system would look like and are engaging with First Nations peoples, organisations, and communities to do the ground-breaking work around transforming those systems, particularly in the areas of health, education, justice, and social service delivery. A decolonising agenda aims to rectify the ways that solutions can often ignore the voices of, and realities faced by, First Nations peoples and discount the structural inequalities that are continually being reproduced through colonial relations and processes in Australia, Canada, New Zealand, and the United States. There is growing acceptance that decolonisation is fit for purpose because it effectively addresses the multiple facets of the disconnect between systems and First Nations outcomes. For example, culturally safe strategies invite the decolonisation of systems through awareness of colonialism, racism, and discrimination (Schill & Caxaj, 2019). Decolonisation invites a commitment to building partnerships and sharing power and decision-making in the design of law, policy, funding, and service arrangements (Schill & Caxaj, 2019). It is a new way of working that privileges Indigenous knowledge, cultures and voices in the design, development and implementation of law, policy, funding, and service arrangements. That new way of working requires 'the sharing of power, provision of resources, culturally informed reflective policy making, and program design …' (Parter et al., 2021, p. 1).

Conclusion

The chapters in this volume show that the current government Indigenous service system is ill-equipped to close the gap in socio-economic disadvantage between Indigenous and non-Indigenous Australians. Indigenous service delivery systems need to be integrated with decolonised approaches that address the complex issues of service delivery alongside economic development, and Indigenous governance and rights. Public officials need to meaningfully decolonise the systemic, cultural, and individual service delivery practices that presently exist to exploit, racialise, and colonise First Nations organisations.

As Puska et al. note, 'like colonisation, decolonisation is a process of transforming material and political relations with consequences for institutional practices and everyday lived experience' (2022, p. 5). Of course, decolonisation requires changing power relations within government institutions and transforming their conceptual underpinnings and practices. Importantly though, decolonisation requires not only the reconfiguration of government Indigenous services, but a decolonising of the dynamics of that system in relation to the place of controlled First Nations organisations within it. Decolonisation will lead to a better, transformed Indigenous service system and that improved system will lead to better outcomes for First Nations people, organisations, and communities.

References

Australian Government (2004). Chapter 5 – Mainstreaming of service delivery. *Council of Australian Governments (COAG) national framework for government service delivery to Indigenous Australians.* www.aph.gov.au/Parliamentary_Business/ Committees/Senate/Former_Committees/indigenousaffairs/report/final/c05

Australian National Audit Office (2012). *Capacity development for Indigenous service delivery: Department of Families, Housing, Community Services and Indigenous Affairs, Department of Education, Employment and Workplace Relations and Department of Health and Ageing.* Audit Report 26, 2011–2012. Australian Government. www.anao.gov.au/sites/default/files/201112%20Audit%20Report %20No%2026.pdf

Begum, N., & Saini, R. (2019). Decolonising the curriculum. *Political Studies Review*, *17*(2), 196–201. doi.org/10.1177/1478929918808459

Bendell, T. (2016). *Building anti-fragile organisations: Risk, opportunity and governance in a turbulent world.* Routledge. doi.org/10.4324/9781315570426

Commonwealth Grants Commission (2001). *Indigenous funding inquiry final report.*

Cooms, S. (2022). *Decolonising disability: Quandamooka weaving* [Doctoral dissertation]. Central Queensland University.

Cross, H. (2021, 13 April). Non-Indigenous organisations receiving 40% of Indigenous Advancement Strategy funding. *National Indigenous Times.* web.archive. org/web/20210922183614/https://nit.com.au/non-indigenous-organisations -receiving-40-of-indigenous-advancement-strategy-funding/

Delgado, H.L. (2015). *Institutional racism.* Salem Press Encyclopedia.

Griffith, D.M., Childs, E.L., Eng, E., & Jeffries, V. (2007). Racism in organizations: The case of a county public health department. *Journal of Community Psychology*, *35*(3), 287–302. onlinelibrary.wiley.com/doi/pdf/10.1002/jcop.20149

Howard-Wagner, D. (2020). *Indigenous invisibility in the city: Successful resurgence and community development hidden in plain sight.* Routledge. doi.org/10.4324/ 9780429506512

Howard-Wagner, D., Riemer, J., Leha, J., Mason, C., Martin, D., Soldatic, K., Hunt, J., & Gibson, J. (2022). *Looking beyond Indigenous service delivery: The societal purpose of urban First Nations organisations*. CAEPR Discussion Paper No. 301. The Australian National University.

Howard-Wagner, D., Soldatic, K., Spurway, K., Hunt, J., Harrington, M., Riemer, J., Leha, J., Mason, C., Fogg, R., Goh, C., & Gibson, J. (2022). First Nations organisations and strategies of disruption and resistance to settler–colonial governance in Australia. In K. Soldatic & L. St Guillaume (Eds), *Social suffering in the neoliberal age: State power, logics and resistance*. Routledge. doi.org/10.4324/9781003131779-16

Howard-Wagner, D., & Markham, F. (2023). *Preliminary findings of the OCHRE local decision making evaluation stage 2* (CAEPR Commissioned Report No. 1/2023). Centre for Aboriginal Economic Policy Research, ANU College of Arts and Social Sciences. doi.org/10.25911/YPGB-E627

Howard-Wagner, D., Soldatic, K., Riemer J., Leha, J., Mason, C., Goh, C., Hunt, J., & Gibson, J. (2023). Organisational fragility among urban FNOs in the era of New Public Management. *Australian Journal of Social Issues*, *58*(3), 523–549. doi.org/10.1002/ajs4.243

Leong, N. (2013). Reflections on racial capitalism. *Harvard Law Review*, *127*, 32. doi.org/10.2139/ssrn.2329804

Meagher, G., Perche, D., & Stebbing, A. (2022). Introduction: Designing markets in the Australian social service system. In G. Meagher, D. Perche, & A. Stebbing (Eds), *Designing social service markets: Risk, regulation and rent-seeking*. ANU Press. press-files.anu.edu.au/downloads/press/n10374/pdf/introduction.pdf

Melamed, J. (2015). Racial capitalism. *Critical Ethnic Studies*, *1*(1), 76–85. doi.org/10.5749/jcritethnstud.1.1.0076

National Agreement on Closing the Gap (2020). *Joint Councils of Australian Governments agreement between all Australian Governments and the Coalition of Peaks*. www.closingthegap.gov.au/national-agreement

Page, A. (2018). Fragile positions in the new paternalism: Indigenous community organisations during the 'Advancement' era in Australia. In D. Howard-Wagner, M. Bargh, & I. Altamirano-Jiménez (Eds), *The neoliberal state, recognition and Indigenous rights: New paternalism to new imaginings*. ANU Press. doi.org/10.22459/CAEPR40.07.2018.10

Parter, C., Murray, D., Mohamed, J., Rambaldini, B., Calma, T., Wilson, S., Hartz, D., Gwynn, J., & Skinner, J. (2021). Talking about the 'r' word: A right to a health system that is free of racism. *Public Health Research and Practice*, *31*(1) doi.org/10.17061/phrp3112102

Productivity Commission (2023). *Review of the National Agreement on Closing the Gap: Draft report.* www.pc.gov.au/inquiries/current/closing-the-gap-review/draft/closing-the-gap-review-draft.pdf

Productivity Commission (2024). *Review of the National Agreement on Closing the Gap: Final report.* www.pc.gov.au/inquiries/completed/closing-the-gap-review/report

Pulido, L. (2016). Flint, environmental racism, and racial capitalism. *Capitalism Nature Socialism, 27*(3), 1–16. doi.org/10.1080/10455752.2016.1213013

Puszka, S., Walsh, C., Markham, F., Barney, J., Yap, M., & Dreise, T. (2022). Towards the decolonisation of disability: A systematic review of disability conceptualisations, practices and experiences of First Nations people of Australia. *Social Science & Medicine 305*, 115047. doi.org/10.1016/j.socscimed.2022.115047

Robinson, C. (2000). *Black Marxism: The making of the black radical tradition.* University of North Carolina Press.

Sanders, W. (2018). Missing ATSIC: Australia's need for a strong Indigenous representative body. In D. Howard-Wagner, M. Bargh, & I. Altamirano-Jiménez (Eds), *The neoliberal state, recognition and Indigenous rights: New paternalism to new imaginings.* ANU Press. doi.org/10.22459/CAEPR40.07.2018.06

Schill, K., & Caxaj, S. (2019). Cultural safety strategies for rural Indigenous palliative care: A scoping review. *BMC Palliative Care 18*, 21. doi.org/10.1186/s12904-019-0404-y

Taylor, P., & Tremblay, C. (2022). *Decolonising knowledge for development in the Covid-19 era* (IDS Working Paper 566). Institute of Development Studies. doi.org/10.19088/IDS.2022.018

Tuck, E., & Yang, K. W. (2014). R-words: Refusing research. In D. Paris & M. T. Winn (Eds), *Humanizing research: Decolonising qualitative inquiry with youth and communities,* Sage. doi.org/10.4135/9781544329611.n12; static1.squarespace.com/static/557744ffe4b013bae3b7af63/t/557f2ee5e4b0220eff4ae4b5/1434398437409/Tuck+and+Yang+R+Words_Refusing+Research.pdf

Index

Page numbers in *italics* indicate information contained in an interview quote on that page.

In keeping with the text, this index uses 'community-controlled organisations' to describe First Nations–run organisations that provide services to First Nations communities.

Abbott Government, 49–50
Aboriginal and Torres Strait Islander Commercial Development Corporation (CDC), 42, 47
Aboriginal Disability Network (ADN), 63–65
Albanese Government, 114
alcohol and drug rehabilitation, 19–20, 160–161, 165–172, 178–179
    see also Glen, The
antifragility, 12, 19–20, 161, 175–177, 178–179, 190
    see also fragility
ATSIC (Aboriginal and Torres Strait Islander Commission), 31–32, 35, 39–41, 93
Australian Productivity Commission, 14
autonomy, 11, 12, 47, 182–183
    see also self-determination

black cladding, 19, 136, 151, 154, 191
Bostock, Uncle Lester, 63–65, *66*
bureaucratic burden
    administrative capacity, 100–101, 139–140

compliance, 6, 8, 97, 193–194
    reporting, 73–74, 96
Butucarbin Aboriginal Corporation, 16–17, 183–184
    background, 83–84, 86–91
    community connection, 90–91, *97*, 102, 103–106
    funding, 87–88, 95–99

closing the gap (Australian Government policy), 43, 184, 195, 197
    impediments, 12, 13
    National Agreement on Closing the Gap (CTG 2020), 1–2, 39, 78–79, 195
    reviews, 14
colonialism
    disability impacts, 61–63, 79–80
    employment impacts, 121–122
    health and wellbeing impacts, 62
    social enterprises, 129–130
community services *see* social services
community services vs individualised services, 2, 13, 35–36, 186–187, 195

community-controlled organisations
  as businesses, 49, 116, 123–125,
    129
  commitment to communities,
    11–12, 17–18, 68–69,
    103–106, 183
  corporations, contrast with, 92, 96,
    98, 106, 143, 154
  disempowerment, 13, 45–46, 47,
    99–108, 109, 186
  experiences, 4–5
  government requirements, 96–99
  infrastructure support, *76*
  intellectual property, 191
  loss of, 84, 92–94
  mismatch with government
    models, 103–108
  response to community needs, 90
  sports, 91, 170
  see also bureaucratic burden; non-
    Indigenous organisations
competition, 2, 30–31, 99
  National Competition Policy
    (NCP), 28
competitive tender processes, 2, 18–19,
  95–96, *145*
cost efficiency, problems with, 127–128
Council of Australian Governments
  (COAG), 38, 43, 44
criminal justice services, 160, 166
cultural competency, 106–107, 183

data sovereignty, 60, 85, 114
decolonisation
  Indigenous service delivery sector,
    182, 195–198
  research practices, 10, 59–60, 85,
    114
  social services, 184–185, 188–189
deficit mentality, 36, 92, 94–95, 161
Department of Families and
  Community Services (FACS)
  NSW, 9
deregulation, 27–29

disability among Indigenous
  Australians
  advocacy and support, 65–69,
    76–77
  disability advocates, 77–78
  settler colonial context, 61–63, 79
  see also First Peoples Disability
    Network (FPDN)
disability services, 6–7, 16
  Aboriginal Disability Network
    (ADN), 63–65
  access challenges, 66–68
  advocacy, 60
  costs, 72–79
  funding, 64
  NDIS (National Disability
    Insurance Scheme), 6–7
drug and alcohol rehabilitation, 19–
  20, 160–161, 165–172, 178–179
  see also Glen, The

economic individualism, 35–36
education support, 89, 117–118
embedded specialist knowledge, 69–70,
  72, 79–80, 102, 118–119
employment support, *104–105*,
  119–122, 140, 172
  settler colonial impacts, 121–122
eugenics, 62

federal–state government relationship,
  28
financial support services, 151–152,
  167
First Peoples Disability Network
  (FPDN), 15–16, 60–61
  advocacy and support, 65–69,
    76–77, 79
  background, 63–65
  Bostock, Uncle Lester, 63–65, *66*
  community connection, 68–69,
    75–76
  expertise, 69–72, 79–80
  funding, 65, 73–75, 78–79, 189

remote communities support,
68–69, 76–78
settler colonial impacts, 61–63, 79
fragility
definition, 161
funding precarity, 12, 84
NPM impact, 109–110, 190
recovery from, 173–177, 178
staff stress levels, 73
see also antifragility
funding, 189
co-contribution arrangements, 9
community-controlled
organisations, 12, 16–17,
19–20, 190–192, 194–195
precarity, 12, 84, 95–99, 173–177
shortfalls, 7–8, 9

Glen, The, 19–20
background, 159–160
Chambers, Kasey, 170
community connection, *174*,
177–178
cultural connection, 162–172
funding, 173–179, 192
governance, 173–175, 178–179
rehabilitation approach, 162–172,
175, 176–177
yarning circles, 162–163
government administration, 14
government Indigenous service
provision
funding shortfalls, 7–8, 9
initiatives and programs, 13–14

Hawke Government, 27, 31–32, 33
health services, 93–94, *97*
see also Glen, The
Howard Government, 2, 14–15,
28–30, 31
abolition of ATSIC (Aboriginal
and Torres Strait Islander
Commission), 39–41, 47
Indigenous Australians policy,
32–39, 46–49, 92

Indigenous Advancement Strategy
(IAS), 136, 183
Indigenous Business Australia (IBA),
42
Indigenous business sector, 42
Indigenous expertise, 19, 102–103
appropriation of, 70–71, 75, 79,
85, 95, 192–193
knowledge colonialism, 16, 61
recognition, 161
valuing, 185, 189, 191, 193–194
ways of knowing, 10, 46, 187
Indigenous Land and Sea Corporation
(ILSC), 114, 115–116, 123, 129
Indigenous rights, 32
Indigenous service delivery sector
failures of market approach, 3–4,
20, 48, 154, 185–193
fragmentation, 5, 129
goals, 185
government inquiries, 9
individualised services vs
community services, 2, 13,
35–36, 186–187, 195
mainstreaming, 43–44, 45–46, 47,
49–50
Māori context comparison, 48
marginalisation of Indigenous
voices, 3
marketisation, 41–46, 80, 92–93,
181–182
non-Indigenous organisations, 50,
68, 70–72
reforms, 6–7, 193–197
underfunding, 176
see also bureaucratic burden
individualised services vs community
services, 2, 13, 35–36, 186–187,
195
institutional racism, 14, 187–188
see also racial capitalism

Keating Government, 28

land rehabilitation, 138, 142–145
Local Aboriginal Land Council
    (LALC), 139

Māori service delivery, 48
market mentality, 50
mentorship, 121–122
Morrison Government, 1
Mount Druitt region, 86–87, 91,
    93–94, 104, 105, 108–110, 187
Muru Mittigar, 18–19, 184
    activities, 139, 140–141
    background, 138–141
    bushfire risk management,
        145–146
    community connection, 149–153
    Community Finance Hub,
        151–152
    cultural awareness training, 140,
        150
    Dharug Country native title, 139
    employment and training, 146–
        149, 154
    funding, 138, 141, 192

National Agreement on Closing the
    Gap (CTG 2020), 1–2, 39, 195
    disability funding, 78–79
National Centre for Indigenous
    Excellence (NCIE), 17–18
    background, 114–115
    community connection, 121–122,
        124, 127–130
    core principles, 118–119
    disinvestment, 114
    funding, 115–118
    profitability, 123–125
    services, 117
    skills development, 119–120
    social impact, 125–128
native title system, 139
NDIS (National Disability Insurance
    Scheme), 6–7

neoliberalism, 6, 15
    deregulation, 27–29
    ethics, 36–37
New Public Management (NPM), 2–3
    colonising effects, 195
    contracting, 18–19, 30, 100,
        134–136, 140–149, 153–154
    disability services, 60–61
    fragility of community
        organisations, 176, 190
    impacts of, 7–8
    Indigenous service sector
        mismatch, 20, 182
    introduction of, 29–31
    post-NPM period, 13
non-Indigenous organisations, 183
    advantages, 72–73, 79, 100–101
    knowledge exploitation, 70–72, 75,
        101, 102, 108, 191
    public service, 105
    Reconciliation Action Plans
        (RAPs), 137
    reconciliation employment
        commitments, 137, 146–149
    staff, competition for, 146–149
    see also community-controlled
        organisations

OCHRE Local Decision Making
    (NSW), 13–14
organisational fragility
    definition, 161
    funding precarity, 12, 84
    NPM impact, 109–110, 190
    recovery from, 173–177, 178
    staff stress levels, 73

People With Disability Australia
    (PWDA), 63–64
policy failures, 2, 14–15, 185–193
privatisation, 28–29
procurement processes, 18–19, 186
    Indigenous procurement policies
        (IPPs), 136, 154, 192

racial bias, 106–108

racial capitalism, 85, 100, 108, 187, 192–193

see also institutional racism

reconciliation, 137, 144, 146–149

self-determination
  ATSIC (Aboriginal and Torres Strait Islander Commission), 31–32
  community organisations, 11–12, 93, 108–110, 141, 183
  service delivery sector, 42, 46, 194
  see also autonomy

settler colonial impacts
  disability among Indigenous Australians, 61–63, 79–80
  employment support, 121–122
  health and wellbeing, 62
  social enterprises, 129–130

Shergold, Peter, 29–30

Shorten, Bill, 64–65

social enterprises
  business approach, 116–117
  challenges, 153
  community commitments, 149–153
  objectives, 19, 134–136, 138, 144
  partnerships, 142–145, 151
  settler colonial context, 129–130

social services, 29, 31, 184
  criminal justice services, 160, 166
  disability services, 6–7, 16, 60, 64, 66–68, 72–79
  drug and alcohol rehabilitation, 19–20, 160–161, 165–172, 178–179
  employment support, *104–105,* 119–122, 140, 172
  financial support services, 151–152, 167
  health services, 93–94, *97*

strengths-based approach, 175, 178–179, 188

surveillance, *107*

trauma and trauma-informed care, 162, 171

Turnbull, Malcolm, 175–176

unemployment, 86–87

United Nations Committee on the Rights of Persons with Disabilities, 65

United Nations Declaration on the Rights of Indigenous People, 37

urban context, 5, 10–11
  Mount Druitt region, 86–87, 91, 93–94, 104, 105, 108–110, 187
  Redfern, 121, 126, *128*
  Western Sydney Region, 84–85, 133, 137, 152

volunteerism, 3, 95, 140, 190

welfare failure, 15, 29

wicked problems, 7, 35, 45, 46

yarning circles, 91, 162–163

www.ingramcontent.com/pod-product-compliance
Lightning Source LLC
Chambersburg PA
CBHW070844300326
41935CB00039B/1437